Did Monetary Forces Cause the Great Depression?

ALSO BY PETER TEMIN

Iron and Steel in Nineteenth-Century America

The Jacksonian Economy

Causal Factors in American Economic Growth in the Nineteenth Century

Did Monetary Forces Cause the Great Depression?

PETER TEMIN

MASSACHUSETTS INSTITUTE OF TECHNOLOGY

NEW YORK

 Published simultaneously in Canada by George J. McLeod Limited, Toronto. Printed in the United States of America.

FIRST EDITION

✧ *The text of this book was typeset in Times Roman on the Variable Input Typesetter. Composition, printing, and binding are by the Vail-Ballou Press, Inc.* ✧

Library of Congress Cataloging in Publication Data
Temin, Peter.
Did monetary forces cause the Great Depression?
Bibliography: p.
Includes index.
1. Depressions—1929—United States. 2. Money supply—United States. 3. Monetary policy—United States. I. Title.
HB3717 1929.T45 338.5′42 75–28367
ISBN 0–393–05561–2
ISBN 0–393–09209–7 pbk.

1 2 3 4 5 6 7 8 9

For my parents

CONTENTS

TABLES AND FIGURES

Tables

Figures

PREFACE

THE ECONOMIC CONTRACTION that started in 1929 was the worst in history. Historians have compared it with the downturns of the 1840s and the 1890s, but the comparison serves only to show the severity of the later movement. In the nineteenth-century depressions, there were banking panics, deflation, and bankruptcy, in various proportions. But there is no parallel to the underutilization of economic resources—to the unemployment of labor and other resources—in the 1930s.

The value of goods and services in America fell by almost half in the early 1930s. Correcting for the fall in prices, the fall in the quantity of production fell by approximately one-third. Unemployment rose to include one-quarter of the labor force. And investment stopped almost completely. It was the most extensive breakdown of the economy in history.

The effects of this collapse are still evident. It shattered people's faith in the ability of the economy to run smoothly without interference—the liberal credo of the nineteenth century; the stage was set for a major expansion of the role of government in the economy. A revolution in economic thought accompanied and justified this expansion.[1] And in Europe, political changes following the onset of the Depression began the progression toward the Second World War.

Given the magnitude and importance of this event, it is surprising how little we know about its causes. The reactions of people to the Depression, the policies undertaken during the Depression, and the effects of the Depression have all been the object of extensive study. But the economic collapse itself has suffered a form of intellectual neglect.

1. Stein, 1969, chronicles the spread of the new, Keynesian, ideas.

Too long ago to be part of the study of the current economy, too recent to be included in most courses in economic history, economists have—with a few prominent exceptions—left the study of the Depression to others. The inevitable result has been a neglect of the economic aspects of the Depression. While economists have advanced a variety of hypotheses to explain how depressions can take place, little attention has been given to the explicit application of these competing theories to the biggest depression in history. It is to this task that I turn in this volume. The brief introduction serves to place the analysis that follows in a historical context. A capsule history of the economic collapse will be followed by an attempt to characterize succinctly the two schools of thought to be discussed in Chapter II and by an outline of the tests to be performed in subsequent chapters.

In Chapter II, the economic literature on the Depression is surveyed, showing that it can be grouped into two classes. The division goes along both substantive and methodological lines, for economists with different views have attempted to substantiate them by different methods. It will emerge, however, that the two groups have been talking past each other and that there is in fact no debate between them. The remainder of the book attempts to initiate such a discussion by performing a series of tests designed to discriminate between the two schools of thought described in Chapter II.

Several tests are performed, none of them as conclusive as might be desired. Some reasons for this inconclusiveness will be given in the concluding chapter, but the collection of tests tells more than any single test could. Given the complexity of the questions involved and the limitations of economic theory, it is unreasonable to expect to find a single overwhelming test that will separate the sheep from the goats. Instead, a series of tests must be utilized to construct a picture that is coherent and most nearly consistent with the data.

The story that emerges is composed of economic events, and the methods of analysis also are economic in nature. The purpose of this book, in fact, is precisely the application of modern macroeconomic tools to the analysis of the Great Depression. Every effort has been made to make the methods and tests used here accessible to readers with only a knowledge of undergraduate economics. And the interested layman who finds it possible to thread his way through a few technical passages should have no problems following the main thrust of the argument.

It is a great pleasure to acknowledge the help I have received along the way in the course of this research. I have learned a lot about the Depression in the context of classes, seminars, and informal discussions. But being unable to name all the participants in these varied contacts, I must make do with a generalized thanks to them. In addition, I would like to thank the following people who read and commented on some draft or some part of the manuscript: Moses Abramovitz, Paul A. David, Stanley Fischer, Franklin M. Fisher, Duncan Foley, Philip Friedman, R. A. Gordon, Charles P. Kindleberger, Peter A. Lindert, Joseph D. Reid, Paul A. Samuelson, Myron C. Scholes, Anna J. Schwartz, Robert M. Solow, and Hal Varian. The book has benefited from their comments; all errors remain mine. Finally, I want to thank Robert Taggart and Michael Weinstein for their invaluable research assistance, Katherine Eisenhaure for her able and unflagging secretarial services, and the National Science Foundation for its generous financial support.

PT

Cambridge, Mass.
June 1975

I

Introduction

THE DEPRESSION began in 1929. Conventional dating of the downturn based on evidence from a variety of sources puts it near the middle of the year. But in the popular consciousness—then and now—nothing happened until the stock-market crash in the fall. Stock prices, which had increased at an exciting rate in 1928 and 1929, collapsed suddenly in October; Black Thursday, October 24, 1929, has become the symbol of the Depression.

The decline in industrial production started slowly, almost imperceptibly. It has taken subsequent research to find the high points of production in 1929 and to isolate cyclical movements from normal seasonal trends. But the change in the financial markets produced by the stock-market crash was dramatic indeed. Short-term interest rates, which had been high in 1928 and 1929 as the Federal Reserve tried to dampen the stock-market boom, fell rapidly to unprecedented levels in late 1929. The Fed, which had been debating whether to keep the discount rate stable or raise it in the middle of the year, found itself rapidly lowering it at the end. The discount rate fell from 6 per cent to 2.5 per cent in one year—a most significant turnaround.

The dramatic financial developments and the curtailment of production that was apparent by the last quarter of 1929 brought forth a variety of reassuring statements from government officials. The Hoover administration simultaneously assured the country that there was no emergency and moved to consult with businessmen and avoid the occurrence of one.[1] There seemed to be some response in early 1930. Stock prices stopped declining, production appeared to pick up slightly, and wage rates were maintained in response to Hoover's urg-

1. Hoover, 1952; Schlesinger, 1964.

ing. But by the end of 1930, it was clear that recovery was hardly on the way. Several developments in the course of 1930 acted to change the outlook.

Agricultural prices had declined during the 1920s in response to a large increase in the supply of agricultural goods. Non-European producers expanded during the interruption of European production caused by the First World War, and they did not retire from the market when the war was over. The resulting competition was muted by the attempts of exporting nations to support the prices of their exports. They accumulated large stocks and with them the need to finance their carrying costs. Increasing loans from industrial countries helped ease these costs before 1929, but the exporters could not continue to acquire stocks forever. The break came at the end of the 1920s, produced by poor wheat crops in the principal non-European exporting countries, the decline in lending by the industrial countries, and the extent of the accumulation of debt. Prices which had been declining slowly, fell rapidly in 1930.[2]

While the fall in agricultural prices was the most dramatic decline, other prices fell too. And while agricultural production did not typically fall in response to the fall in prices—in many cases it actually rose—industrial production did decline. The earnings of firms fell, bankruptcies rose, employment fell. Somewhere around the middle of 1930, perhaps when the expected fall upsurge in business failed to materialize, it became apparent that production had fallen dramatically. The declines in construction and automobile production symbolized the general decline.

As agricultural prices fell and businesses failed, banks who financed agricultural trade and some aspects of industrial production found themselves under increasing pressure. The rate of bank failures jumped dramatically in the last quarter of 1930, scaring both depositors and banks and leading to an increase in the demand for currency and for excess reserves that continued throughout the Depression.

Despite all these deflationary forces, a recovery again appeared to be in the making in early 1931. But the collapse of the European financial system more than offset any expansionary tendencies. The difficulties became apparent with the failure of the Credit Anstalt, the largest bank in Austria, in May 1931. The Austrian government guaranteed its liabilities and the bank's foreign creditors agreed to stop

2. Timoshenko, 1953.

withdrawals. This meant, however, that the assets of the creditors lost liquidity. German banks were affected particularly, and their creditors started to withdraw deposits in anticipation of further trouble. The loss of foreign reserves by Germany was so severe that currency controls were instituted in July. A ''domino effect'' began to be apparent. As each currency experienced difficulty and as free markets in these currencies were suspended in one way or another, anticipations that other currencies would experience difficulties also increased. Holders of these currencies attempted to protect themselves by selling these currencies, and the resulting pressure helped speed the anticipated alteration of the markets. With the imposition of German controls, the pressure shifted to Britain. The British did not impose controls on international currency movements; they abandoned the fixed exchange rate between the pound and gold that had been the cornerstone of international finance for a century. Britain went off the gold standard, and the pound depreciated.

If anyone had any lingering doubts by this time that the economic system was collapsing, this event erased them. The effects on America, though, were more immediate than any such change in expectations. With the pound depreciating, holders of dollars began to speculate against a similar movement of that currency. American policy differed both from the German and Austrian policies of imposing controls and the British policy of devaluing; the Federal Reserve raised interest rates enough to stem the outflow of funds. This difference of policy owed something to ideology, but it undoubtedly reflected also the relative strength of the speculation against the various currencies. The pressure on the dollar was mild enough to be diverted by the classical remedy of raising interest rates; it is unlikely that the European currencies could have effected a reasonable policy using interest rates alone.

The deflationary pressure in America coming from the international collapse and the further decline in expectations from the same source, squashed any incipient recovery, and the Depression continued to deepen. Prices, wages, and production all fell, while short-term interest rates and bankruptcies rose. Expectations of future declines were by this time powerful forces leading to further declines.

A bottom of sorts was reached in the summer of 1932, but recovery was again aborted during the presidential campaign and the long lame-duck period between the election and Roosevelt's inauguration.

Confidence in the banking system finally collapsed altogether during this last period, and Roosevelt was inaugurated in the midst of a convulsive banking panic. Roosevelt proclaimed a federal bank "holiday," that is, he closed all banks, immediately upon taking office in March 1933, and he undertook a whirlwind of activity to restore confidence and to counteract a variety of deflationary pressures. While the efficacy of the New Deal has been widely questioned, the long economic contraction was over.

The extent of the collapse is shown in the data in Tables 1 through 3. Gross national product in constant dollars fell by 29 per cent between 1929 and 1933. Consumption expenditures fell by 18 per cent, and gross investment practically ceased. Accompanying this fall in production was a fall in the stock of money of 27 per cent if a narrow definition of money (M_1) is used and 33 per cent if a broader definition

TABLE 1 • *Real GNP and Selected Components, 1919–39 (billions of 1929 dollars)*

	Total Consumption Expenditures	Gross Investment	Construction	Gross National Product
1919	50.2	10.7	4.8	74.2
1920	52.7	12.8	5.0	73.3
1921	56.1	7.4	4.9	71.6
1922	58.1	10.6	7.1	75.8
1923	63.4	15.6	8.2	85.8
1924	68.1	12.4	9.0	88.4
1925	66.1	16.4	10.0	90.5
1926	71.5	17.1	10.7	96.4
1927	73.2	15.6	10.4	97.3
1928	74.8	14.5	9.8	98.5
1929	79.0	16.2	8.7	104.4
1930	74.7	10.5	6.4	95.1
1931	72.2	6.8	4.5	89.5
1932	66.0	.8	2.4	76.4
1933	64.6	.3	1.9	74.2
1934	68.0	1.8	2.0	80.8
1935	72.3	8.8	2.8	91.4
1936	79.7	9.3	3.9	100.9
1937	82.6	14.6	4.6	109.1
1938	81.3	6.8	4.1	103.2
1939	85.9	9.9	4.9	111.0

SOURCES: Kendrick, 1961, Table A-11a, pp. 294–95; Pilgrim, 1969, p. 161.

(M_2) is used. This fall took place in the face of a continuing rise in the monetary base (high-powered money) as both the ratio of deposits to bank reserves and of deposits to currency in the hands of the public fell. And it was accompanied by a dramatic fall in prices. The wholesale price index fell by 31 per cent from 1929 to 1933, the consumer

TABLE 2 • *The Money Stock and Related Quantities, 1919–39 (billions of dollars)*

	M_1	M_2	High-powered money	D/R	D/C
1919	21.7	30.8	6.6	10.2	6.7
1920	23.5	34.5	7.2	11.0	6.7
1921	21.2	32.5	6.5	11.3	7.1
1922	21.5	33.6	6.3	11.4	8.2
1923	22.7	36.4	6.7	11.8	8.3
1924	23.5	38.4	6.9	11.7	8.8
1925	25.5	41.8	7.0	12.3	9.6
1926	25.9	43.3	7.1	12.5	9.9
1927	25.9	44.5	7.2	12.6	10.3
1928	26.2	46.1	7.1	13.0	10.9
1929	26.4	46.2	7.1	13.0	11.0
1930	25.4	45.2	6.9	12.8	11.2
1931	23.6	41.7	7.3	11.8	9.2
1932	20.6	34.8	7.8	10.3	6.2
1933	19.4	30.8	8.2	8.2	5.1
1934	21.5	33.3	9.1	6.4	6.3
1935	25.5	38.4	10.7	5.6	7.1
1936	29.2	42.9	12.2	5.4	7.3
1937	30.3	45.0	13.4	5.0	7.1
1938	30.0	44.9	14.6	4.3	7.2
1939	33.6	48.7	17.6	3.7	7.1

NOTE: All yearly figures are the averages of the respective monthly figures.

M_1 Currency held by the public and (adjusted) demand deposits helf in commercial banks.

M_2 Currency held by the public and (adjusted) demand and time deposits held in commercial banks.

High-powered money Currency held by the public plus bank vault cash plus bank deposits at Federal Reserve banks.

D/R Commercial bank deposits (demand plus time) divided by bank reserves (member bank deposits minus float plus nonmember bank clearing account, seasonally adjusted by Shiskin-Eisenpress method).

D/C Commercial bank deposits divided by currency held by the public.

SOURCE: Friedman and Schwartz, 1963a, Tables A-1, B-3, pp. 709–16, 801–05.

price index fell by 25 per cent, and the implicit GNP deflator fell by 25 per cent. The pervasive decline in all of these macroeconomic variables—except the quantity of high-powered money—was an awesome and awful event.

The magnitude of the Depression is clear; the reasons for its severity are less apparent. One reason, often and correctly given, is the absence of a concerted expansionary macroeconomic policy between 1929 and 1933. The monetary and fiscal policies that we now think could have been effective in moderating or eliminating the contraction were not used to any perceptible extent.[3]

TABLE 3 • *Aggregate Price Indexes, 1919–39*

	Wholesale Price Index (WPI) 1947–49 = 100	Consumer Price Index (CPI) 1947–49 = 100	Implicit GNP Price Deflator 1929 = 100
1919	90.1	74.0	106
1920	100.3	85.7	121
1921	63.4	76.4	103
1922	62.8	71.6	98
1923	65.4	72.9	100
1924	63.8	73.1	99
1925	67.3	75.0	101
1926	65.0	75.6	101
1927	62.0	74.2	99
1928	62.9	73.3	100
1929	61.9	73.3	100
1930	56.1	71.4	96
1931	47.4	65.0	85
1932	42.1	58.4	77
1933	42.8	55.3	75
1934	48.7	57.2	80
1935	52.0	58.7	79
1936	52.5	59.3	82
1937	56.1	61.4	83
1938	51.1	60.3	83
1939	50.1	59.4	82

SOURCE: *Historical Statistics,* Series E25, E113, F5, pp. 117, 125, 139.

3. For the failure of monetary policy to be used, see Friedman and Schwartz, 1963a, and the discussion of this work in Chapter II. For the failure of fiscal policy, see Brown, 1956, and Table 24, below. Norman, 1969, argues that a successful macroeconomic policy would have had to approach the size of government expenditures during the Second World War.

It is not surprising that the policies we now recommend for similar conditions were not tried. For if they had been tried and found wanting—if the Depression had occurred despite the imposition of expansionary monetary or fiscal policies—we would no longer count them as effective. Given the existence of the Depression, only policies that were not tried could escape with untarnished reputations.

But the negative argument that macroeconomic policies were not used is hardly the same as the positive argument that these policies would, in fact, have been effective. This latter assertion is difficult, most likely even impossible, to prove, and the debate about it revolves on questions about the structure of the economy rather than the occurrence of specific historical events.

The question posed here is not whether some alternative policy would have worked, but rather what happened to make such a corrective policy desirable. What happened at the end of the 1920s that (in the absence of offsetting governmental policies) led to the historically unique events just described?

As the title to this book suggests, this question can be narrowed down further. It turns out that explanations of the Depression can be classified into two groups, one group offered generally by those who believe that monetary policy would have been the best tool to alleviate the Depression and the other by adherents of fiscal policy. While this correspondence of views is apparent, there is no logical need for it. One can believe that the Depression was caused by events having nothing to do with the financial markets and yet that monetary policy would have been effective in offsetting the deflationary shocks. Or one can equally well believe that the economy declined due to financial developments, but that fiscal policy is the most effective expansionary tool. The question of what happened in the early 1930s is distinct from the question of what policy an omniscient economic dictator should have pursued.

The two classes of explanations for the Depression have different events at their cores. What I have called "the money hypothesis" asserts that the collapse of the banking system was the primary cause of the Depression, while "the spending hypothesis" asserts that a fall in autonomous aggregate spending lay at the root of the decline. The following chapters represent an attempt to discriminate between these two hypotheses.

The difference between them can be suggested by reference to the familiar *IS-LM* diagram of macroeconomic textbooks. These two curves jointly determine the equilibrium level of operation of the economy. For this equilibrium level to shift, one or the other of the curves has to shift. The money hypothesis asserts it was the *LM* curve; the spending hypothesis, the *IS* curve.

But although the two hypotheses may be distinguished by this stark statement, a simple test of their empirical merits does not emerge from it. There are several reasons for this unhappy fact. First, the simple model of *IS* and *LM* curves assumes that the economy is continuously in equilibrium. But adjustment to changes in the economic environment is never instantaneous. At any moment of time, the economy is in transition from one equilibrium to another, and it may never reach an equilibrium if the external influences change sufficiently rapidly. In any empirical test, therefore, the mechanism by which the economy adjusts to changes needs to be given as much prominence as the location of equilibrium points.

Second, the conventional *IS-LM* model is static. It assumes, for example, that income would stay constant in a stable equilibrium. But if investment is positive at this equilibrium—as it is in most actual economies—income must be growing. And if one important variable like income is changing, then others must be changing too, and the way they change will have important repercussions.

One possibility is that prices will change in response to the interaction of changes in income and movements of other variables. The *IS* and *LM* curves typically are drawn under the assumption of constant prices, and the tendency of prices to change is another reason why the simple *IS-LM* model does not lead directly to a test of the two hypotheses.[4]

The Depression was a complex historical event. It took place over time and developed complexity as it went along. And as it unfolded, the economic magnitudes that are assumed to stay constant when we do our textbook analysis changed sharply. The textbook framework therefore can provide a guide to thinking and a shorthand mode of expression; but the actual tests used to choose between the competing hypotheses need to take account of events and developments not found in the textbooks.

The tests to be performed here can be outlined by means of a

4. The nominal stock of money fell in the early 1930s, but the real stock did not. See Tables 2 and 23. It makes a big difference whether the curves are defined in real or nominal terms.

simple device. Two brief narratives of the Depression may be given, depending on whether the money hypothesis or the spending hypothesis is assumed to be true. The stories may then be compared, and tests will be appropriate at points where the stories differ. The skeletal narratives, then, are as follows.

According to the spending hypothesis, the Depression was generated by a fall in autonomous spending. At a given level of income, desired investment and consumption fell. Various reasons for this fall can be given, but the two most frequently cited focus on construction and the stock market. Construction—which was a substantial component of investment—fell because the housing stock exceeded the demand after 1925. And consumption fell sharply after 1929 in response to the stock-market crash. The fall in these components of autonomous spending then produced a fall in real income and prices by the multiplier process. The Depression was severe because the fall in autonomous spending was large and sustained.

The fall in income and prices resulting from the decline in autonomous spending led to a decrease in the demand for money. Interest rates fell to equilibrate the demand and supply of money. Had the supply of money been completely interest-inelastic, the quantity of money would not have been affected. But the supply of money was partly a function of interest rates, and the movement along the supply curve occasioned by the fall in the demand for money for any given interest rate led to a fall in the stock of money as well as a fall in interest rates. The monetary base (high-powered money) continued to increase during the Depression except for a brief dip in 1930, as can be seen in Table 2. The fall in the stock of money then was largely a movement along the supply curve of money in response to changes in interest rates, not a shift in the curve itself.

The movement along the supply curve of money was not accomplished without difficulty, and the banking panics of the early 1930s show how hard it is to completely restructure the pattern of interest rates in a short time. The banking panics reduced the quantity of money that a given monetary base could support, and they therefore led to a decrease in the supply of money at a given interest rate. But, according to the spending hypothesis, this shift was small relative to the other movements taking place. The banking panics were a part of a larger process that started with the decline in autonomous spending. They provided a way to help equilibrate the money market in the face of precipitously falling demand and an increasing monetary base. Had they not taken place, the market would have been equilibrated in other ways, but the overall story of the Depression would not have been much different.

As the Depression deepened, adverse expectations kept autonomous spending low. The international collapse intensified the Depression in the United States by further depressing expectations and by diminishing exports. In the face of a small aggregate demand, the economy settled down to an underemployment position.

The money hypothesis leads to a rather different tale. In this story, a "normal," short-lived depression was converted into a major continued downswing in income and prices by the collapse of the banking system. The first banking panic in late 1930 led to a fundamental change in behavior that was encouraged by the banking panics of the following years. The demand for deposits (bank liabilities) on the part of the public fell, and the demand for excess reserves on the part of banks rose, as both individuals and banks sought to protect themselves from bank failures and panics.

This change in behavior by both banks and individuals led to a decrease in the supply of money for a given quantity of high-powered money and a given level of interest rates. This downward shift in the supply curve of money then led to downward pressure on real income and prices which fell to equilibrate the money market.[5] The direction of causation was clear. The banking panics led to a downward shift in the supply curve of money which led in turn to a fall in nominal income composed partly of deflation and partly of a decline in production and employment.

The decline in real income was severe and sustained because the decline in the supply of money was severe and sustained. The international Depression intensified the American one through the pressure it put on the dollar and the deflationary monetary policy adopted to counteract this pressure.

There are many differences between these two stories—although they both purport to explain the same macroeconomic data—but three differences will be given major attention in the following chapters. First, the Depression was precipitated by a fall in autonomous spend-

5. See Chapter IV for a description of how this downward pressure can spread from the money market to the economy as a whole.

ing according to the spending hypothesis and by banking panics according to the money hypothesis. Stated differently, the spending hypothesis sees the banking panics as results of the Depression rather than as causes, while the money hypothesis sees them as primary causative events. And the money hypothesis sees the fall in investment and consumption as the result of the Depression, while the spending hypothesis views them as independent deflationary events. One way to discriminate between these stories, therefore, is to see to what extent the falls in investment and consumption on the one hand and the banking panics on the other can be seen as independent of the fall in income that composed the Depression. If either one was independent of the fall in income, then the relevant hypothesis is consistent with the data. But if these events were caused by the fall in income, they cannot have precipitated this fall.

Second, in the story generated by the spending hypothesis, the stock of money fell because the demand for money fell. In the alternative story, the stock of money fell because the supply of money fell. If we could identify these curves to find out whether the demand or the supply curve fell, we would be on the way to test the validity of these stories. We could then see if the changes in the money market were the results of changes in the rest of the economy or whether they were the causes of changes elsewhere.

Third, the two stories give different reasons for the extent of the Depression and emphasize different parts of the international decline. We can ask which story is more consistent with the data, although not much discriminatory power can be expected from this test. Once the downward movement of the economy was well under way, all variables declined in a mutually interactive manner, and the decline in the United States interacted with economic troubles in other countries. It is highly unlikely that we will be able to disentangle the causal elements in this complex story. Nevertheless, as a minimum test, a successful story should be consistent with the data.

Having noted these differences, it should be acknowledged that the two stories have been given here in "pure form" and that the actual history cannot be expected to correspond with one or the other of the simple stories narrated just above. Most people would agree that the Depression, once well under way, acquired a momentum of its own, that is, that the multiplicity of events occurring together had effects that each one acting alone might not have. And there is no logical or historical reason why the Depression needed to have been caused by a single event or unfavorable influence.

Nevertheless, it is useful to keep the two hypotheses separate in this investigation. While this procedure runs the risk of examining straw men, it also permits more clarity in the discussion than would otherwise be possible. And it is important to see if we can disentangle the complex events that allowed such a large process to get underway. For while it may be true that "everything happened at once," this bland observation does not provide many clues to either historical understanding or policy formation.

The three differences between the stories just described will be examined in Chapters III, IV, and V of this book. Before performing the tests, the existing economic literature will be surveyed in Chapter II to show that the hypotheses being tested here are appropriate ones, that they have not yet been adequately tested elsewhere, and that they cannot be tested by the techniques used by previous authors.

II

The Role of Assumptions and Econometrics in the Analysis of the Depression

THE EXISTING economic literature on the Depression exhibits no agreement on the causes of the Depression. Instead, there are several schools of thought whose views seldom are brought into direct conflict. Friedman and Schwartz have given the best exposition of what I have called the "money hypothesis," and this view will be represented by their exposition. Most other analyses of the Depression have concentrated on one or another of the hypotheses I have grouped together under the name of the "spending hypothesis." Econometric models of the interwar economy have been used extensively to define and refine this hypothesis. But while the implications of the spending hypothesis are brought out, the issue of choosing between the money hypothesis and the spending hypothesis typically is raised only tangentially, if at all. In fact, neither the approach adopted by Friedman and Schwartz nor the econometric approach is a good way to analyze this choice.[1]

The discussion will be divided into three parts. First, Friedman and Schwartz's account of the money hypothesis will be analyzed. Second, econometric models of the Depression will be compared to each other and to Friedman and Schwartz's account. Third, a model of the supply and demand for money which incorporates features of both hypotheses will be tested against the data. For reasons that will emerge during the

1. Writers on the international Depression have asserted uniformly that the Depression in the United States was caused within the United States. See Lewis, 1949, p. 52; Lundberg, 1968, p. 74; Kindleberger, 1973, p. 117.

discussion, this exercise can only provide a limited test of the money hypothesis.

The Money Hypothesis: Friedman and Schwartz

The account of "the Great Contraction" in Chapter 7 of Friedman and Schwartz's classic *Monetary History of the United States* stands without peer among narratives of the early 1930s.[2] It is scholarly, detailed, insightful, and fascinating. As might be expected, it has had an enormous influence on our views of the Depression. It has become something like the standard history of the Depression for students of economics. Any account of the economic literature on the Depression, therefore, must give disproportionate weight to this study.[3]

The *Monetary History* appeared at the same time as two articles coauthored by Friedman that provide a context for the historical analysis in the book. In one article, Friedman and Meiselman showed that the level of income was more closely correlated with the stock of money than with a measure of "autonomous spending" over almost a century. While a correlation is not evidence for causation, the results were striking and suggestive. Significantly, however, they held true in every decade but one. In the 1930s, the level of income was not more closely correlated with the stock of money than with "autonomous spending."[4]

The argument was carried further in an article by Friedman and Schwartz. They rejected the idea that the correlation found between income and money could be coincidence and asked how the two could be related. The choice they presented was simple: Either changes in the stock of money caused income to change, or vice versa. The resolution was equally simple. The stock of money was determined by a variety of forces independent of the level of income, according to Friedman and Schwartz, and the direction of causation therefore must be from money to income, not the other way.[5]

2. Friedman and Schwartz, 1963a.

3. Although it is one chapter in a long book, this chapter may be discussed independently of the rest of the book. There are comparatively few references in the narrative to other parts of the book, although the methodology is, of course, the same. And the authors thought that Chapter 7 was sufficiently independent of the rest of the book to issue it as a separate book by itself. Friedman and Schwartz, 1965.

4. Friedman and Meiselman, 1963.

5. Friedman and Schwartz, 1963b.

The *Monetary History* completed the argument. The historical determinants of the stock of money were only briefly sketched in the article, and the encyclopedic discussion of the book provided the details. The book thus contains the evidence on which the conclusions of the article are based; to evaluate the whole discussion, it is necessary to examine this evidence. Since the Depression is the most important single episode discussed and since the correlation reported by Friedman and Meiselman was least good during the Depression, consideration of this historical episode tests the whole argument at a critical point.

The conclusions of the study of the Depression in the *Monetary History* are shown by the words used by Friedman and Schwartz to describe it in other publications. They summarize it as follows:

> An initial mild decline in the money stock from 1929 to 1930, accompanying a decline in Federal Reserve credit outstanding, was converted into a sharp decline by a wave of bank failures beginning in late 1930.
>
> The quantity of money . . . fell not because there were no willing borrowers—not because the horse would not drink. It fell because the Federal Reserve System forced or permitted a sharp reduction in the monetary base, because it failed to exercise the responsibilities assigned to it in the Federal Reserve Act to provide liquidity to the banking system.[6]

The quantity of money fell, in other words, because of a fall in the supply of money, not a fall in the demand. The fall in the supply of money was caused in the first instance by a decline in Federal Reserve credit outstanding in 1930, but far more importantly by the effects of the banking failures starting in late 1930. The clear—but unstated—implication is that the fall in the quantity of money caused the level of income to fall. Given a stable demand for money, a fall in the supply of money required a movement along the demand curve, that is, a fall in income, to equilibrate the supply and demand for money. The banking panics then were the proximate cause of the Depression, and the behavior of the Federal Reserve System was the underlying causal factor.[7]

What evidence do Friedman and Schwartz muster to support these propositions? Their narrative is long and complex, but it offers far less

6. Ibid., p. 52; and Friedman, 1968, p. 3. Alternatively, Friedman, 1969, pp. 97 and 218.

7. These views were presented earlier, in much abbreviated form in Warburton, 1945 and 1966.

support for these assertions than appears at first. In fact, it assumes the conclusion and describes the Depression in terms of it; it does not test it or prove it at all. A detailed analysis of their narrative will show why.

Three strands can be identified in the discussion by Friedman and Schwartz. First, the determinants of the stock of money in the United States were analyzed. The Federal Reserve System was an important part of the mechanism determining the stock of money, and its actions were described in great detail. Second, the effects of the movements of the stock of money on the rest of the economy were described. And third, Friedman and Schwartz described the possible effects of policies that could have been followed but were not. This part of the narrative is qualitatively different from the others, for while the rest of the chapter deals with the explanation of events that actuallly happened, this part deals with the effects of events that did not happen. The propositions, in the current jargon of economic history, are counterfactuals.[8] These strands will be disentangled from the overall narrative in turn.

Friedman and Schwartz identified three determinants of the stock of money. They are the quantity of high-powered money or the monetary base (that is, those kinds of money that can be used either as currency or as bank reserves), the ratio of bank deposits to bank reserves, and the ratio of bank deposits to currency held by the public.[9] In an appendix to the book, Friedman and Schwartz showed how the stock of money is a function of these three ratios. High-powered money, H, is the sum of reserves, R, and currency in the hands of the public, C. The stock of money, M, is the sum of currency, C, and bank deposits, D. From these two relations, the following equation can be derived:[10]

$$M = H \frac{\frac{D}{R}(1 + \frac{D}{C})}{\frac{D}{R} + \frac{D}{C}} \tag{1}$$

The relation in equation (1) is purely definitional. And while changes in economic magnitudes can be analyzed in terms of definitional relations, we generally find it more interesting to use behavioral

8. See Hempel, 1965.

9. Since the stock of money was defined to include all deposits of commercial banks, the ratios must be interpreted to include these deposits also.

10. Friedman and Schwartz, 1963a, p. 791.

relations. The discussion, then, can be carried on in terms of the actions of identifiable groups in response to identifiable influences. Friedman and Schwartz did not claim that equation (1) is anything more than a definition, but they did claim that there are behavioral grounds for formulating equation (1) in terms of H, D/C, and D/R. The argument is that each of these three magnitudes was determined by the actions of a separate and independent group of people. The stock of high-powered money, H, was determined by the monetary authorities, that is, the Federal Reserve System. The deposit-reserve ratio, D/R, was determined by the actions of banks, and the deposit-currency ratio, D/C, was determined by individuals.[11]

This separation of influences appears to be rather different than the normal separation used by economists. A more traditional decomposition of influences determining prices and quantities of economic goods separates them into supply and demand components. It is appropriate, therefore, to ask if the behavioral relations underlying equation (1) relate to the supply of or the demand for money to see if this equation can be identified either with the supply of or the demand for money.

The monetary authorities and banks are suppliers of money. A description of their behavior accordingly is a description of the supply of money. Individuals (and nonfinancial businesses) are holders of money, and their behavior normally is considered to be on the demand side. In the formulation by Friedman and Schwartz, however, individual's preferences for a monetary ratio—the deposit-currency ratio—is relevant, not their desires about their total money balances. There appears to be an implicit argument that individuals make two independent decisions. They decide how much money they want to hold and they decide in what form, currency or deposits, they want to hold it. For each individual, the decisions are separate, although for the economy as a whole they are related by equation (1). The first decision clearly is part of the demand for money, but the second decision is harder to place.

This issue can be resolved by consulting other writings of Friedman. He has talked extensively about the demand for money and formalized the demand function in different ways. The deposit-cur-

11. Ibid., pp. 784–91. This separation was done in the context of a specie standard, and then extended without discussion to a mixed specie and fiduciary standard. Consequently, the extent to which the Fed is responsible for H was determined by extension from the specie case rather than directly.

rency ratio never figures in any of these formulations. The implication is that the determinants of this ratio are not a part of the demand for money. They therefore must be part of the supply.[12]

Equation (1) then is a supply function for money. To the extent that the analysis of changes in the stock of money is conducted in terms of this equation, it treats only the supply side of the market for money. There is no reason not to detail changes in the supply of any good over time, but we do not normally speak of the supply alone as the determinant of quantities on the market.

Yet Friedman and Schwartz consistently referred to the variable on the left-hand side of equation (1) as the stock of money, not the supply of money. And they referred to the arguments on the right-hand side of equation (1) as the determinants of the money stock. They clearly assumed that the stock of money was determined by supply alone.

The reasoning behind this assumption is indicated by the persistent use of the word *stock*. Consider the stock of bonds. The size of this stock is the product of past decisions about corporate and government finance. It is fixed at any moment of time by these previous supply decisions. If the demand for bonds shifts, it will not change the number of bonds in existence immediately; it will change their prices. In the short run, therefore, the quantity of bonds is determined by the supply, and the price is determined by the demand. In the longer run, the price will be a function of both the supply and the demand working through a recursive relationship.[13] Friedman and Schwartz employed the short-run part of this argument; they appear to have rejected the long-run part.

The implicit model of Friedman and Schwartz therefore starts with the arguments on the right-hand side of equation (1): H, D/C, and D/R. They determined the supply of money, which was equal to the stock of money by assumption. The demand function is not specified, but there is no reason to think it is in any way unusual. The demand

12. See Friedman, 1956, 1970. This argument implies that individuals affect both the supply and the demand for money by independent decisions. Their decisions about the quantity of money determine the demand, and their decisions about the composition of money affect the supply. The discussions of desired money balances in Friedman's other work do not deal with their composition. The narrative about the desired composition of money balances in the *Monetary History* does not include treatment of their desired total holdings. The two decisions are considered completely independent, and there is no contradiction in placing the actions of individuals on both the supply and demand sides of this market.

13. See Foley and Sidrauski, 1971, for an extended analysis of this kind of market.

for money is taken to be a function of income and interest rates by virtually everyone who writes on the subject, and such a function is consistent with the exposition by Friedman and Schwartz. Once the stock of money was determined, therefore, the level of income and interest rates had to move to bring the demand side of the money market into balance. (The market was assumed to be in equilibrium at all times.) The arguments of equation (1) were the determinants of the stock of money; the stock of money was the determinant of income and interest rates.

This is the first half of the usual specification of market dynamics for an asset. It describes what happens in the short run, where the duration of the short run is a function of the period of production of the asset. Since the stock of money can change rapidly in a matter of weeks, the short run in this market is very short indeed. The usual specification of long-run behavior allows for the influence of the price on the supply, but the model used by Friedman and Schwartz does not seem to. The supply of money was assumed to be determined by forces independent of income and interest rates. This assumption is critical to their argument and needs to be considered carefully.

The interest rate is not usually thought of in connection with the determination of the deposit-currency ratio by individuals,[14] but banks are thought to determine their reserve ratios and the volume of their borrowing from the Federal Reserve at least partly by reference to interest rates. The reserve ratio is just the inverse of Friedman and Schwartz's deposit-reserve ratio; bank borrowing from the Fed is a component of high-powered money. In addition, international gold movements, caused in part by interest rates and movements of income, also affected the quantity of high-powered money. To the extent that these magnitudes were affected by interest rates and income, the stock of money was not independent of the demand for any substantial period of time. Equation (1) then is only one part of a recursive relationship. It shows the movements of the supply of money, without providing information on whether movements of the supply curve or of the demand curve were responsible for any particular changes in the stock.

Friedman and Schwartz seem to have assumed that D/R and H

14. Note that Tobin's analysis of the demand for currency implies that the deposit-currency ratio could be a function of interest rates. Tobin, 1959; Brainard and Tobin, 1968.

were not responsive to interest rates and income on two grounds. The first argument asserts that other determinants of *D/R* and *H* were much more important. Far and away the most important single determinant of *D/R*—and *D/C*—in the early 1930s, according to Friedman and Schwartz, was the sequence of banking panics in those years. These banking panics must have been independent of interest rates and income for Friedman and Schwartz's argument to hold. Yet the first banking crisis was stated by Friedman and Schwartz to be related to agriculture (which is a part of income) and subsequent ones to be related to the rise in yields of relatively low-grade bonds, that is, to the fall in their price. In addition, foreign currency problems induced by the fall in income in the United States compounded the banks' difficulties.[15] The argument that the banking panics were independent of interest rates and income will not stand.

The second argument for the separation of supply and demand is rather different. (It applies only to the period after 1914, which includes the chapter under discussion here.) According to this argument, the Federal Reserve had the power to offset any market change. It could have offset changes in interest rates by changing the discount rate, and it could have avoided the banking panics by changing its procedures. To borrow a term from international finance, it could have "sterilized" changes in market variables. To the extent that it did not, Friedman and Schwartz said that the changes in the money supply were due to the Fed's failure to sterilize the market forces, rather than to the changes in the market forces themselves.

The effect of this attribution is to blur the distinction between history and policy analysis. All historical events came about because of the success or failure, the commission or omission, of various policies, according to this view. There are no other possibilities. In particular, the changes in the economy that called for changes in policies fade into the background. Their place is taken by the discrepancy between what the Fed actually did and what it might have done.

While the actions of the Federal Reserve are of undoubted importance, the events that induced these actions are of interest also. Given that the Fed did not sterilize all market forces—whether or not it could have—these market forces then had effects on the supply of money. The historical path is the result both of actions by the Fed and changes elsewhere in the economy. Neither should be ignored by exclusive at-

15. Friedman and Schwartz, 1963a, pp. 308, 314, 355; Chapter III, below.

tention to what might have been if history had been different. The influence of market forces on the supply of money cannot be forgotten. Equation (1) is only a part of the recursive relationship between money, interest rates, and income.

A specific example from the narrative of Chapter 7 will illustrate the point at issue. The stock of money fell between August 1929 and October 1930. In terms of equation (1), the decline was due to a decline in high-powered money, which was due in turn to a decline in bills discounted by the Fed. Friedman and Schwartz concluded from this, "Ultimately then, it was the failure of the Reserve System to replace the decline in discounts by other credit outstanding that was responsible for the decline in the stock of money." [16] They did not deny that changes in interest rates led banks to decrease their discounts at the Fed. Instead they asserted that the Fed was "responsible" for the decline. How does this judgment help us to decide if interest rates affected bank behavior?

The discount rate was reduced dramatically in this period. The Fed apparently was using its traditional tools to discourage the fall in discounts. But, said Friedman and Schwartz, "Though the discount rate fell absolutely, it probably rose relative to the relevant market interest rates, namely, those on short-term securities with essentially zero risk of default." [17] Even though the Fed moved in the right direction to discourage the decline in discounts, it did not move far enough or fast enough to discourage it completely. There were, in other words, two events behind the fall in discounts. The relevant market interest rates fell, and the discount rate fell less. It only makes sense to dismiss the market interest rates as irrelevant if the Fed had pegged the discount rate to these relevant market interest rates in the fashion of some central banks today. Changes in market rates then would have been sterilized as far as their influence on bank borrowing from the Fed went.

But the discount rate was not pegged to any other rates in an explicit way. The Fed was conscious of market interest rates when it set the discount rate, and it is possible to assert that the decisions were taken on the basis of relative interest rates, even though discussions within the Federal Reserve System were conducted in terms of the absolute level of the discount rate. Friedman and Schwartz did not try

16. Ibid., pp. 340–41. This is the "initial mild decline in the money stock" referred to in the summarizing quotation given above.

17. Ibid., p. 341.

to characterize the decision-making process of the Fed in any abstract way, however, and the attribution of responsibility for the fall in discounts to the Fed does not seem to rest on such a formulation. The argument for dismissing the role of income and interest rates in the determination of the stock of money consequently is not a historical one.

Friedman and Schwartz's descriptions of the determinants of the stock of money then is seriously incomplete. It looks only at one side of the market and ignores effects coming from the demand for money. An account of the supply alone cannot tell us how much of the variation in the quantity came from changes in supply conditions and how much from demand conditions. An account of the whole market is necessary for this separation. How else are we to know if the change in the quantity supplied was a shift of the supply curve or a movement along the supply curve?

Since Friedman and Schwartz assumed that the stock of money was determined by forces independent of the level of income, they could infer that the stock of money then determined the level of income. If the assumption is not valid, the inference may not be either. If the stock of money was determined by both the supply and demand for money, then the stock of money and the level of income were jointly determined by other variables. And it is possible that these other variables had more direct effects on income than on money, so that the line of causation ran from changes in income to changes in money in the early 1930s, rather than the reverse. The second strand of Friedman and Schwartz's discussion treats the relationship between the stock of money and the rest of the economy. A discussion of their comments on the nonmonetary parts of the economy will permit an evaluation of their arguments that the direction of causation ran from the stock of money to the level of income and not the other way.

The initial downturn of industrial production, wholesale prices, and personal income—Friedman and Schwartz's indexes of events outside the monetary sector recorded in their Chart 28—"coincided" with the stock-market crash. Friedman and Schwartz reported the turning point without any causal statements at all. They then asserted, "Even if the contraction had come to an end in late 1930 or early 1931, as it might have done in the absence of the monetary collapse that was to ensue, it would have ranked as one of the more severe contractions on record." [18] While no explicit statement was given, the

18. Ibid., pp. 303, 306.

passage reads as if Friedman and Schwartz believed that the initial downturn was caused by events outside the monetary sector and that this nonmonetary downturn was turned from a severe contraction into a catastrophic depression by the monetary collapse starting at the end of 1930.

Evidence both for and against this inference exists elsewhere in the narrative. In the previous chapter of the *Monetary History,* the decline in high-powered money and in the stock of money itself during 1928 and 1929 before the crash was noted, and Friedman and Schwartz argued that Federal Reserve policy during the boom was "too easy to break the speculative boom, yet too tight to promote healthy economic growth."[19] These comments suggest that the downturn in 1929 was due to a prior monetary restriction.

Yet no explicit statement that the previous decline in the stock of money caused the downturn in production and prices is to be found. The analysis of the money stock in the 1920s appears in a separate chapter of the *Monetary History* without explicit connection with the Depression and it was not included in the separate publication of Chapter 7. In Chapter 7 itself, the only reference to the previous monetary events also lacks a causal statement: "As noted in the previous chapter, no other contraction before or since has been preceded by such a long period over which the money stock failed to rise."[20] Friedman and Schwartz did not say whether this was a historical curiosity or a cause of the initial downturn. Since they referred in their discussion of the stock-market crash to "the underlying forces making for a severe contraction in economic activity," without further specification, the reader takes away the impression that it was merely a curiosity.[21]

In any case, the stock-market crash "helped to deepen the contraction," and this pressure was "strongly reinforced" by a decline in the stock of money. Whatever the effects of the decline in the stock of money before the stock-market crash, the decline in the stock of money after the crash exerted a "downward pressure on income."[22] As we have just seen, Friedman and Schwartz held the Fed responsible for the decline in the stock of money after the crash, but they did not

19. Ibid, pp. 241–42, 290–91, 297–98.
20. Ibid., p. 299.
21. Ibid., p. 306.
22. Ibid., pp. 306–07.

ask whether it was a fall in the demand for money that made more vigorous action by the Fed desirable. The fall in income may have decreased the demand for money, leading to lower interest rates and therefore smaller borrowing from the Fed. In other words, the decline in the stock of money may have been a result of the fall in income.

The account of the first banking crisis in late 1930 details its effects on the banking system, but notes that it "left no clear imprint on the broad economic indicators shown in Chart 28 [personal income, industrial production, and the wholesale price index]." In fact, industrial production and personal income reversed their downward trends briefly in early 1931 and began to rise. Friedman and Schwartz said these movements "have many of the earmarks of the bottom of a cycle and the beginning of revival." [23] There is no suggestion that the first banking crisis had any harmful effect on income at all. Yet the presumed effects of this banking crisis on the supply of money and on the level of income lie at the heart of Friedman and Schwartz's story.

A new banking crisis started in March 1931, and "a month or two later, a renewed decline started in economic activity in general." [24] It is clear that Friedman and Schwartz wanted to suggest that the second banking crisis caused the renewed decline in economic activity. But there is no explicit statement to that effect. No cause for the abortive revival in 1931 was given, and the causes of the revival's failure could have been related to its unspecified causes. No argument one way or the other is given.

Britain's decision to abandon the gold standard in September 1931 produced major changes in financial variables within the United States. Yet, stated Friedman and Schwartz, "The broader economic indicators in Chart 28 show little effect of the financial developments that followed Britain's departure from gold." [25] The effects of the changes in the monetary sector on income and production, if any, do not seem to be apparent in the indicators Friedman and Schwartz used for the economy in general.

In sharp contrast to their treatment of income and production, Friedman and Schwartz discussed the effects of the banking crises on interest rates at several points. In these discussions, changes in interest rates are spoken of repeatedly as the "effects" of the banking crises.

23. Ibid., pp. 303, 308–11.
24. Ibid., p. 313.
25. Ibid., p. 322.

Similarly, the "effects" of the Fed's open-market purchases in 1932 on interest rates are described.[26] These discussions abound in causal statements. The absence of causal statements in the discussions of income and production therefore cannot be attributed to an excessive delicacy about causal statements in general. Amid many other strong arguments, the argument that changes in the stock of money caused changes in production and income appears to be missing.

This lacuna is confronted directly only in the discussion of the open-market purchases of 1932. An improvement in the general economic indicators in the summer of 1932 followed the start of these purchases. Friedman and Schwartz argued that the improvement in the economic indicators could not have initiated the open-market purchases; the Fed did that. Rejecting the possibility that the purchases and the economic improvement were unrelated to each other, they concluded, "The timing relations, previous experience, and general considerations all make it highly plausible that the economic improvement reflected the influence of the monetary improvement." [27]

This is a very cautious conclusion indeed, and the three subjects of this statement are rather vague. Yet, even if the conclusion is accepted as firmly established, it must be appreciated how special it is. No one disputes that the Fed has the power to undertake open-market operations. And most people agree that these actions have effects on the economy. But very few of the monetary changes in the early 1930s were the results of conscious decisions to undertake open-market operations. Friedman and Schwartz argued that the decline in the stock of money in 1930 was the result of a fall in discounts at the Fed in response to a fall in market rates not fully duplicated by the discount rate, and that the fall in 1931 was due to a decline in the two deposit ratios produced by the banking crises. These events are not the same as open-market purchases.

The parallel between open-market operations and a fall in market interest rates or banking crises is hardly exact. To show that the Fed could exert an independent influence on the stock of money and that it did exert such an influence in the summer of 1932 to some small degree does not imply that all changes in the stock of money were the results of actions by the Federal Reserve. This single example leaves open the general question of whether the decline in the stock of money

26. Ibid., pp. 312, 315, 323.
27. Ibid., p. 324.

caused the decline in income or whether the causation ran the other way. And as the discussion here has shown, Friedman and Schwartz's analysis of events other than the open-market purchases of 1932 carefully avoids direct statements on this issue.

Two additional examples may be given to show how pervasive this ambiguity is. First, the recovery in 1932 was again aborted. Friedman and Schwartz commented, "Once again, banking difficulties were a notable feature of the relapse." But were they cause or effect? Friedman and Schwartz asked explicitly about the causes of the relapse. They attributed it to the weak capital position of banks, the presidential election campaign of 1932, uncertainty about the incoming administration after the election, and general uncertainty about the economy.[28] One can read this description to mean that these factors caused a banking crisis which caused a renewed decline in the economy as a whole through its effect on the stock of money. But one can also read it to mean that the last three factors produced a renewed decline in the economy by themselves and that this decline, coupled with the weakness of banks, led to the banking crisis. Friedman and Schwartz did not say in their narrative which story they preferred.

Second, a comparison with Canada later in the chapter illuminates the treatment of monetary changes. Friedman and Schwartz introduced Canada into the discussion in order to make the point that the banking crises by themselves were unimportant: Their effect on the stock of money was what mattered. Canada offers a good contrast to the United States because income and the stock of money both fell sharply in Canada, but there were no banking crises. Why then did the stock of money fall? According to Friedman and Schwartz, "Because Canada kept its exchange rate with the United States fixed until Britain left the gold standard in September 1931 and then maintained its exchange rate at a new level involving a smaller depreciation than that undergone by the pound sterling, *its internal level of income and its stock of money had to adjust* to maintain external equilibrium."[29] The level of income and the stock of money apparently were jointly determined by the requirements of Canada's balance of payments. As with all other arguments in Friedman and Schwartz's narrative, save their discussion of the open-market purchases of 1932, the relationship between money and income is left ambiguous.

28. Ibid., pp. 324, 330–32.
29. Ibid., p. 352, emphasis added.

This ambiguity, it must be remembered, lies at the center of their argument. Friedman and Schwartz noted in the article published contemporaneously with the *Monetary History* that there was a strong historical correlation between changes in the level of income and changes in the size of the stock of money. They then said there were three possible explanations of this correlation. It could have been a coincidence, changes in the level of income could have determined changes in the stock of money, or changes in the stock of money could have determined changes in the level of income. The first possibility was rejected out of hand. And the second was rejected because the third could be accepted. It was accepted on the basis of an abbreviated narrative showing that changes in the stock of money were not the results of changes in the level of income.[30]

The *Monetary History* can be seen as providing the details of this argument. The purpose of the narrative, therefore, was primarily to show that the determinants of the stock of money were independent of the level of income. It attempted to do this by looking exclusively at the supply of money. But, as was argued earlier, this procedure is satisfactory only under special assumptions. The comments about income and production in the narrative seem to be designed to give indirect support to these assumptions without stating them directly. As a result, there is nothing in the narrative in Chapter 7 of the *Monetary History* to refute the following story: Income and production fell from 1929 to 1933 for nonmonetary reasons. Since the demand for money is a function of income, the demand for money fell also. To equilibrate the money market, either interest rates, the stock of money, or both, had to fall. And since the supply of money was partly a function of the interest rate, this movement down along the supply curve of money meant a decrease in both. In the absence of banking crises, the decline in the stock of money would have been "caused" primarily by a fall in the deposit-reserve ratio. In the presence of banking panics, the deposit-currency ratio fell too.

In this story, the banking panics acted to lower the deposit-currency ratio. But the decline in this ratio was not complementary to the decline in the deposit-reserve ratio; it was a substitute for it. The argument in Chapter 7 of the *Monetary History* implies that the deposit-reserve ratio would have fallen less than it did in the absence of the banking crises. This story implies that it would have fallen more.

30. Friedman and Schwartz, 1963b.

Given the almost complete indifference to income determination in Friedman and Schwartz's description of the Depression, their narrative does not indicate which story is preferable.

The third strand of Friedman and Schwartz's discussion—their counterfactual arguments—needs to be seen in light of this unresolved choice. Friedman and Schwartz assumed that the stock of money was determined exclusively by its supply, and conducted their counterfactual thought experiments on the basis of this assumption. These thought experiments, therefore, do not and cannot add more support to this assumption.

This can be seen clearly in those counterfactual statements that deal with the relationship between monetary and nonmonetary events. For example, Friedman and Schwartz stated at the outset of their discussion, "Had a decline in the stock of money been avoided, velocity also would probably have declined less and thus would have reinforced money in moderating the decline in income." Speaking of the abortive recovery of 1931, they said, "Perhaps if those tentative stirrings of revival had been reinforced by a vigorous expansion in the stock of money, they could have been converted into sustained recovery." [31] These brief statements exhaust the counterfactual assertions about the impact of monetary changes on the economy in general. The other counterfactuals refer only to the stock of money, making at best tangential references to the rest of the economy. These statements clearly are based on the assumption that a change in the stock of money would change the level of income. But they just as clearly do not constitute evidence in favor of such a proposition.

Other counterfactual assertions in the course of the narrative deal only with the stock of money. The relative constancy of the deposit-reserve ratio during the first three-quarters of 1930 is taken as evidence that "additional reserves would almost certainly have been put to use promptly." [32] But this, of course, is a *non sequitur*. The constancy of the deposit-reserve ratio shows that the events of 1931 as they actually happened did not lead banks to accumulate excess reserves. It is impossible to tell from this observation whether or not different events would have sufficiently changed the incentives to make them desire excess reserves. If the demand for money, for example, was interest-

31. This assertion is repeated later in slightly different terms. Friedman and Schwartz, 1963a, pp. 303–05, 313, 343.

32. Ibid., p. 341.

inelastic and falling very rapidly at more or less the same rate as the actual rate of decline of bank reserves, then a slower fall in bank reserves might well have resulted in a rise in excess reserves.

Similarly, Friedman and Schwartz inferred from the fact that bank deposits fell in the months following Britain's abandonment of the gold standard by fourteen times as much as bank reserves, that "the provision of $400 million of additional high-powered money to meet the currency drain without a decline in bank reserves could have prevented a decline of nearly $6 billion in deposits." [33] If the actual decline in deposits had come about, however, because of a decline in the demand for money rather than because banks called in or refused to renew loans in order to keep their deposits and reserves in balance, then this conclusion would not follow. Only if the demand for money acted to determine the level of income and not the stock of money will this conclusion be valid.

Near the close of their exposition, Friedman and Schwartz gave sustained attention to three alternative policies they said could have been adopted by the Fed. They considered open-market purchases of $1 billion each in three periods: the first part of 1930, the first part of 1931, and the period following Britain's abandonment of the gold standard. These periods were the subjects of the counterfactual statements made during the narrative cited just above. The discussions made in the course of the narrative therefore were collected together and expanded in this section.[34]

The descriptions of the effects of the policies recommended by Friedman and Schwartz are confined almost entirely to the effects on the stock of money. And these effects were calculated solely by reference to equation (1), that is, by reference to the supply of money. The implicit assumption is that the stock of money was determined by supply considerations alone. If it was determined also by demand considerations, then the hypothetical paths described by Friedman and Schwartz are invalid. The calculations in these pages are the results of assuming that supply conditions alone matter; they do not provide additional evidence for this proposition.

Characteristically, the effects of the alternative policies on nonmonetary variables are listed only tangetially and tentatively. They intrude on the discussion only because the problem of international gold

33. Ibid., p. 346.
34. Ibid., pp. 391–99.

flows cannot be treated without some discussion of the economy as a whole. So one finds the following statement in the analysis of 1930: "The change in the monetary situation might have affected the gold movement, reducing the gold inflow or even converting it into a gold outflow." The mechanism by which it might have done this is given also: "Only if the change in the monetary climate had lessened the severity of the economic contraction and made the capital markets easier, would it have affected gold flows." These conditional statements were replaced by a stronger one in the discussion of 1931: "Again, the change *would have produced* a reduction in the inflow of gold and might have converted it into an outflow with a resulting easing of the financial difficulties in Europe." [35] No reason for the contrast between 1930 and 1931 is given. And no evidence is given that a change in the monetary climate would have had an impact on the economic contraction. These statements are not an argument that it would have; they are the results of assuming that it would have.

Friedman and Schwartz's history of the Great Contraction therefore is a description of the supply of money during the contraction. It is accompanied by statements based on the assumption that the supply of money determined the stock of money without reference to the demand and, further, that movements in the stock of money determined the level of income. The latter assumption figures much less strongly in the narrative than the former and plays a far less important role in the formulation of the counterfactual thought experiements.

Friedman and Schwartz's main conclusions are that the level of income fell as sharply as it did in the early 1930s because of a massive fall in the stock of money. This stock in turn fell primarily because of the sustained effects of multiple banking crises, that is, because of a restriction in the supply of money. But an account of the supply of money cannot be taken for an account of the stock of money unless it is known that demand plays no role. The *Monetary History* appears to have been designed to show just this—but it turns out to be a narrative based on such an assumption, not an argument for it. Friedman and Schwartz referred elsewhere to the *Monetary History* to show that the stock of money was historically determined independently of income and that the correlation between money and income therefore must be interpreted to mean that movements in the stock of money determine

35. Ibid., pp. 393–95, emphasis added.

movements of income.[36] The *Monetary History,* however, does not provide independent evidence for this proposition. It follows that the hypothesis about the cause of the Depression must be regarded as unproven as well.

The Spending Hypothesis: Econometric Studies

The view of the Depression espoused by Friedman and Schwartz had been a minority view among economists at least since the Second World War. Running through almost all postwar theoretical exercises and textbook explanations of the Depression—or more commonly, of depressions in general—is the belief in some version of the spending hypothesis. But, despite the volume of extensive theoretical elaboration and repetition of this idea, there have been comparatively few studies attempting to show that it explains the Depression of the 1930s.

Keynes gave what may be the first expression of the spending hypothesis. In the *Treatise on Money* he said, "The boom of 1928–29 and the slump of 1929–30 in the United States correspond respectively to an excess and deficiency of investment." Looking for the cause of this change from excess to deficiency, he continued, "I attribute the slump of 1930 primarily to the deterrent effects on investment of the long period of dear money which preceded the stock-market collapse and only secondarily to the collapse itself. But the collapse having occurred, it greatly aggravated matters, especially in the United States, by causing a disinvestment in working capital." [37]

Subsequent writers adopted Keynes's framework of thought without attributing the same importance to the level of interest rates. Keynes himself presented a modified position in *The General Theory* when he said that the marginal efficiency of capital, as he then termed it, fell because of the large previous investment.[38] This is the form in which the spending hypothesis has received support from later investigators, although the stock-market crash reappears in some studies as an explanatory factor in the Depression. The first serious studies of the Depression to embody the Keynesian point of view were done by Han-

36. Friedman and Schwartz, 1963b; Friedman, 1968. See the quotations from these sources at the start of this discussion.

37. Keynes, 1930, vol. 2, pp. 194, 196.

38. Keynes, 1936, p. 323.

sen and Wilson at the start of the 1940s.[39] Their conclusion, in Wilson's words, was that "The collapse [of income] occurred only because the development of underconsumption was accompanied by a declining demand for houses and a serious exhaustion of investment opportunities." [40]

With the exception of the archaic term, *underconsumption,* this sentence ably summarizes most of the succeeding empirical literature on the spending hypothesis. The hypothesis has been stated in several different ways, but an emphasis on the decline in housing expenditures or in investment opportunities in general or in both identified a proponent of the spending hypothesis. (The concept of *underconsumption* has been abandoned in modern discussions of macroeconomics, although the idea that consumption was depressed before the onset of the Depression by an unfavorable distribution of income occasionally reappears. A glance at Table 1, above, however, shows that the ratio of consumption to national income was not falling in the 1920s. An underconsumptionist view of the 1920s therefore is untenable.) [41]

The informal approach used by Hansen and Wilson was extended by Gordon in a series of studies published approximately a decade later.[42] His work contains what is probably the most comprehensive statement of the spending hypothesis, giving due allowance for a variety of factors, but concentrating on housing and the exhaustion of investment opportunities. A paragraph from a recent restatement of his position will show the direction his elaborations took:

> It is possible to find in the situation prevailing in 1929 important elements of weakness that were sufficient to create a depression more severe than that of 1924 or 1927. It is clear that the rise in output of durable goods in 1928–1929 was too rapid to be long maintained. Excess capacity was developing in a number of lines, and this meant a decline in demand for capital goods. As a matter of fact new orders for some types of durable goods declined fairly early in 1929. The automobile market was clearly oversold; in addition, the industry's capacity exceeded even the peak production of 1929. The tire industry had been overbuilt, and the tire production had fallen sharply in the latter part

39. Hansen, 1941, Chapters 1, 2; Wilson, 1942.

40. Ibid., p. 156.

41. For a recent statement of the underconsumptionist view, see Schlesinger, 1964, pp. 159–60. For an analysis of the distribution of income in the 1920s, but not the presumed connection to consumption, see Keller, 1973. The behavior of consumption during the opening stages of the Depression will be considered in Chapter III.

42. Gordon, 1949, 1951, 1955, 1956.

of 1928. The textile industries had been suffering from overcapacity for some time. Residential construction had been declining sharply since the beginning of 1928, and an overbuilt situation obviously existed in that area. Some of these developments may be described as a result of the belated and rough working of the acceleration principle, although it should be emphasized that we can trace no simple correlation between the short-term changes in the rate of increase in output and the demand for capital goods.[43]

Writing at about the same time as Hansen and Wilson, Schumpeter embedded his views in such a complex overlay of repetitious cycles that a brief summary of his views is impossible. His contribution to the succeeding literature has consisted largely of a single metaphor: Although consumers and producers made plans in 1930 on the basis of the solid footing provided by the functioning economic system, the ground gave way under their feet.[44]

Klein's first econometric models also date from the end of the 1940s, and subsequent work on the spending hypothesis has stayed largely within the veins explored by Klein.[45] Despite the appearance of several summary statements of the spending hypothesis,[46] there have been few empirical studies that strayed from the path of the econometricians. And two recent studies that have eschewed the use of aggregate econometric models still based their conclusions on the results of estimating consumption and investment functions.[47]

The recent literature on the spending hypothesis therefore consists almost exclusively of econometric work.[48] But, for reasons that will emerge shortly, this methodology does not lead toward a comparison of the spending and money hypotheses. Instead, in parallel with the procedure adopted by Friedman and Schwartz, it assumes the validity of the spending hypothesis and leads toward the construction of a story

43. Gordon, 1974, pp. 43–44.

44. Schumpeter, 1939, vol. 2, pp. 794, 911. See Kindleberger, 1973, p. 137.

45. See below.

46. Burck and Silberman, 1955; Duesenberry, 1958; Galbraith, 1955; Chandler, 1970.

47. Dorfman, 1967; Green, 1971. Only the consumption function was estimated (by Dorfman). Green relied upon Dorfman's consumption function and Klein's investment function. See Chapter III for a discussion of the consumption function in this period.

48. Kindleberger did not use econometric techniques in his recent analysis of the world Depression. Nevertheless, he accepted the spending hypothesis in his discussion of events in the United States. See Kindleberger, 1973, p. 117, and his frequent jibes at Friedman and Schwartz.

on that basis.[49] Since monetary data are available on a daily or weekly basis, Friedman and Schwartz decomposed their story chronologically. In the absence of such detailed temporal breakdowns of data on consumption, investment, and similar quantities, proponents of the spending hypothesis have decomposed their story along analytical and formal lines.

Even though the econometric studies assume the validity of the spending hypothesis, the results of estimating these models do not provide an overwhelming case in favor of this view. This may reflect in part the shortcomings of the specific models that have been estimated, but it also suggests that the formulation and estimation of econometric models may not be the best way to approach the Depression. Since almost all the variables in which one might be interested rose in the 1920s and fell in the 1930s, there is very little diversity of movement among them. Consequently, the time series do not contain the kind of information needed to choose between alternative hypotheses. It is at once too easy to show that a model is consistent with the data and too hard to use the data to reject hypotheses.[50] The important contribution of the econometric models lies in their specification, and the rigors of specifying an aggregate econometric model have restricted the econometricians to the causative factors listed by Keynes, Wilson, and Gordon.

The limitations of the econometric literature can be seen clearly in the seminal econometric models of Klein. Even though they were written in the late 1940s, they are not the earliest econometric models to deal with the Depression—being antedated most notably by Tinbergen's classic work—but they, more than Tinbergen's, set the tone of succeeding econometric models, and they typify both the strengths and weaknesses of later models.[51]

An econometric model is a series of equations representing the interrelationships between economic variables. The equations are specified by the analyst, and then the magnitudes of the coefficients in the different equations are estimated from the data. Two types of variables in an econometric model may be distinguished. Some variables are

49. Dorfman utilized the *IS-LM* framework to attempt such a test, but detailed discussion of her procedure must await full publication of her study. See Dorfman, 1968.

50. See Tables 1 through 3 and the discussion of the econometric model of the money market later in this chapter.

51. See below for a description of Tinbergen's model.

considered to be determined within the model, that is, by the other variables of the model. These are the variables whose movements are "explained" by the model. The level of income will be such a variable in any model describing the economy in the Depression. In the language of econometricians, it will be an endogenous variable.

Clearly, not all variables can be explained within the model; there must be something in the model that explains their movements. Variables that are not determined within the model are either exogenous or predetermined. Exogenous variables are those that are determined outside the model in question; predetermined variables are past observations of variables which may have been determined within the model in the past, but cannot be altered by an current movements. The endogenous variables, therefore, may be spoken of as functions of the exogenous and predetermined variables as long as we remember that these functions may be very complex in large econometric models. In particular, the functions may involve dynamic behavior that lasts over long periods of time. Both the range of exogenous and predetermined variables and the nature of the dynamic behavior allowed by the model affect the view of the Depression expressed by any econometric model.

Klein presented a sequence of econometric models in his 1950 book on interwar economic fluctuations. The first of these models, Model I, was characterized as "a simple three-equation model." [52] It was purely real (that is, neither money nor prices entered the model), highly aggregative, and designed to be only a first approximation to a complex reality. The three equations referred to are as follows:

The first equation states that consumption (C) is a function of private and government wages (W_1 and W_2, respectively), profits (Π), and an error term (u_1).

$$C = a_0 + a_1(W_1 + W_2) + a_2\Pi + u_1 \tag{2}$$

The second equation states that investment (I) is a function of current and lagged profits, the lagged capital stock (K_{-1}), and an error term (u_2).

$$I = b_0 + b_1\Pi + b_2\Pi_{-1} + b_3K_{-1} + u_2 \tag{3}$$

The third equation states that private wages are a function of current

52. L. Klein, 1950, p. 58.

and lagged income (Y) adjusted for the difference between taxes (T) and government wages, a time trend (t), and an error term (u_3).

$$W_1 = c_0 + c_1(Y + T - W_2) + c_2(Y + T - W_2)_{-1} + c_3 t + u_3 \qquad (4)$$

These are the only behavioral equations, but three definitional equations are needed to close the system. The first two relate income to consumption and investment on the one hand and to wages and profits on the other. They reflect the expenditure and income sides of the national income accounts.

$$Y + T = C + I + G \qquad (5)$$

$$Y = W_1 + W_2 + \Pi \qquad (6)$$

The last one identifies investment as the change in the capital stock.

$$\Delta K = I \qquad (7)$$

The completed system, therefore, has six equations. Being linear, it can then determine the value of six endogenous variables. The first three of these endogenous variables clearly are the left-hand variables in equations (2) through (4). The other three can be identified by a simple rearrangement of the definitional equations.

$$Y = C + I + G - T \qquad (5')$$

$$\Pi = Y - (W_1 + W_2) \qquad (6')$$

$$K = K_{-1} + I \qquad (7')$$

Income and the capital stock are determined as the obvious sum of other endogenous variables. The level of profits is found as a residual after wages have been deducted from income.

All the other variables in these equations therefore must be either exogenous or predetermined variables. The former group consists of government wages (W_2), taxes (T), and the time trend (t). The latter group contains lagged profits, the lagged capital stock, and lagged adjusted income.

All of the endogenous variables declined in the early 1930s. An econometric model like this one advances our understanding of this pervasive movement if it leads us to see changes in the economy that lie behind it. It makes sense therefore to work backward through the model. The values of the endogenous variables are determined within the model. For the values of these variables to have changed, something else within the model must also have changed. The question, then, is what else changed?

The most obvious possibility is that an exogenous variable changed. The exogenous variables in this model, however, consist only of a time trend and two variables reflecting government finance. Since the time trend could not have changed to produce the Depression, the only possibility is that the government started the Depression by raising taxes or dismissing government employees. These actions could start a depression, and actions like these have been blamed for many depressions, but no one alleges that the government did either of these things in 1929. Yet there are no other possible exogenous changes within this model.

This curious result betrays the origin of Klein's Model I. It was derived from a simple Keynesian income-determination model like those appearing in most macroeconomics textbooks. These models are designed to show the effects of government policies, and variables reflecting those policies are the only exogenous variables included. Klein took such a model and showed that it could be used to describe the world. This, of course, was a notable achievement. But in a book about economic fluctuations, the presumption is that the models will inform the reader about the causes of such fluctuations. Unhappily, the only possible cause of the Depression coming from a change in an exogenous variable in Model I is the government.

Looking for exogenous variables is not the only way to use an econometric model. The movements of the endogenous variables may not have been due to unusual movements of the exogenous variables, but rather to the dynamics of the system itself. If a system generates cyclical behavior without external pressure, then the movements of the exogenous variables may not be important.

Klein's Model I is a very simple model. It contains only first-order lags, and it does not have too many of these. Yet it has the capacity to generate cyclical behavior. The multiplication of variables increases the complexity of the possible dynamic behavior in exactly the same way as increasing the order of the lags. If one solves Model I for a difference equation in Y, for example, a third-order equation is found despite the absence of any lags longer than one period.

Klein found the general solution to this equation and verified that it did not produce cumulative divergences from equilibrium. The model therefore is not unstable in the sense of responding to any shock by setting off on a monotonically increasing or decreasing path. The model is also not "stable," however, in the sense that it approaches a stable value once it is disturbed. Instead it oscillates with very little damping.[53]

Klein did not analyze the cyclical characteristics of his model, apparently because he did not think they were important. Even though the model might have produced a depression through oscillations deriving from some distant shock, Klein did not assert that this was the explanation of the Depression.

There are good reasons for Klein's reticence. The model is highly schematic. Given the limitations of this very small-scale model, it would be dangerous to infer conclusions from its dynamic structure. In addition, the dynamics of this particular model do not appear to generate the proper movements. Simulating Klein's Model I for the interwar period, using historical values for the exogenous variables and values generated within the model for the lagged endogenous ones, does not produce anything that looks like the Depression. Simulated income reaches a trough in 1927–28, below which it never goes during the 1930s.[54]

This discussion poses a problem. If the Depression cannot be explained by movements of the exogenous variables in Model I and if it is not reproduced by simulating the dynamic behavior of the model, then how does the model describe the Depression? By a process of elimination, the Depression must show up in the model as a set of unusual error terms in equations (2) through (4). This, in fact, is the way it appears in Klein's estimation. But this finding does not help us to understand the Depression. It amounts to saying that the Depression was caused by factors not included in the model. It was the result of nonsystematic forces whose identity and quality have not been explored.

Model I evidently is too simple to be of much help in analyzing the causes of the Depression. Nevertheless, the analysis of this simple model exposes problems inherent in the use of econometric models to understand the Depression that remain problems when far more complex models are considered.

An econometric model can generate fluctuations in two ways. The

53. These statements are based on Klein's solution to the homogeneous equation. He did not obtain a complete solution to the total equation. L. Klein, 1950, p. 77.

54. Kempson, 1972.

exogenous variables can move perversely at the time of the fluctuations, or the dynamic characteristics of the model may cause the effects of changes in variables or parameters in early years to show up at a later date. The first alternative can only be as important as the specification of the model allows it to be. Variables must be selected and labeled exogenous or endogenous before any estimation can take place. At this point, the possible candidates for exogenous causes of the fluctuation have been determined. A simple check of the movements of these variables over time will show which ones have the potentiality to cause the movements of the endogenous variables. The resulting set of variables—while not empty in more complex models—typically is very small and very standard.

Klein's Model I, for example, is purely real. Changes in the supply of money could not have caused the Depression within this model because money does not even appear in this model. Klein's model shows how a simple version of the spending hypothesis can be quantified, but it does not test it in any serious fashion. No other explanation of the Depression is considered, and no choice is involved. Even though the model has serious drawbacks as a description of the economy, it was not evaluated relative to an alternative.

The dynamic characteristics of models are equally problematical. Unlike the set of exogenous variables with the "proper" time path, the class of dynamic behavior permitted by even the simplest econometric models is quite large. Given appropriate values of the parameters, various kinds of cycles could be generated by most models. But, for reasons that appear to be very complex, easily recognizable cyclical behavior does not seem to appear in the estimated forms of these models. And, even if it did, this evidence would not be used intensively. The view of business fluctuations that sees them as some form of deterministic oscillation has been abandoned by most economists. The models that generate these oscillations do not capture accurately the dynamic relations between the variables in them, and the resulting oscillations are no more than a curious artifact. The dynamic properties of econometric models, therefore, have been neglected, even when they might potentially furnish an explanation of fluctuations in economic activity.

Since these problems are general, they reappear in econometric models of the Depression that are more complex and more complete than Klein's Model I. These models are more extensive both in the range of possible exogenous causes they allow and in their dynamic behavior, but none of them provides a test of the money hypothesis.

For example, the third model in Klein's book, Model III, was described as "a large structural model." [55] It included over a dozen endogenous variables, including several types of investment, and it contained a monetary sector. How did this expansion increase the range of possible causes of the Depression?

The exogenous variables—of which there are many—can be placed into four groups. The first group consists of the governmental variables: revenues, expenditures, wages, taxes. As with Model I, movements of these variables could have caused the Depression, but did not. The second group consists of variables needed to close the model. They include farm construction variables, a time trend, and exports. Neither changes in farm construction nor the time trend caused the Depression, and they can be ignored. Exports fell sharply in the early 1930s. Inclusion of this variable therefore provides a way in which the world Depression could have intensified the Depression in the United States.

The third group of exogenous variables in Model III concerns nonfarm housing, that is, residential construction. The most important of these variables for our purposes is the number of new nonfarm families. This variable reached a peak in 1929 and fell to one-quarter of its 1929 value in 1932. The number of new families affects the demand for housing in an obvious way, and the decline in this variable provides another possible cause of the Depression.

The final group of exogenous variables contains only one: excess reserves. This is the only exogenous variable impinging on the monetary sector in this model. Its movements cannot help to explain the Depression because excess reserves increased in every year from 1926 to 1936.[56]

Model III therefore permits the investigation of many more hypotheses than did Model I. In particular, declines in two exogenous variables—exports and new nonfarm families—caused income to fall

55. L. Klein, 1950, p. 84.

56. L. Klein, 1950, p. 145. If the level of excess reserves in these years acted to increase the sensitivity of the model to certain events, then this variable would help to explain the Depression by showing how a given shock could have a greater effect on the economy in the late 1920s than at another time.

in the early 1930s. A third area—money—was introduced into the model, but not in a way that allowed its influence to be examined. The model acknowledges the existence of money; it does not permit it an important role in income determination. It cannot be used to compare the money and spending hypotheses.

More recent econometric models of the interwar period have followed in the directions indicated by Klein's Model III. Investment behavior has been scrutinized closely, either by decomposing it into its constituent parts or by finding a new aggregate description. And the monetary sector has been expanded to become a more detailed representation of that part of the economy. The treatment of exports, however, has languished. Instead of exports, most models include only net exports, that is, the trade balance. This variable moves far less than exports alone. And since imports fell in response to the fall in income in the 1930s, the influence of events outside the United States is understated.[57]

Any model containing a single equation for total investment will be dominated by that equation. With any reasonable consumption function, the large fall of investment will be translated into an even larger fall in income. The factors causing investment to decline will therefore appear as the primary determinants of the Depression. If investment is seen as insensitive to monetary conditions, for example, the movements of income in the early 1930s will be seen as substantially independent of changes in the financial sector. Thus it would not be much of an overstatement to say that the other equations of the model do not matter at all once the investment equation is specified.

In particular, the level of income in such a model will not be determined by the demand for money. Investment normally is taken to be function of interest rates and a variety of nonmonetary variables. And in all cases, the nonmonetary variables play much more important roles in the decline in investment than interest rates. This may reflect the course of history, but it may also reflect the choice of interest rates used to reflect monetary condtions. In every case, some approximation to a risk-free nominal interest rate has been used, and none of these

57. Of course, to the extent that the world Depression was the result of events within the United States, including exports as an exogenous variable would overstate the importance of events outside the United States.

approximations rose in the early 1930s in a manner that could explain the fall in investment.[58]

It can be argued that an interest rate of this sort is a poor indicator of monetary conditions. Some index of the risk-free interest rate plus a risk premium might be preferable. An index of the real interest rate might be appropriate. Some measure more closely related to the quantity of money might also be a possibility. It is hard to know what would be the results of using variables like these, but they could be quite different than the results actually found in the econometric models that have been estimated.[59]

If this substitution makes a difference, it will show how important the specification of the model and the choice of variables is. To a considerable degree, the results of estimating an aggregate econometric model of the interwar period can be predicted before the estimation. Econometricians to date have chosen specifications that do not permit the money hypothesis to be tested.

For example, in a recent model by Kirkwood, the investment equation was formulated in such a way that the level of stock-market prices is the only exogenous variable that could have caused a decline in investment through this equation.[60] The stock-market crash appears therefore as the cause of the Depression. To evaluate the validity of this inference, we must examine the behavior that is being described.

Kirkwood said that stock prices were a factor in investment decisions because equities were a source of capital for firms contemplating investment, but he discounted this connection because of the importance of other sources, both internal and external. Instead, he asserted, "Their central importance for investment decisions is as a barometer

58. In one extreme case, investment was taken to be exogenous! Monetary conditions obviously are not an important determinant of income in this model. See Morishima and Saito, 1964.

59. See Chapter III for a discussion of the risk premium; Chapter V, for a discussion of the real interest rate. The discussion of interest rates in Chapter IV concerns their short-run paths. The appropriate rate for the inquiry of Chapter IV need not be the one appropriate for an econometric model.

60. Kirkwood, 1972. The lagged capital stock and the interest rate on Aaa bonds also appear in this equation. Neither variable changed enough in the early 1930s to be an important cause of the fall in investments in those years. If other exogenous variables had caused income to fall through their effects on other equations, then they would have been exogenous determinants of the fall in investment through the effect of income on investment. Examination of the model as a whole, however, shows that stock prices were the most important exogenous determinant of investment.

of future business." [61] Stock prices fell, in other words, because expectations about the course of future business changed. People who had been optimistic before October 1929 suddenly became pessimistic. Stock prices fell as a result, causing investment and income to decline. *The Depression occurred because people expected it to occur!*

This is hardly an explanation of the Depression. Either the conclusion just articulated is empty—in the sense that the Depression is stated to have happened without any ascertainable cause—or else there must have been something happening to change people's expectations. But we are left completely in the dark as to what this unknown process might be. At its best, therefore, Kirkwood's model provides no candidates for the causes of the Depression.[62]

In addition, the fall in stock-market prices may not have been the result of changing expectations. That is, it may not have been caused by events other than the fall in income. For not only did the value of stocks fall, the earnings of the corporations they represented fell also. Price-earnings ratios did not fall at all. The logic of treating stock prices as an exogenous variable therefore may be questioned.

Data on stock prices and price-earnings ratios are presented in Table 4. The two sets of indexes differ for two reasons. First, of course, they represent different samples of firms. And it can be computed from the table that the earnings of the firms in the Cowles sample fell much more than the earnings of the firms in the Standard and Poor sample. Second, the Standard and Poor prices are for the end of the year, while the Cowles prices are yearly averages. The decline in the 1929 price shown in the Standard and Poor series therefore reflects events after the stock-market crash, not before.

Despite the enormous fall in stock-market prices documented in the top half of Table 4, the bottom half of the table shows that price-earnings ratios were stable or rising. The hypothesis that stock prices fell because firm earnings fell cannot be rejected on the basis of these data. And if this hypothesis is accepted, then stock prices can hardly be used as an exogenous variable or, a fortiori, as a cause of the Depression.

61. Ibid., p. 815.

62. An opposing view was presented by Green, 1971. He rejected the stock market as an important factor in the Depression because Klein's investment equation (equation [3], above) and a permanent-income consumption function were able to explain the data without using data on the stock market. On the relation between the stock market and consumption, see Chapter III.

To formalize this argument, the fall in stock prices could be decomposed by some rule into the part caused by the fall in earnings and the remainder. Only the latter part would be a true exogenous variable.[63] The movements of this variable clearly would depend on the way in which the decomposition was done. Table 4 shows one way. Assuming investors based plans on stock yields rather than earnings would give another. Or investors may have used some kind of average of past earnings to value stocks, refusing to make plans on the basis of

TABLE 4 • *Prices and Price-Earnings Ratios of Common Stocks, 1927–32*

Prices	1927	1928	1929	1930	1931	1932
Standard and Poor—Composite	17.66	24.35	21.45	15.34	8.12	6.89
Standard and Poor—Industrials	14.82	20.85	16.99	11.90	6.32	5.18
Cowles—Composite	118.3	149.9	190.3	149.8	94.7	48.6
Cowles—Industrials	118.5	154.3	189.4	140.6	87.4	46.5
Price-Earnings Ratios						
Standard and Poor—Composite	15.91	17.64	13.32	15.81	13.31	16.80
Standard and Poor—Industrials	15.77	17.38	13.07	15.66	13.74	16.71
Cowles—Composite	13.21	13.70	16.05	21.10	33.67	138.89
Cowles—Industrials	13.89	14.25	16.31	22.22	46.51	172.41

NOTE: Prices for the Standard and Poor series are for the end of the year, 1941–43 = 100. Prices for the Cowles series are averages of monthly figures, 1926 = 100. Earnings in both cases are annual.

SOURCES: Standard and Poor's, 1974, p. 131; Cowles, 1938, pp. 67, 69, 405.

the abnormally low earnings of the 1930s. If so, then the exogenous variable would have fallen, but the fall would have been smaller than the fall in prices alone. The path of this new variable over time therefore might or might not resemble the time path of stock prices. It might or might not have been correlated with the level of investment. In short, no evidence has been presented to show that changes within the stock market had an important effect on the economy.

To be sure, no evidence has been presented either way. The preceding discussion says that the data are consistent with the hypothesis

63. Cagan, 1971.

that the stock market decline was a result of the Depression, but it is also consistent with the reverse. If the stock-market crash had a depressing effect on consumption and the resulting reduction in demand reduced business profits, then we might not observe a fall in the price-earnings ratio. If this process worked slowly, there would be an initial decline in the price-earnings ratio followed by a rise as the price of stocks fell first and earnings fell later. But if the process worked quickly, no such dip in the price-earnings ratio would be observed.[64]

Some evidence will be presented in Chapter III to suggest that the level of stock-market prices did indeed affect the level of consumption. This link, unlike the link between stock prices and investment in Kirkwood's model, has a firm basis in the theory of consumption. Its presence supports the hypothesis that the declines in the stock market and in business activity interacted with each other, and it therefore is not correct to say either that the entire decline in spending was due to the stock market or that the entire fall in the stock market was due to the decline of business. Instead the initial fall in stock prices helped to depress business, and the overall decline in demand—from this and other sources—depressed earnings and prices still more.

An alternative approach to the treatment of investment in the interwar period follows Klein's lead and the practice now used in constructing large econometric models by decomposing investment into various categories and assuming that investment within each of these categories was determined by variables specific to it. The change from a single investment equation to several equations for the components of investment does not change the function of investment in an econometric model. If investment is determined by a variety of factors other than the supply of money, the level of income will be, too. Therefore, if a model is constructed in which the determinants of investment are taken to be risk-free nominal interest rates and various other variables specific to the type of investment being considered, it cannot test the money hypothesis. The causes of the Depression are sure to be found in the behavior of investment, not in the supply of money.

This approach was adopted in a recent model by Bolch and Pilgrim. The level of residential construction is an important determinant of income in their model. Of its determinants, only an occupancy

64. Data on prices are available daily, but earnings are only available by year. It therefore is not possible to test this hypothesis by looking at fine breakdowns of the data in order to spot this lag.

index, which is in part demographic, appears to be independent of the level of income. Bolch and Pilgrim subjected this variable to extensive analysis which showed that if no other exogenous variables had changed, the historical fall in this variable would have produced a fall in income almost as large as the actual fall. They concluded that their work "offers direct confirmation of the thesis that the residential construction cycle, which is directly associated with population, played a prominent role in the determination of the course of income during the 'twenties and 'thirties." [65]

This conclusion follows from the structure of their model. The occupancy index is said to be exogenous. It therefore has the capacity to determine the course of income. But if it was in fact not exogenous, that is, if it was determined by the level of income, then the conclusion of Bolch and Pilgrim does not follow. If the occupancy index was a function of the level of income, then the fall in income would be both a cause and a result of the change in this index. It would not make sense to discuss the one without the other; it would be more accurate to say that they were jointly determined by other forces.

This change has been made in a model by Hickman. His model of the housing sector is similar in structure to the model of Bolch and Pilgrim, but it contains an additional equation.[66] The new endogenous variable is the rate of family formation, which is a major determinant of changes in the occupancy index. The rate of family formation is said to be a function of various endogenous variables, of which the level of income is the most important, and a new exogenous variable called "standardized households" which converts the vector of demographic characteristics of the population into a single index.[67] The rate of family formation, then, is the result both of demographic changes—as shown by changes in the number of standardized households—and of economic changes—which show up primarily as changes in the level of income. Holding income constant in this model eliminates

65. Bolch and Pilgrim, 1973, p. 337. The occupancy index was the ratio of nonfarm families to nonfarm housing units.

66. B. Hickman, 1973. The model is even more similar to an elaboration of the housing sector of Bolch and Pilgrim's model in which rents are also explained. See Bolch, Fels, and McMahon, 1971.

67. The number of standardized households is the number of households that would have existed in a population of the actual size and age structure in any year if the number of households bore the same relationship to the size and age structure of the population that it did in 1940. Changes in this variable, therefore, record purely demographic changes.

most of the fall in construction in the 1930s by eliminating the observed fall in the rate of family formation in that decade.[68]

Bolch and Pilgrim said that the fall in construction investment caused the fall in income in the 1930s. Hickman asserted that the fall in income in the 1930s caused the fall in construction (by reducing the rate of family formation). These statements need not be inconsistent. We can interpret them as statements about the structural relations within the economic system. Together, they say that the movements of income and of construction were related. It was not possible for one to move without the other. Interpreted this way, of course, neither of these assertions tells us about the causes of the Depression in the sense of supplying exogenous variables whose movements determined the movements of income. In other words, neither of them identifies an external cause for the decline in income.

The monetary sector of recent models of the interwar economy shows much greater uniformity than investment. Klein's Model III had a single exogenous monetary variable: excess reserves. In later models of Klein's applied to this period, this model has been expanded to include an additional monetary variable: the discount rate.[69] These variables are the natural ones to include from Klein's point of view. Two of the traditional policy tools of the Federal Reserve, open-market operations and changes in the required reserve ratio, operate on the reserve position of banks. The third, changing the discount rate, operates directly on an interest rate. It is natural to provide a variable showing the effects of Fed policy on the reserve position of banks and the discount rate as exogenous variables. But if these are the only exogenous monetary variables, the monetary sector of the resulting models is restricted in the same way that Klein's entire Model I was restricted. There are no ways for monetary forces to cause a depression in these models except through actions by the Federal Reserve. Changes in the demand for money that affect the reserve position of banks are not shown in the model. Therefore, if the Fed caused the Depression by raising the discount rate in 1929, these models have the potential for showing that connection. But if the banking panics of 1930 and 1931 were the critical monetary events of these years, these models miss the important events. They will show up only as errors in the estimated equations.

68. B. Hickman, 1973, pp. 309–10.
69. L. Klein, 1966, pp. 227–53.

These models, consequently, can tell us whether monetary policy caused the Depression by raising the discount rate or by depriving banks of reserves. They cannot tell us whether monetary events in general caused the Depression. And to the extent that bank reserves are a function both of Fed policy and events in the economy, the use of reserves as a proxy for the Fed's actions will give a distorted picture of these actions.

Most other models have been designed in the same spirit as Klein's. Where additional exogenous variables have been added, they have not been in the monetary sector. The models typically include the discount rate and a variable giving the reserve position of banks, although it is more common to find free reserves than excess reserves in recent models. These variables affect the short-term interest rate, which then has a very damped effect on the long-term rate. The effects on the economy all come through the movements of this single long-term interest rate.[70] Any changes in the supply of money that come from factors apart from changes in excess reserves or the discount rate or that have effects communicated through channels other than the long-term interest rate (on relatively safe financial assets) will be ignored. If the banking panics had a "disastrous effect on confidence," for example, this would not appear in these econometric models.[71]

Many more connections between the real and monetary sectors of the economy have been recognized in theory and in econometric models designed to deal with the postwar period. The only model of the interwar period to approach the standards of theory and of recent large-scale model building is the first econometric model constructed for this period: Tinbergen's classic study, published in 1939. We cannot begin here to do justice to the complexity of Tinbergen's model, but some dimensions of the analysis in it can be suggested.

Tinbergen's model distinguishes between several different kinds of investment and is unique among the models of the interwar period in recognizing different costs of capital for different kinds of investment as well. There are separate costs of capital for business investment, residential housing, and inventory investment.[72]

70. See Kirkwood, 1972; Bolch and Pilgrim, 1973.

71. The phrase is Wilson's, 1942, p. 170.

72. This can be compared with the MPS model, which recognizes four separate costs of capital. There are two for business investment (plant and equipment), two for residential construction (single family and multifamily), but none for inventory investment. See de Leeuw and Gramlich, 1968.

In addition, monetary factors can affect consumption through the stock market. Nonfarm consumption is a function of income and capital gains from changes in the price of equities, and the price of equities is endogenous. It is a function of the dividend rate, the long-term interest rate, a time trend, and—sometimes—past capital gains. The last term becomes operative only when the rate of change of the price of equities exceeds an arbitrary threshold. It was above this threshold only in 1928 and 1929, and the last term in the function for share prices therefore introduced a factor into their determination for 1928–29 that was not present at other times. The gradual increase of dividends before 1929 and decrease after then was converted by use of this term into a dramatic rise and fall of stock prices. It is hard to distinguish this description of the stock market from one that simply assumes the boom and crash to have been exogenously determined and uses a dummy variable to explain the high prices in 1928 and 1929.

Despite all the attention given to monetary factors in Tinbergen's model, however, they did not turn out to be important in determining the course of the Depression. The influence of short-term interest rates was found to be very small. The influence of long-term rates was larger, but it was overshadowed by changes in profits and in the existing stock of housing. In general, the movements of the financial variables were not closely in touch with changes in real variables. The general impression given by the model is that the monetary sector was, in Tinbergen's term, "elastic." [73]

But it is hard to tell exactly what was important in causing the downturn of income. Consumption fell because wages, other income, and capital gains all fell, with the fall in wages having the largest effect. Business investment fell because profits fell and—to a lesser extent—because the yield on equities rose. Residential construction fell because the stock of housing four years previously was high. Inventories fell because sales fell. But wages, profits, and sales all fell because consumption and investment fell. The model is recursive, and there are few important exogenous variables. The two variables that seem critical are the acceleration effect of the stock market and the previous stock of houses. The fall in the stock market decreased consumption directly and investment indirectly by raising the yield on shares. The large existing stock of houses acted to depress construction after 1925. Tinbergen's model, for all the richness of its construc-

73. Tinbergen, 1939, pp. 128, 184.

tion and monetary sector, does not contain exogenous explanations of the causes of the Depression absent in simpler models. Its primary value appears to be negative—that is, in showing that a complex financial sector does not enhance the importance of monetary forces.[74]

The pursuit of exogenous variables whose movements can be said to have caused the Depression therefore must be judged unsuccessful at this time. The exogenous variables that have been proposed to fulfill such a role in econometric models either cannot be taken seriously as explanations of the Depression because their use is too arbitrary or they are better thought of as endogenous in a more completely specified model. And it is more likely that we are observing a general phenomenon rather than examples of bad workmanship. The aim of econometric model building has been and is to include as much complexity as possible within the model. Model builders try to take variables that have been treated as exogenous by others and provide explanations for their movements. Exogenous variables become endogenous ones as our models get more and more complete.

But as stated above, there are ways to view econometric models other than as guides to exogenous variables. These models all describe behavior over time, and there may be aspects of the dynamic behavior itself that will help us to understand the Depression.

The deterministic parts of all the econometric models of the interwar period—with the exception of Tinbergen's—have a very standard structure.[75] Like Klein's Model I, they are collections of linear equations, where the value of each variable depends on current and lagged values of other variables. A set of simultaneous difference equations can describe a wide variety of dynamic behavior, and these models, therefore, have the potential of describing a cyclical pattern that could fit the facts of the Depression. But the models in fact do not seem to follow paths of this sort in response to shocks imposed in sim-

74. The conclusion about the effect of the stock-market boom is not subject to the same objections as Kirkwood's, 1972, since stock prices are endogenously determined. The logic behind the term explaining high prices in 1928 and 1929, however, is not at all clear. And, as noted in the text, it leads to a formulation not too different than Kirkwood's.

75. Clark, 1949, constructed a model with a highly unusual and highly unstable inventory investment equation. The model as a whole is also unstable, but hardly descriptive of the historical process.

ulations. They tend to return rather quickly to a region around equilibrium, where they stay.[76]

It is hard to understand why the models behave this way, since solution of the underlying difference equations produces characteristic roots near one.[77] In other words, the models appear to describe cyclical behavior when viewed in the abstract, but the cycles do not show up when the models are simulated with approximations to historical data. This phenomenon is unexplained, and the authors of these models have not been interested in it. When they paid attention to dynamic behavior of their models at all, it was to show that the response to a shock is not explosive. The range of behavior of stable models has not been explored.[78]

It has not been explored because no serious student of economics believes that a deterministic model of the economy can be formulated that will capture accurately the dynamic interactions between the different parts of the economy. But many economists recognize that there are substantial lags and similar processes giving rise to autocorrelated behavior of time series. And it has been well known at least from the time of Slutsky's classic article that autocorrelated series exhibit behavior that appears to be cyclical.[79] They are not cyclical in the sense of reproducing repetitive oscillations, but they give the appearance of such behavior for periods covering a few oscillations. The use of the stock-adjustment model in some investigations suggests that there may have been lags in the system that produced autocorrelation in the variables and "cyclical" behavior as a result.[80] There also are other ways to introduce lags and autocorrelation into an economic model; lags can

76. Bolch and Pilgrim, 1973, p. 336, demonstrate this behavior for their model. It is likely that the other models of the interwar period behave similarly.

77. L. Klein, 1950, p. 77; Bolch and Pilgrim, 1973, pp. 336–37.

78. But see the analysis of dynamic aspects of postwar econometric models in B. Hickman, 1972.

79. Slutsky, 1937.

80. Bolch and Pilgrim, 1973, used this model to explain inventory investment; Mercer and Morgan, 1972, used it to ask whether "overcapacity" in automobile production could have caused or accentuated the Depression. Mercer and Morgan defined the market as "saturated" when the actual stock of cars exceeded the desired stock. The desired stock was assumed to be a function of economic variables: income and prices. It follows that market saturation is endogenous to the model. Either prices have to rise or income fall to cause the desired stock to fall below the actual. In the first case, we are observing an excess of demand or a restriction of supply; in the second, a result of the Depression. In neither case is the cause of the Depression illuminated.

be introduced into a variety of equations, and the presence of autocorrelation can be acknowledged without deriving it explicitly from assumed behavior.

There is a school of thought which maintains that these characteristics are basic to the operation of the economy. The cycles they produce are called "long swings" or "Kuznets cycles," and they are said to have an average duration of about twenty years. The interwar period therefore would have been the appropriate length to have a complete cycle, that is, an upswing followed by a downswing. A model of these swings has not been formulated, but the discussions involve precisely the interaction of economic and demographic forces and the stock-adjustment models that have been discussed here.[81]

To build these thoughts into an explanation of the Depression would require two things. First, the existence of the appropriate lags in the economy would need to be demonstrated. Everyone recognizes that there is substantial autocorrelation in economic time series. But there is no standard by which to evaluate this autocorrelation in order to say if it was strong enough to cause the appearance of a large cycle in income. Given the econometric problems present in the estimation of lag structures, the usefulness of econometric models in the investigation of this approach may be questioned.[82] Second, the nature of the shocks that caused the economy to diverge from a smooth path needs to be elucidated. The theory of long swings does not trace the swings back to specific shocks. The fluctuations are thought to be the results of the cumulated impact of myriad small shocks, by their nature invisible to the economic historian. This approach, while a possible one, does not seem appropriate to the interwar period, where the question is why the fluctuations were so much more severe than they have been before or since. Even though a specific shock may not have been needed to generate such a large swing, the presumption is that there was in fact such a shock. The only event that can be interpreted as such a shock is the First World War, and this theory ultimately sees the Depression as a delayed response to the war.[83] The two parts of the explanation then boil down to an explanation of how an admittedly large shock to the economy could generate a downturn a decade later.

81. Easterlin, 1968, part I. See also the earlier discussion of long cycles in Schumpeter, 1939, vol. 1.

82. Griliches, 1961; Jorgenson, 1971.

83. Duesenberry, 1958; Kindleberger, 1973.

Econometric models, to summarize this discussion, have not been and cannot be expected to be useful in pinpointing exogenous variables whose movements can be called the causes of the Depression. Explicit government policy does not seem to have precipitated the Depression according to the existing models, and the trend is toward making the other important variables endogenous to the model. If a new exogenous variable was proposed as the cause of the Depression, the impulse of econometric model builders would be to make it endogenous.

In addition, while the models demonstrate the importance of lags in shaping the reaction of the economy to events, the econometric models of the economy do not appear to have interesting dynamic characteristics. This, no doubt, reflects the interests of the model builders and is at least potentially avoidable. But in view of the evident difficulty of testing the validity of complicated lag structures, it may be doubted whether econometric models of the economy will prove useful in the exploration of dynamic behavior in the interwar years.

Despite these drawbacks, the econometric models of the interwar period embody the most precise descriptions of the various forms of the spending hypothesis, that is, they pinpoint most clearly the falls in autonomous spending that are thought to have caused the Depression. As noted above, none of these models can be considered to have proved its point, in the sense of showing that the view of the Depression embodied in it is superior to the alternatives. They should be seen instead as analogues of Friedman and Schwartz's history. Instead of testing their hypothesis, they state it and show that it is consistent with some selection of data. Just as Friedman and Schwartz assumed that the stock of money was determined solely by the supply, so these models assumed that investment and hence the level of income was not affected by the banking panics. The important job of testing these assumptions has not been done.

Bank Failures in a Model of the Money Market

The effects of the banking crises, according to Friedman and Schwartz, operated through their effect on the supply of money. As a result of the increased probability of a run on banks, banks tried to increase their reserve ratios and individuals tried to increase the proportion of currency in their cash balances. These changes in preferences decreased the supply of money in two ways. As individuals withdrew currency from banks, it ceased being available for bank reserves. And each dollar of bank reserves gave rise to fewer dollars of bank deposits as banks raised their reserve ratios (see equation [1]).

But, as Friedman and Schwartz noted, bank failures and the risk of more bank failures could have had an effect on the demand for money also. As deposits became riskier assets, and people tried to reduce the amount of bank deposits they held, they might have bought other assets for them instead of or in addition to currency. To the extent that they bought other assets, like U.S. government securities or diamonds, they were reducing their total cash balances—as opposed to simply changing their composition. We do not know what people bought when they "sold" bank deposits, and the possibility that the bank failures reduced the demand for money cannot be dismissed.[84]

In order for the banking crises to have had the effects attributed to them by Friedman and Schwartz, therefore, two conditions must have been fulfilled. The bank failures must have decreased the supply of money. And they must have decreased it more than they decreased the demand for money. The general problem of which curve shifted more—the supply or the demand for money—in the early 1930s clearly is an identification problem. As such, it should be amenable to the wide range of techniques developed by econometricians for just such purposes.[85] But, as we have seen, the specification of the demand and supply curves for money involve issues central to the explanation of the entire Great Depression, and they cannot be treated in isolation.

The arguments of the preceding pages may be gathered together here to demonstrate this point. According to Friedman and Schwartz, the supply of money was determined by the forces underlying equation (1). The demand function for money was not out of the ordinary, but since the stock of money was fixed by the supply, the direction of causation ran from the stock of money to its determinants on the demand side rather than the other way around. The determinants of the

84. The effect of bank failures on the demand for money was discussed by Friedman and Schwartz, 1963a, pp. 352–53, and estimated statistically from cross-section data by Gandolfi, 1974.

85. See Fisher, 1966.

demand for money therefore were endogenously determined within the money market. Since the level of income was an important—if not the sole—determinant of money demand, it was determined in this fashion.

The alternative view of the money market seen in econometric models of the Depression views the interest rate as the price of money. This market then cleared in the same way that other markets did. There was a supply curve and a demand curve, and the price moved to bring the market to their intersection. The level of income was not determined in this process. The level of income was one of the determinants of the demand for money, but it was not determined directly by the stock of money. In this view, the price established in this market—the interest rate—was an important determinant of the level of income, but the relation between the stock of money and the level of income was indirect. In a model of the money market alone, therefore, the level of income could be taken as exogenous.

It would be preferable, of course, to have a larger model, in which the level of income and perhaps also the rate of bank failures were endogenously determined. In such a model, it might turn out that the nonmonetary determinants of income were very weak and that the interest rate did not or could not equilibrate the money market. The level of income then might be determined within the money market. Alternatively, the direction could go the other way through an endogenously determined bank failure rate. Use of an aggregate econometric model thus offers hope that the different views of the money market can be directly compared.

But, as we have seen, the specification of such a model involves many choices and typically prejudges the important questions at issue. For example, the use of an investment equation which sees investments as determined by a variety of forces extraneous to the money market and a few interest rates clearly is inconsistent with the formulation of Friedman and Schwartz. The level of income cannot have been determined by the stock of money if important components of income (like consumption and investment) were determined by factors outside this market. And the use of a single interest rate or a small collection of interest rates to connect the money market with the volume of investment assumes that the markets were not connected by more diverse and complex paths. The specification of the model determines which view the results will illustrate.

For this reason, the identification problem will be approached in Chapter IV by noneconometric means. By examining the mechanism by which a change in the stock of money is thought to communicate its effects to the rest of the economy, a test of the influence of supply may be developed. Here the role of bank failures in the money market is examined within a model of the money market that assumes that both the level of income and the rate of bank failures were determined outside this market. The role of bank failures therefore is subjected to only a partial test.

The first step in this test is the specification of demand and supply functions for money. The dependent variable in the demand function is taken to be the real stock of money, that is the stock of money divided by the price level. This formulation follows the accepted practice of assuming that any change in the price level produces an exactly equivalent change in the demand for money in nominal terms.[86] The quantity of real balances (Real M) is a function of the short-term interest rate (r_s), real income (Real GNP), the bank failure rate (f), and an error term (u_1):

$$\text{Real } M = a_0 + a_1 r_s + a_2(\text{Real GNP}) + a_3 f + u_1 \tag{8}$$

The supply of money was formulated in nominal terms, again following the literature and reflecting the behavior of banks who deal in nominal quantities. The supply of money is assumed to increase when the short-term interest rate rises and to fall when the discount rate (r_d) rises. It is larger, for a given level of interest rates, when the unborrowed component of the monetary base, unborrowed reserves (RU), is larger. And we assume that the rate of bank failures affects the supply of money also. Adding an error term (u_2), the supply function looks like this:

$$M = b_0 + b_1 r_s + b_2 r_d + b_3 RU + b_4 f + u_2 \tag{9}$$

An alternate form of the supply curve was also used as a check. In this formulation, only the supply of bank deposits is modeled. And since required reserves are proportional to deposits, and free reserves are just unborrowed reserves minus required reserves, it is convenient to set up a function for free reserves (RF) that is directly comparable

86. Friedman, 1970; Goldfeld, 1973. A narrow definition of the money stock, M_1, was used. The results using a broader definition, M_2, were qualitatively the same.

to equation (9). The only addition is a lagged term allowing the influence of the independent variables to be spread out over time: [87]

$$RF = c_0 + c_1 r_s + c_2 r_d + c_3 RU + c_4 f + c_5 RF_{-1} + u_3 \qquad (10)$$

Table 5 reports the effects of estimating simultaneously these supply and demand curves for money for the interwar period. The policies of the Federal Reserve as reflected in the discount rate (r_d) and the volume of unborrowed reserves (RU) are taken as exogenous. The failure rate of banks (f) is also taken to be exogenous, as are the price level and real GNP.[88] It would be preferable to have prices and income endogenous, but that would require a complete econometric model. The equations shown in Table 5 therefore were estimated using real GNP as an exogenous or an instrumental variable. Since GNP does not enter the supply function, the only effect of assuming income exogenous on the supply equation was on the choice of instrumental variables. The use of different instruments in the supply equation did not have much effect on the size or the significance of the coefficient of failure rate, although it did alter the interest-rate coefficients. The effects of taking GNP to be exogenous on the assessment of the role of bank failures therefore are largely confined to the demand function.

The demand for money is shown as the first equation in Table 5. As expected, the demand for money rose when the short-term interest rate (r_s) fell and when GNP rose. Both of these effects were significantly different from zero. The coefficient of the failure rate also has the expected sign, but it is not significantly different from zero. The hypothesis that the failure rate had no effect on the demand for money in the interwar period cannot be rejected.[89]

The estimated supply function for money is shown as the second equation in Table 5. As expected, the supply of money expanded when the short-term interest rate (r_s) or unborrowed reserves (RU) rose

87. This is a common formulation in the literature. See Hendershott and de Leeuw, 1970.

88. The actual failure rate for 1933 was not used because the Bank Holiday gave *failure* a different meaning in this year than in other years. In the absence of a more appropriate figure, the mean of the failure series was used for 1933 in order not to bias the results.

89. This conclusion is not altered if the demand function is estimated in nominal terms or if the stock of money is defined to include time deposits as well as demand deposits, that is, if M_2 is used in place of M_1. Gandolfi, 1974, reached the same conclusion using cross-section data.

and when the discount rate (r_d) fell. All of these effects were statistically significant. As in the demand function, the effect of bank failures also has the correct sign, but it is not significantly different from zero. The hypothesis that the bank failures had no effect on either the supply or the demand for money in the interwar period cannot be rejected.[90]

The alternate supply function of money, expressed as an equation for free reserves (RF) is shown as the third equation in Table 5. Since more free reserves mean fewer deposits and therefore a smaller supply of money, all the coefficients in the third equation except the coefficient of RU should have the opposite sign from those in the second equation.

All of the coefficients have the expected sign, but none of the ef-

TABLE 5 • *Regression Results on the Effects of Bank Failures, 1921–41*

Dependent Variable	C	r_s	r_d	Real GNP	RU	Failure Rate	RF_{-1}	R^2	DW
Real M_1	4035	−2673		.473		−652		.926	.634
	(.632)	(−5.91)		(8.24)		(−.676)			
M_1	26207	11059	−13095		1.64	−1751		.817	1.63
	(4.17)	(2.80)	(−2.40)		(4.51)	(−1.39)			
RF	−1271	−54	260		.72	105	.30	.99	
	(−1.56)	(−.1)	(.35)		(7.4)	(.65)	(2.4)		

NOTE: All these equations were estimated by use of instrumental variables. The dependent variable and the short-term interest rate (r_s) were treated as endogenous. All other variables were taken to be exogenous, and those absent from any equation (except RF_{-1}) were used as additional instruments. Quasi t-statistics are shown below the coefficients.

SOURCES: The definitions of the variables and their sources are as follows:

Real M = M_1/CPI
M_1 = demand deposits plus currency in millions of dollars (Friedman and Schwartz, 1963a, Table A-1)
CPI = consumer price index (*Historical Statistics,* series E113, p. 125)
r_s = interest rate on prime commercial paper, New York City (ibid., series X306, p. 654)
r_d = discount rate, New York City (*Banking and Monetary Statistics,* 1943, pp. 439–42)
Real GNP = GNP in 1929 prices (Table 1, above)
RU = unborrowed reserves (*Banking and Monetary Statistics,* 1943, pp. 346–50, 399–400)
Failure rate = per cent of deposits in suspended banks, except in 1933. For 1933, the mean of the series was used (ibid., pp. 17, 283)
RF = free reserves (ibid.)

90. As with the demand equation, this conclusion is not affected by varying the form of the supply equation or altering the definition of the variables.

fects just discussed are significant. The influence of interest rates therefore appears to be less systematic in the third equation of Table 5 than in the second; that is, it is clearer in the full supply curve of money than in the component of the supply that should be most responsive to interest rates. Further work would be needed to explain why the influence of interest rates shows up more strongly in the former than the latter.

Fortunately, there is no conflict about the evidence on bank failures in the second and third equations of Table 5. Both coefficients of bank failures have the right sign, but neither coefficient is significantly different from zero. There is no evidence in Table 5 that allows one to reject the hypothesis that bank failures were totally without effect on the market for money.

Inability to reject a hypothesis, however, is hardly compulsion to accept it. There are several possible reasons for this result. The first one, of course, is that the hypothesis of no effect is correct. But this is not the only alternative. As noted above, the specification of this model of the money market is not neutral, and a different specification might yield different results.[91] And even if the specification were absolutely correct, there might not be enough information in the data to provide a reliable indication of the effect of bank failures.

The level of bank failures—as measured by the percentage of deposits in failed banks—remained more or less constant during the 1920s. It jumped to a far higher level in 1930–33 and then fell to a low level for the rest of the 1930s.[92] Compared to the jumps between these periods, the variation within them was negligible. There are therefore only three distinct observations on the level of bank failures, and normal econometric approaches require more information to discriminate between alternative hypothesis. As noted above, this is a general problem for the interwar period.

If one cannot reject the hypothesis that bank failures had no effect on the money market in the early 1930s from the regressions in Table 5, one also cannot reject the hypothesis that the point estimates shown in this table are correct estimates of the appropriate parameters. What

91. As noted in the preceding footnotes, a variety of experimentation with the specification did not alter the results shown here. Nevertheless, it cannot be shown that further experimentation would be similarly fruitless.

92. It was between 0.2 and 0.6 through 1929, between 1.6 and 11.3 from 1930 through 1933 (or between 1.6 and 3.6 if 1933 is excluded as in the regressions), and below 0.1 thereafter.

are the implications of assuming this to be the case? The size of the estimated coefficients of bank failures—as opposed to their significance—is completely in accord with the narrative of Friedman and Schwartz. First, the bank failure variable rose by just over one from 1929 to 1930 and by just under two from 1930 to 1931. Multiplying these changes by the coefficient in the second equation in Table 5 (the supply-of-money equation) indicates the presence of a depressing effect on the supply of money of just under $2 billion in 1930, of over $3 billion in 1931. The actual fall in the stock of money in those years was about $1 billion and $2 billion respectively.[93] The rise in bank failures can account for the full fall in the supply of money under this hypothesis.

Second, the coefficient of bank failures in the demand equation is smaller in absolute value than the coefficient in the supply equation. The demand equation was deflated by a price index that was less than one for this entire period; multiplying the demand equation by this index to make the two equations comparable therefore reduces the size of the bank-failure coefficient even further. The point estimates of Table 5 consequently support the second part of Friedman and Schwartz's story also: The effect of bank failures was to depress both the supply and demand for money, but it had a stronger depressing effect on the supply than on the demand.

The results shown in Table 5 thus are consistent both with the money hypothesis and with the spending hypothesis as far as they go. The confidence intervals on the coefficients of bank failures are so wide that both stories can be told without assigning values to coefficients outside these reasonable limits. But the model underlying Table 5 is not really consistent with either the money or the spending hypothesis, and the test is only partial. As noted above, the money hypothesis asserts that the level of income is determined within the money market, but the specification of this model has income exogenous. Under the assumptions of the model, therefore, the absence of bank failures would have resulted in a larger stock of money and a lower interest rate—but not in a higher income. Similarly, the spending hypothesis asserts that bank failures were partly the result of income movements, not exogenously determined as shown in the model.

While the imprecision of this test derives from the particular model estimated here, the argument of this chapter suggests that the outcome

93. Table 2, above.

may be typical. Accordingly, the rest of this study adopts a sympathetic but distinct approach. We ask first whether the decline in GNP and the rise in bank failures assumed to be exogenous in these equations should better be regarded as endogenous. We then approach the identification problem in the money market in a noneconometric fashion.

III

Precipitating Factors

THIS CHAPTER begins the task of confronting the alternate explanations of the Great Depression in the spending hypothesis and the money hypothesis. It examines the initial parts of the stories where the factors that precipitated the Depression are described. These factors need to be examined from two points of view. First, were they independent of the fall in income, so that they could have been a cause—as opposed to a result or a part—of the Depression? And second, what were their effects? The two hypotheses are tested in turn.

The Spending Hypothesis: Housing and the Stock-Market Crash

A problem arises immediately when we turn to this test. It is not at all clear what it means to precipitate a depression. In particular, there are two meanings one could attach to this term with respect to the Great Depression. One could ask either about the causes of the downturn in 1929 or about the causes of the great severity of this downturn relative to others the economy has experienced. In one case, the deviation of the economy from a trend path is being explored; in the other, the deviation from a "normal" depression.[1]

Since our interest lies in explaining why the Great Depression was different than other economic downturns, we choose the second definition. The downturn which started in the second quarter of 1929 might not have turned into the Great Depression.[2] The economy is always deviating in one way or another from its trend. And we do not lavish equal attention upon all deviations. The 1930s are of interest because

1. For a similar division, see Lundberg, 1968, p. 77; Gordon, 1974, p. 70.
2. For the traditional dating of the downturn, see Burns and Mitchell, 1946, p. 78.

they show a considerably larger deviation from trend than usual, and it is this aspect of the experience that we want to illuminate. Hence, the second definition of *precipitate* is appropriate. We ask how events in 1930 differed from those in a short-term depression. Alternatively, what happened in 1930 that did not happen in, say, 1921 or 1938?

We start with the fall in autonomous spending cited in the spending hypothesis. And as stated above, we need to scale the data on spending to analyze them. Income, consumption, and investment always fall in depressions; without some calibration, there is no way to say if a given fall is large or small. The standard of comparison used here is the size of the depressions of 1920–21 and 1937–38. The structure of the American economy changed during the first half of the twentieth century, and there is no way of knowing in advance if these changes were important for cyclical stability—although, given the record of the postwar years to date and man's incurable optimism, we believe they were. Therefore, a comparison with fluctuations outside the immediate temporal environment of 1929, that is, outside the interwar period would be inappropriate.

The two depressions in 1921 and 1938 were of short duration. The comparison made here therefore compares 1930 to depressed years followed by recovery. Implicitly, the question posed is as follows: Is there anything in the macroeconomic data to suggest that 1930 was different from 1921 or 1938? Can these data provide clues for the failure of the economy to recover in 1931?

Data on the GNP and some of its components are shown in Table 6. The top half of the table shows the percentage change over a one-year span which is also the span from peak to trough (on an annual basis) for 1920–21 or in 1937–38.[3]

Most discussions of the Depression following the spending hypothesis take the fall in investment to be the determinant of the Depression's severity. The data in the top half of Table 6 suggest, however, that the fall in investment in the initial year of the Depression was not as large as the fall in the other two (short-lived) interwar depressions. One therefore cannot argue that the severity of the Great Depression was due simply to the multiplier effects of a severe fall in investment. There appear to be two possibilities. The time path or the composition

3. These recessions were not of equal length when monthly data are used, but the length of the downturn in each case can be rounded to one year. See Burns and Mitchell, 1946, p. 78.

of the fall in investment may have been different and more deflationary in 1930 than in the other years. Or the large falls in consumption and exports may have been important in driving income to even lower levels.

These inferences, of course, are highly tentative. There is a considerable margin of uncertainty in the data. They are only on an annual basis. And the data shown relate the changes in 1930 to the magnitudes of 1929, which was not a very typical year of the period. The

TABLE 6 • *Changes in Real Macroeconomic Variables in Three Periods (percentage changes)*

	1920–21	1929–30	1937–38
GNP	−2.4	−8.9	−5.4
Consumption	+6.4	−5.4	−1.6
Investment	−41.7	−35.6	−53.1
Exports	−14.2	−19.1	+1.7
	1919–21	**1928–30**	**1936–38**
GNP	−3.5	−3.4	+2.3
Consumption	+11.6	−0.2	+2.1
Investment	−30.7	−27.8	−26.4
Exports	−19.7	−15.7	+29.8

NOTE: All variables are in 1929 prices. Investment and Exports refer to Gross Private Domestic Investment and Merchandise Exports.

SOURCE: Kendrick, 1961, pp. 294–95; *Historical Statistics,* 1960, pp. 117, 537.

first two problems are insoluble given the current state of the data, but the last one can be avoided by a simple device. The bottom half of Table 6 shows the same comparisons as the top half taken over a two-year span. The data shown in this part of the table are the percentage changes of the variables from the year before the peak of the cycle to the year after. Data from the peak year itself do not appear here at all.

The ranking of periods by the size of the fall in real income is completely different on this basis than on the previous one. The depression of 1921, which earlier appeared to be the mildest, now appears to be the severest. And the fall in real GNP in 1930, which earlier appeared to be the largest of the three, now appears to be almost the same size as the fall in 1921. In 1938, the fall in investment was partially offset by rises in consumption and in exports. In 1921, the declines in investment and exports were offset by the large rise in consumption. But in 1930, all three components of the national product fell.

The decline in income in 1930 therefore looks different from the other two interwar depressions whether a one-year or a two-year perspective is taken. Investment fell no more in this decline than in other declines, and the difference does not lie here. It lies rather in the combined behavior of consumption and exports. Consumption fell in 1930 while it rose in 1921. The difference is quite striking, quite large, and not offset by the behavior of exports. Consumption fell in 1938, but nowhere near as much as it fell in 1930. And the failure of exports to fall in 1938, which resulted in a large rise in exports over the two-year period, 1936–38, helped to buoy up the economy. In short, the rise in consumption in 1921 and the combination of a small change in consumption and a rise in exports in 1938 contrast sharply with the combination of sharply falling consumption and exports in 1930. And while the fall in consumption was partly induced by the simultaneous fall in income, the movement in 1930 appears to bear a different relation to income than the changes of the other years shown.[4]

Turning to the composition of investment, a significant difference between 1930 and the other two depression years is apparent here, too. Table 7 shows a breakdown of the change in gross private domestic in-

TABLE 7 • *Proportion of the Change in Investment in Various Components in Three Periods*

	1920–21	1929–30	1937–38
Construction	.06	.42	.10
Equipment	.19	.22	.28
Inventories	.75	.36	.62
	1919–21	1928–30	1936–38
Construction	−.09	.82	−.33
Equipment	.20	.18	.28
Inventories	.89	0	1.06

SOURCE: Swanson and Williamson, 1972, p. 70.

4. Government expenditures did not change much in 1930 or 1938, as shown in Table 24, below. They fell dramatically from their wartime peak in 1919 to 1920, which was an important factor in the 1921 depression. They did not, however, fall much from 1920 to 1921. *Historical Statistics,* 1960, p. 718.

vestment for the same periods shown in Table 6. Unlike Table 6, these proportions are of investment in current prices because of the absence of suitable deflators. Since one normally uses the same deflator for total investment and for inventory investment, the share of inventories in the total would be unaffected by deflation.

Whether one takes a one-year or a two-year perspective, the share of the investment decline accounted for by business equipment is roughly the same for all three periods. But the share of inventory investment is much smaller in the 1930 change, and the share of construction is correspondingly larger.[5] There are two distinct reasons why the fall in construction expenditures could have been important for the economy.

Inventory investment is an unstable component of national income, both because the size of desired inventory investment varies sharply from year to year and because actual inventory adjustment adjusts rapidly to changes in desired inventory adjustment. Desired construction investment, by contrast, is a function of variables that change relatively slowly. And actual construction investment adjusts to changes in the desired level more slowly than inventory investment. The greater than normal fall in construction in 1930 therefore suggests that some underlying parameter changed in a way injurious to the health of the economy.

However, the work surveyed in Chapter II, above, showed that the major part of the fall in construction in the 1930s can best be seen as the result of the fall in income rather than as the result of a change in some alternative variable. This explanation of the fall in construction in the 1930s obviously does not extend to the fall before 1929. Private construction fell by $2 billion between 1926 and 1929, and this movement could not have been the result of a fall in income, for the simple reason that the level of income was rising in these years.[6] An alternative explanation is needed.

Restrictive immigration laws in 1921 and 1924 reduced the rate of immigration into the United States. A smaller number of new immigrants meant fewer new families and therefore a smaller demand for new homes. It is tempting to attribute the decline in construction to the fall in demand from this source, but the data do not support such an

5. As noted above, these results would not be changed significantly by conversion to constant-price estimates.

6. See Table 1.

inference. Immigration was small relative to the increase in the domestic population, and even major increases in the rate of immigration would not have made a noticeable change in the rate of family formation. Estimates of what immigration might have been in the absence of the immigration laws show that housing investment would have been increased by less than 1 per cent during the 1920s by the absence of these laws.[7]

In light of this finding, the explanation for the pre-1929 downturn must be sought within the housing market itself. Given the long lags that characterize this market, it is not surprising to find temporary disequilibria and long wavelike movements. The cycle of the 1920s must have been such a movement, initiated, no doubt, by events in and around World War I.[8]

But if such a wave was washing over the economy in the 1920s, it seems to have had remarkably little impact. The economy was not noticeably more expansionary before 1926 when this wave was advancing than it was after then when it was receding. In any economy, some industries will be expanding while others are stagnating. So it was in the 1920s. As long as total demand was high, it did not seem to matter in which sector it was concentrated.

Income began to fall in 1929, and the rate of decline of construction increased. Having fallen by $2 billion in the three years from 1926 to 1929, it fell by $2.3 billion from 1929 to 1930.[9] This acceleration probably reflects the effects of the general economic decline rather than some influence specific to the construction sector. In other words, when national income began to fall, this change in the economic environment depressed construction below what it would have been if the general expansion had continued beyond 1929. The difference between 1929 and 1930 was not the result of changes within construction. The volume of investment was more important than its composition, and construction is best seen as just another industry.

Before leaving the subject of construction, one effect of a fall in this activity (and of any other activity characterized by long lags) may be noted. The long lags inherent in the construction process imparted a

7. Galster, 1972, estimated three alternative econometric models of immigration. They all showed that the immigration restriction was not an important determinant of the level of construction.

8. This is the most usual interpretation. See Duesenberry, 1958, pp. 288–90; Bolch, Fels, and McMahon, 1971; Gordon, 1974, p. 31.

9. See Table 1.

smoothness to the volume of construction that was not present for many industries. If inventory investment was low in one year, it was no more likely to be low the following year also than if it had been high. But if construction was low in one year, then it was likely to be low also in the next year. The decline in construction therefore may have depressed expectations of investment spending in 1931 more than an equivalent fall in inventory or other investment would have done. The magnitude of this effect is hard to know.[10]

The supposed fall in autonomous investment therefore does not seem to offer strong support for spending hypothesis. The fall in construction in the late 1920s was deflationary, but too small to precipitate a major depression. The fall in 1930 was larger, but the magnitude of this decline was not—so far as can be seen—independent of the fall in income taking place at that time. And the fall in total investment in 1930, as Table 6 shows, was not at all unusual for an income movement of the size experienced in 1930. The much larger declines of subsequent years were part of the Depression; they did not precipitate it in any meaningful sense of the word.

The combined fall in consumption and exports, however, does suggest that a fall in autonomous expenditures helped to deepen the Depression. The fall in exports was the smaller of the two movements; it is important because it moved with consumption, rather than against it as in 1921. And it was not induced by events within the United States. It resulted from the deepening world agricultural depression and from European troubles independent of the United States.[11] Events outside the United States therefore exerted a deflationary impact within this country.

The fall in exports was small relative to the fall in consumption.

10. Another effect of the fall in construction could not be found in the data. Easterlin, 1968, asserted that durable purchases were tied to family formation which was tied in turn to construction activity. A fall in construction could have inhibited durable purchases and thereby have depressed aggregate economic activity. Inserting a construction variable into the consumption functions shown in Table 8, below, did yield a significant coefficient, but this coefficient was significant also in the regression for nondurable consumption—where Easterlin's hypothesis predicts its absence. The construction variable clearly acted as an indicator of the interwar business cycle in the regressions; it did not show the effect of construction on durable purchases.

11. See Chapter V for support of this statement. In any period but the 1930s, the exogeneity of exports would not be a matter of dispute; but during the Depression, no country was unaffected by events in the United States. Nevertheless, the Depression in the United States did not spread immediately to the rest of the world, and exports can be taken to be exogenously determined for 1930.

And as Table 6 shows, the fall in consumption was larger than might have been expected from the fall in income alone. While part of the fall in consumption was the consequence of the decline in income, not all of it can be explained in this way. The stock-market crash has been offered as a possible cause for the sharpness with which consumption fell, and it is worth examining this story in some detail.[12]

There are two ways in which the stock-market crash could have operated to decrease consumption. First, the fall in stock-market prices decreased personal wealth, which could have decreased consumption. Second, the crash may have changed expectations in a way that decreased consumption. We examine these mechanisms in turn. The first will be examined by comparing the explanatory power of consumption functions using wealth as an argument; the second, by an attempt to measure expectations directly.

Economists now agree that consumption is at least partly a function of wealth.[13] The disagreements center on the form of the relationship, the nature of the data to be used, and the magnitude of coefficients, rather than on the concept itself. In order to test the proposition that the stock-market crash accounted for the drastic fall in consumption in 1930, a consumption function using measured wealth explicitly as a determinant of income was used. The function was estimated on an annual basis because of the paucity of data for the interwar period; it consequently resembles closely the original function of Ando and Modigliani.[14] A few alternative definitions of the data were used to avoid capricious results, although the results do not differ much among themselves. In addition, further experimentation with the form of the function and the parameters involved is reported in Appendix 1.

The dependent variable in the life-cycle consumption function, as the function estimated here is known, is not consumption expenditures as reported in Table 1. The data reported in Table 1 show the sum of consumer purchases of durables and nondurables. But while nondurable goods are consumed immediately, durables are not. Only a fraction of the value of a durable good is consumed, that is, used up, in the

12. Almost all analyses of the Depression mention this effect, although different authors assign it different weights in their explanations of the Depression. For the extreme views, see the work of Kirkwood, 1972, and Green, 1971, analyzed in Chapter II, above.

13. Modigliani, 1973.

14. Ando and Modigliani, 1963.

year the good is bought. The rest is consumed slowly over the life of the good. The correct dependent variable is the sum of expenditures on nondurables and the current consumption from the stock of durable goods. Purchases of durables then need to be explained separately.

The data do not exist to construct a reliable set of estimates of this variable for the full interwar period, and the regressions were run on two proxies: nondurable expenditures and total consumption expenditures. The former is smaller than the true variable, but it moves closely with it. The latter may be larger or smaller than the true variable and may contain movements resulting from purchases of durable goods that do not relate to the function estimated. Nevertheless, it is the variable we are seeking to explain, and so it was used. The results were virtually identical for the two variables.[15]

One of the independent variables, wealth, is also known only imperfectly. All economic historians must be grateful for the pioneering work of Goldsmith who compiled wealth estimates for benchmark years.[16] But it is necessary to interpolate between these benchmarks, and the interpolations are subject to considerable error. The interpolations constructed for this study are compared with those of Ando and Brown for 1929 and later years in Appendix 1.[17] The regressions were run both with the new wealth series and with a combination of the new series before 1929 and the Ando-Brown series thereafter. Again, the change did not make much difference.

The regressions are shown in Table 8. Four functions were estimated, since there was a choice both of the dependent variable and of the wealth variable. As can be seen, the results were not very sensitive to the choice. Total consumer spending exceeds nondurable consumption, of course, and at least one of the coefficients explaining it therefore has to be larger. The difference appears to be concentrated entirely in the income coefficient, suggesting that spending on consumer durables was more responsive to changes in income than changes in wealth.

15. In addition, depreciation on consumer durables was estimated crudely, and a rough series of nondurable consumption plus the use value from durables was constructed. No drastic changes in parameter values (and, hence, in residual patterns) resulted. This alternative consumption variable was abandoned because of the low quality of the estimated use value from consumer durables.

16. Goldsmith, 1955, vol. 1, Tables W1, W22, W27.

17. Ando and Brown, 1963.

These estimates are compared with two others in Table 8. The original estimates of Ando and Modigliani, which were for a period that started in 1929 and ended in 1959 with a gap for the war years, is shown first. An estimate for the postwar years alone is shown in the last line. It can be seen that the wealth coefficient increases as the change is made from interwar data to a period starting in 1929 and then to one starting after World War II. It is possible that the wealth

TABLE 8 • *Estimated Consumption Functions, 1919–41*

	Constant	Current Income	Wealth	R^2
Nondurable consumption				
Temin data	9947	.594	.0229	.929
	(3.16)	(12)	(2.36)	
Ando-Brown data	10413	.596	.0209	.926
	(3.28)	(11.6)	(2.12)	
Total consumer spending				
Temin data	7512	.762	.0165	.935
	(2.06)	(13.2)	(1.46)	
Ando-Brown data	7838	.763	.0152	.934
	(2.15)	(12.9)	(1.34)	
Ando-Modigliani (1929–40, 1947–59)	8.1	.75	.042	.998
	(8.1)	(15)	(4.7)	
Arena (1946–58)	60.39	.484	.064	.994
	(1.61)	(3.34)	(2.84)	

NOTE: *t*-statistics are given in parentheses.

SOURCE: Appendix; Ando and Modigliani, 1963; Arena, 1964.

coefficient has been rising over time, and that the original Ando and Modigliani result was an average between a lower interwar coefficient and a higher postwar coefficient. But since it is possible also that the poor data of the interwar period preclude an accurate estimate of the coefficient for that period, the results of Table 9 are compared with analogous results using the postwar coefficients in Appendix 1. The results are not sensitive to the choice.

Some aspects of the difference between actual consumption and the consumption predicted by the estimated interwar consumption functions are shown in Table 9. The first three columns show the residuals for the years compared in Tables 6 and 7. It can be seen that the actual consumption was above the predicted level in 1921 and

1938, but below it in 1930. The unusual nature of 1930 is clearly apparent.

But the level of consumption is not the crucial variable. Table 6 reported the change in consumption, and the aim of using a consumption function was to see if the decline in stock prices can explain this fall. Accordingly, the last three columns of Table 9 show the change in the residual from the peak year of the interwar depressions to the depres-

TABLE 9 • *Residuals from Consumption Functions Using Different Data (billions of dollars)*

	R_{21}	R_{30}	R_{38}	R_{21}–R_{20}	R_{30}–R_{29}	R_{38}–R_{37}
Nondurable consumption						
Temin data	3.82	−.87	1.27	5.11	−1.60	1.79
Ando-Brown data	3.80	−.46	1.99	5.13	−.24	2.45
Total consumer spending						
Temin data	4.04	−.91	.85	6.09	−1.92	1.57
Ando-Brown data	4.02	−.64	1.36	6.10	−.94	2.05

SOURCE: See text.

sion year, or the first depression year in the case of 1930. A negative entry means that the actual fall in consumption was larger than the predicted fall.[18] The fall in consumption in 1930, it will be remembered from Table 6, was large relative to the other years shown. It emerges from Table 9 that it was also large relative to predictions of the fall based on movements of income and wealth.

Upon reflection, it is not surprising to find that wealth changes cannot explain the fall in consumption in 1930. The stock market did not collapse in one day; it declined more or less steadily for three years. Measured wealth therefore had not fallen very much by 1930, and the decline in wealth did not have a major impact on consumption in that year. On the assumption that the overprediction of the decline in consumption shown for 1921 and 1938 is the norm for this function in depression years, the predicted decline in consumption was $5 billion too low in 1930. This is in current prices. Conversion to constant dollars implies that fully $3 billion of the $4.3 billion drop in consumption shown in Table 1 is unexplained.[19]

18. Algebraically, the actual change in consumption was smaller (that is, more negative) than the predicted change.

19. The current value estimate is the average difference between the fifth column

A few caveats are now in order. First, the coefficients reported in Table 8 were estimated by ordinary least squares. They therefore contain a simultaneous-equation bias, since the consumption function is only one equation in an interrelated system. For the reasons outlined in Chapter II, a new econometric model of the economy was not constructed here. But, as noted above, the results reported here were compared with the results obtained by using coefficients derived from postwar data to see if they were sensitive to changes in the coefficients. As was to be expected, the residuals were larger, but the story is the same.

Second, an alternative formulation of the consumption function employs an estimate of "permanent income" in place of current income and measured wealth.[20] The use of permanent income approximates wealth by a weighted average of income—presumably from all forms of capital—at different times. It does not consider the market value of this wealth at all directly, and the stock-market crash affected the consumption predicted by the permanent-income consumption only as it affected various components of consumers' incomes. This function did not show as marked a difference between 1930 and the other interwar depression years as the function using a direct wealth estimate, but it too underpredicted both the level and the fall in consumption in 1930. Both the results of using postwar coefficients and of using a permanent-income consumption function are shown in Appendix 1.

Third, only the simplest type of consumption function was used here. In particular, purchases of durables were not estimated separately, showing the dependence of durable purchases on the stock and possibly the age of the existing stock of durables. But while this omission may be important in obtaining a thorough understanding of the behavior of consumption, it is not important for the present inquiry. As shown in Table 9, the unexplained component of nondurable consumption was almost as large as the unexplained part of total consumer spending. Even if all durable purchases could be explained precisely for 1929 and 1930, there would still be an unexplained drop of between $2 and $3 billion in 1929 prices in nondurable consump-

---

of Table 9 and the average of the adjacent columns. It is two-thirds of the total fall in the current value of consumption. Applying this proportion to the fall in real consumption yields the figure in the text.

20. Friedman, 1957.

tion. This change will not be eliminated by separate estimation of durable expenditures.[21]

The exogenous fall in consumption in 1930 of $3 billion in 1929 prices is in addition to two other changes in spending. Exports decreased by $1 billion in constant prices in 1930, and the decline in asset values following the stock-market crash lowered consumption if the consumption function estimated in Table 8 is used. Imprecise data preclude an exact estimate of this latter effect, but it was under $1 billion and possibly even below $.5 million. The sum of these autonomous falls may then be estimated conservatively at around $4 billion in 1929 prices, or 4 per cent of real GNP.[22]

But even though the consumption function estimated here did not explain the fall of consumption, it could have been due to the stock-market crash through a route different than a decline in measured wealth. It may have altered consumer expectations in a way that caused them to decrease consumption expenditures. In 1929, most people expected good times to continue. By 1933, most people expected bad times to continue. Sometime in the interim, people's vision of what the next few years would bring changed. The question, therefore, is not whether expectations changed in the Depression, but when.

The importance of this question cannot be overestimated. With the advantage of hindsight, we can see 1930 as the beginning of the worst depression in history. But it is by no means clear that contemporary observers could see the same thing. In fact, it would be highly surprising if they did, since the events following 1930 were outside everyone's previous experience. How did people regard the events of 1929 and 1930 as they happened?

The alternatives are clear. Either the collapse of stock-market

21. The function estimated in Table 8 differs from the theoretical specification of the Ando-Modigliani consumption function by including a constant term. Given the quality of the data and the limitations of the estimating technique, it did not seem appropriate to restrict the constant to be zero. The existence of a constant term does not affect the change in residuals noted in the last half of Table 9, and the range of coefficients sampled there and in Appendix 1 is wide enough to include the true value.

22. Exports fell by $1.4 billion in current prices in 1930 and by almost exactly $1 billion in 1929 prices. The wealth effect differs according to which of two wealth series is used and according to whether postwar or interwar regression coefficients are used. The range is from one-third to one billion dollars in current dollars, or somewhat less than this in constant dollars.

prices in 1929 affected people's expectations so that people were very pessimistic about the prospects for the next few years, or people viewed 1930 as another recession—a short fluctuation in business activity similar to the one in 1921. The methods available for discriminating between these alternatives are not so clear. There are, as usual, almost no data on the expectations of consumers. We have various written sources, but they all suffer from one or another defect. If they were written at the time, they tend to be descriptive of the state of business, telling how much of something was sold, rather than people's states of mind. The authors of these pieces had no more insight than we do about motivations. More thoughtful accounts have been written, but in the nature of such writings, they were written reflectively after some years had passed. And anyone writing after the Depression was well underway could hardly help but see the events of 1929 and 1930 as the beginning of the long slide down. But the question here is of foresight, not hindsight.

The problem of hindsight is apparent even by 1931. Fred Allen, writing *Only Yesterday* in the year, betrayed by his title how profoundly he thought the world had changed since late October 1929. The stock-market crash was for him the dividing point between unbounded optimism and equally uncontainable pessimism, and he took it as a matter of course that everyone in 1929 saw the significance of these events that he could see in 1931.[23] But it would be surprising indeed if the consciousness of change had come immediately on Black Thursday and not been affected by events thereafter. The transformation must have come over some period of time; the issue at hand is how long that period was.

In Allen's mind, and in the minds of later writers as well, the stock-market crash became the symbol of the vast discrepancy between the 1920s and the 1930s. And this symbol is not devoid of interest. As we have just seen, the change in wealth produced by the stock-market decline probably had an effect on people's spending. But this limited effect was only a part of the change taking place in consumer spending, and a relatively small part at that. Phrased precisely, the question now is whether the stock-market crash decreased consump-

23. Allen, 1931, p. 338. In his words, "There was hardly a man or woman in the country whose attitude toward life had not been affected by it [the Big Bull Market] in some degree and was not now affected by the sudden and brutal shattering of hope."

tion by more than an equivalent—but less dramatic—change in wealth would have done. And to answer this question, the symbol and the reality must be carefully distinguished.[24]

The search for contemporary evidence is hard. Newspapers in late 1929 were full of reassuring statements by prominent people. The Federal Reserve Board, Alfred P. Sloan, Jr., and many others, saw no connection between the stock-market crash and business conditions in November 1929. Some officials and bankers even said that business would gain from the fall in stock-market prices, since lower prices meant cheaper capital costs for firms.[25]

But this evidence is suspect. For while all the economic news in late 1929 appears to be positive, there was an enormous increase in these reassuring statements. In the second quarter of 1929, few people felt obliged to emphasize the condition of business. Presumably, everyone knew it was good; it was not news. In the last quarter of 1929, by contrast, the press was full of optimistic statements. Is this not evidence that what was once assured was now in question? Should positive statements be taken at face value or as attempts to deny the obvious?

The business press did not report business as usual, but it did not foresee disaster either. The picture that businessmen shared among themselves in late 1929 was one of a mild decline in business activity. Foreboding about the future was absent. On November 16, 1929, *Business Week* observed that "a slow and irregular business recession is going on." The following issue contained an article entitled " 'Off 7%' A Drama of Business" in which it was predicted that business in 1930 would be 7 per cent lower than in 1929. The week after that, the editors reported businessmen's expectations that business during the three winter months would be down 2 per cent from last year, but that the stock market would recover and agricultural conditions would improve. By the middle of December the editors could announce, "We feel that, so far as industrial activity is concerned, the worse will be over in the next six weeks." [26]

24. See Sobel, 1968, p. 391.

25. *New York Times,* November 1, 1929, p. 1; November 2, 1929, p. 2; November 6, 1929, p. 39; November 11, 1929, p. 24; November 25, 1929, p. 43.

26. *Business Week,* November 16, 1929, p. 3; November 23, 1929, p. 22; November 30, 1929, p. 40; December 14, 1929, p. 3. *Business Week* began publishing in the latter part of 1929. It prided itself on its close connections with the business community and the absence of a distinction between its reporting and its editorializing. Even its reporting, therefore, tells its attitudes.

The industry forecasts that appeared through the last quarter of 1929 were in the same vein as these comments about the aggregate volume of business. Business in various lines was expected to be worse than 1929, which was a very good year, but not worse than 1928, which was hardly a bad one. The explicit forecasts that appeared at the start of 1930 compared the expected business conditions in this year favorably with 1927 and about evenly with 1928.[27]

But these forecasts were accompanied by expressions of doubt. There were uncertainties in the situation that exceeded the uncertainty implicit in any prediction of the future. The *New York Times* exposed these doubts to public view in an article giving arguments for and against the continuation of poverty. Entitled "The Financial Outlook for 1930," it would not escape the notice of anyone reading the business section of the *Times* on January 1, 1930.

Five reasons for expecting continued prosperity were given, and an opposing view was given with each one. The stock-market crash, for example, was said to be only a reaction to unreasonable speculation. In the tradition of public statements in late 1929, it would then be considered divorced from the rest of the economy. Not so, said the opposing argument. No matter how the prices of stocks were determined, high stock prices encouraged consumption, and low prices will discourage it.

In that case, replied the optimistic side, the Hoover administration will offset the decline in purchases. The pessimists acknowledged the expansionary effect of President Hoover's proposals, but argued that they were too small and too spread out in time to offset the deflationary influences. Giving a final argument in this vein, the optimists then asserted that industrial expansion is inevitable. Not without purchasers, replied the prematurely Keynesian pessimists.

Turning to another aspect of the current situation, the optimistic side argued that the period of easy money ushered in by the stock-market crash would promote business. But, noted the dissenters, easy money may be the result of reduced industrial activity as much as a cause for revival. And finally, the optimistic side asserted that international agreements had stabilized the balance of payments. The less sanguine opposition questioned the link between politics and economics.

27. *Business Week,* January 1, 1930, pp. 20–22; *New York Times,* January 1, 1930, pp. 1, 33.

The author of the article, having exposed the arguments for depression, ended the article with a ringing assertion that the optimistic side was right. He added a few arguments of his own—without refutations—in which "the indomitable spirit of confidence in the longer trend of American prosperity" figured prominently.[28] He had put the negative views in the article to report the discussion fully, but he did not accept them. In the light of history, we can see that he made a mistake. We would like to know how many people agreed with him at the time he wrote, whatever they came to think later on.

No surveys of consumer attitudes were taken in late 1929 and early 1930, and we know only the expressed sentiments of public officials, businessmen, and financial writers. It is plausible to argue that these men should have been the first to realize that the economy was about to depart from historical precedent. Any consumer looking back over recent history would have seen a series of sharp, but short, depressions.[29] There would be no reason for him to anticipate anything more. Yet one cannot dismiss entirely the argument that the stock-market crash had been something unusual which had set up unusual expectations.

In any case, the optimistic tone of the popular and semipopular press continued through the early part of 1930. The National Business Survey Conference, a blue-ribbon group of business executives formed at the suggestion of President Hoover in December 1929, publicized favorable reports of business conditions in the spring of 1930.[30] *Business Week* chronicled the week-to-week health of the economy in optimistic tones. An example will show the style and attitude of its editors. On March 26, they said, "The early spring showers of easy money that have fallen on the stock and bond markets this week started the speculative sap rising, but the buds on the trees of business evidently need a little more statistical sunshine from industry and trade before they dare open." And on July 9, they gave eight reasons for a business upturn, including the rapid rate of expansion of bank credit, low inventories, low prices for raw-material imports, and good prospects for autos in the fall.[31]

28. *New York Times,* January 1, 1930, p. 33.

29. This comparison was made in a short article appearing next to the one just discussed.

30. *New York Times,* March 24, 1930, p. 1; April 28, 1930, p. 1.

31. *Business Week,* March 26, 1930, p. 5; July 9, 1930, pp. 5–6.

Then during the last quarter of 1930, the tone changed. The September report of the National Business Survey Conference was devoid of optimism and presented without comment. On September 10, *Business Week* said that the country was experiencing a mild depression but that the risk of prolonged depression was not past. A month later they said that the mild recession during the first half of 1930 had become a world-wide depression. On November 12, they commented, "That business activity should continue to seek new low levels at this season is both unexpected and unwarranted," and they analyzed the causes of the depression, attributing it to the monetary and credit conditions surrounding the stock-market boom and blaming the Fed for not using open-market purchases.[32]

Sometime in the fall of 1930, then, businessmen became convinced that prosperity was no longer just around the corner. The timing of this change is not known with precision, but it came approximately one year after the stock-market crash, and it preceded the banking crisis in November and December of 1930 and the failure of the Bank of United States on December 11. The precise events that produced this change are not known, and not everyone appears to have been conscious of it as it happened. Nevertheless, it would appear that businessmen's and probably also consumers' expectations built up during the 1920s about the normal state of business activity were not shattered immediately by the stock-market crash; they only dissolved about a year after the crash.[33]

This kind of evidence is extremely impressionistic, and we would like to have some way to quantify the impressions received from it. We cannot do this for the timing, but we can quantify the amount of pessimism felt in 1930. We do this by means of an analysis of agency ratings of bonds.

A great variety of bonds were rated by agencies (Fitch, Moody's, Poor's, Standard Statistics) who attempted to give investors an index of the riskiness of the bonds. The agencies were not selling bonds, and they were free of the incentive to distort their ratings for self-serving ends. The ratings were done contemporaneously, and they are free also of the taint of latter knowledge. The agencies presumably were staffed by experts in the various fields in which bonds were outstand-

32. *New York Times,* September 29, 1930, pp. 1, 14; *Business Week,* September 10, 1930, p. 40; October 22, 1930, p. 40; November 12, 1930, pp. 45, 48.

33. Schumpeter, 1939, vol. 2, p. 911.

ing, and they therefore were in a position to make informed judgments about the future. We may take their ratings of bonds as an index of informed, unbiased opinion about the future prospects for business.

As an index of expectations during 1930, we use a measure of the extent to which the rating agencies changed their opinion about outstanding bonds. If they had expected a serious depression, they would have changed the ratings of bonds to reflect a greater degree of risk. If they had not expected the bad times to continue, there would have been far less change in bond ratings.

Following W. B. Hickman's monumental study of the quality of corporate bond financing, we may distinguish nine grades of corporate bonds, starting with Aaa and going down through the grades of the various rating agencies.[34] There are eight boundaries between ratings, and we could examine the number of bonds that crossed any or all of them. Since there are always reclassifications going on, we want to use the net movements in a particular direction as our index; that is, the number of bonds reclassified upward minus the number reclassified downward. If economic conditions do not change, this variable should have a mean of zero, although a nonzero variance.

It is not possible to get data directly on the reclassification activities of rating agencies, and the data need to be derived from the magnitudes of the outstanding bonds. The variable we want is not equal to the change in the proportion of outstanding bonds with each classification because the change in these proportions is a result both of reclassification and of differences between the quality of bonds issued and bonds extinguished. Hickman selected a particular boundary between the qualities of bonds (just below Moody's Baa), dividing the population of bonds into "high" and "low" quality. He then corrected the changes in the populations of high and low quality bonds to eliminate the effects of new issues and of extinguishments. The resulting index of net upward movements across the boundary he had selected was called "net upgrading" and is shown in Table 10. The index was derived in two different ways, equivalent in theory but not in practice. Both are shown in Table 10.[35]

When examining the magnitudes in Table 10, it should be remembered that they show the net changes across only one of eight boundaries in bond quality. If the movements across this boundary were typi-

34. W. B. Hickman, 1958.
35. The derivation is described in W. B. Hickman, 1958, pp. 162–70.

cal of the movements across other boundaries, then the total net movements would be eight times the size shown in Table 10. The net downgradings (taken to be the negative of net upgradings) shown in Table 10 for the years 1930–32, total between 2.5 per cent and 3.0 per cent, depending on which index is used. If the true measure was eight times this amount, however, then between one-fifth and one-fourth of all bonds were reclassified downward during these three years.[36] De-

TABLE 10 • *Characteristics of Corporate Bonds, 1915–39*

	Total Bonds Outstanding (billions of dollars)	Net Upgrading (millions of dollars) I	II	Proportion of Bonds Upgraded, Net (percentages) I	II
1915	16.9	73	−69	.43	−.41
16	17.2	44	29	.26	.17
17	17.5	−32	−17	−.18	−.10
18	17.8	−25	−15	−.14	−.09
19	17.9	−15	−40	−.08	−.22
20	18.1	−3	15	−.02	.08
21	18.8	−194	−174	−1.04	−.92
22	19.7	7	36	.04	.19
23	20.3	119	117	.58	.57
24	21.0	−37	1	−.17	.01
25	22.1	−15	40	−.07	.18
26	23.0	22	42	.09	.18
27	24.4	−73	−29	−.30	−.12
28	26.5	−43	21	−.16	.08
29	27.1	−59	−9	−.22	−.04
30	27.2	−150	−100	−.55	−.37
31	28.6	−349	−291	−1.22	−1.02
32	29.1	−339	−305	−1.17	−1.05
33	28.6	−13	26	−.05	.09
34	27.8	−48	−24	−.17	−.09
35	27.2	2	32	.01	.12
36	26.5	24	64	.09	.24
37	26.4	−199	−170	−.76	−.65
38	25.4	−106	−74	−.42	−.29
39	25.9	−54	−22	−.21	.08

SOURCE: W. B. Hickman, 1960, Tables 1, 52, 55.

36. If some bonds were reclassified more than once, the total number of bonds reclassified would have been less.

spite the smallness of the numbers in the last two columns of Table 10, this would represent a major change in perceived bond quality.

As with the indexes of aggregate activity examined earlier, we need to formulate a set of expectations about the behavior of new downgradings during a short depression. Bonds were downgraded in all depressions; we want to ask if the downgradings in 1930 were unusually large. As before, we compare 1930 with 1921 and (in this case) 1937. Bonds were downgraded in each of these years. Net downgrading equaled about 1 per cent in 1921 and about ⅔ or ¾ per cent in 1937. In 1930, net downgrading was smaller than in either of these years. It was about ½ or ⅓ per cent in that year.

This finding that a smaller proportion of bonds were downgraded in 1930 than in either 1921 or in 1937 demonstrates beyond a shadow of a doubt that the bond rating agencies did not expect a major depression in 1930. They reacted rather less sharply than they did in the other short interwar depressions, changing their expectations less than in these other two years. They continued to downgrade bonds in 1931 and 1932, so that the cumulative number of bonds downgraded in this period far exceeded the number downgraded in any other comparable period, but they did not downgrade all of these bonds in 1930. This evidence—from as unbiased a source as it is possible to get—shows that expectations were not more negative in 1930 than they had been in 1921.

These are informed expectations, and most consumers were relatively uninformed. But informed observers would have spotted a divergence from previous patterns more rapidly than less informed observers, and these expectations therefore should have led consumer expectations.

Taken together with the evidence from the contemporary press, the data on agency ratings suggest the following hypothesis on expectations. People responded to the fall in business activity and prices in 1930 in roughly the same way they reacted to the roughly similar fall in 1921. They knew business was bad, but they expected it to recover soon. It was only when business failed to show signs of recovery in the fall of 1930 that expectations changed. As far as one can see, it was the failure of business to pick up in the fall of 1930 rather than the decline of stock-market prices in 1929 that produced the change.

The large fall in consumption in 1930 therefore has no satisfactory explanation. It may have been related to the fall in construction, since construction tends to move in waves and a decline in this activity may have altered expectations adversely. It may have been related to the stock-market crash if the tests of expectations reported here do not capture the thoughts of consumers and it may have been related to the sharp decline in farm income, if farmers responded more quickly to a fall in their incomes than nonfarm consumers did to the rise in theirs stemming from the fall in food prices; [37] but these arguments are pure speculation. The fall in consumption must be regarded as truly autonomous, which in this case means also unexplained. The unexplained component of consumption, therefore, was approximately $3 billion in 1929 prices (out of a total fall of $4.3 billion). When added to the smaller falls in exports and in consumption due to the fall in asset prices, this implies a fall in autonomous spending of about $4 billion in 1929 prices. Compared to a total Gross National Product of approximately $100 billion, this fall—if it was indeed an autonomous fall—could have had multiplier effects large enough to explain the continued downward path of national income.

It is somewhat unsatisfactory to say that the Depression was started by an unexplained event, but this alternative is preferable to statements that are inconsistent with the data. The spending hypothesis is consistent with the data if we accept the autonomous nature of a large part of the fall in consumption in 1930. It is not, however, a complete story.

The Money Hypothesis: The Banking Crisis of 1930

The money hypothesis, it will be recalled, starts off with banking panics, the first of which was in November and December 1930. These panics set in motion the events that differentiated the Depression of the 1930s from all other depressions. The money hypothesis therefore offers no explanation for the downturn in 1929, which is presumed to resemble other, more short-lived downturns more closely than the spending hypothesis admits. The assertion is that the banking panics turned a short depression into a sustained decline in national income.[38] The question to be examined here is whether the banking panics were independent of the fall in income or a result of this fall.

37. See Chapter V for a fuller statement of this argument in the context of the world-wide agricultural depression.

38. See Chapter II.

The sequence of banking crises and failures leading to the Bank Holiday of 1933 are well-known. They are discussed prominently by all historians of the Depression, and Friedman and Schwartz organized their narrative of this period around them. The temporary rise in bank suspensions in November and December 1930 is termed the first banking crisis, and it provides a significant turning point in their narrative. Other banking crises followed, but for various reasons this crisis is central. The ratio of deposits to currency in the hands of the public (the deposit-currency ratio) started to fall at this time and continued to fall into 1933. This fall acted to decrease the stock of money in the economy and, therefore, the size of national income also, according to the money hypothesis. In addition, the reasons usually given for the subsequent crises imply that these crises were the results of the Depression, not a cause. The principal reason given for subsequent bank failures is the decline in the capital value of bank portfolios coming from the decline in the market value of securities. This reason was not listed among the causes of the initial banking panic in late 1930 by Friedman and Schwartz.[39]

They did not include the decline in the value of bonds held in bank portfolios among the causes of bank failures in 1930 because they relied on faulty data. They did not observe the price of bonds directly; they inferred it from data on the yields to maturity of bonds of a given risk class.[40] But, as will be shown in detail in Chapter IV, this inference is invalid. Table 10 shows that bonds were being reclassified into more risky categories in this period, and the price of any single bond fell both because of the change in its own riskiness and because of the fall in the price of bonds of a given risk. The data in Table 12, in Chapter IV, show clearly that the value of bonds had started to fall well before the banking panic of 1930. This decline is one reason behind the panic of that year.

The aggregate evidence cannot tell which banks will fail first, and a look at the incidence of bank failures may provide more insight into the nature of the failures. If bank assets were declining in price, all banks would be weakened. The weakest are likely to have failed first; an examination of the pattern of bank failures, therefore, can indicate sources of bank weaknesses. We return to Friedman and Schwartz for possible hypotheses.

39. Friedman and Schwartz, 1963a, pp. 342, 351–56.
40. They used Baa bonds. Ibid., p. 312.

Friedman and Schwartz gave two separate causes for the initial wave of bank failures in November and December 1930. They are implicit in their description of the events: "A crop of bank failures, particularly in Missouri, Indiana, Illinois, Iowa, Arkansas, and North Carolina, led to widespread attempts to convert demand and time deposits into currency, and also, to a much lesser extent, into postal savings deposits. A contagion of fear spread among depositors, starting from the agricultural areas, which had experienced the heaviest impact of bank failures in the twenties." [41] This description suggests that the bank failures were the results either of changes in the agricultural sector or of factors that had produced failures in the 1920s, although the nature of these presumed causal elements is not specified. The failure of the Bank of United States on December 11, 1930, was the result of the "contagion of fear . . . from the agricultural areas." [42]

In a separate, explicit discussion of the bank failures, Friedman and Schwartz paradoxically made no mention either of agriculture or previous failures. In this rather inconclusive discussion, they said only that "the great surge in bank failures that characterized the first banking crisis after October 1930 may possibly have resulted from poor loans and investments made in the twenties." [43] The evidence they presented on this issue is meager, and it goes against this suggestion. For example, they referred to a calculation that shows that the Bank of United States eventually paid off over 80 per cent of its deposits as evidence that its assets had not fallen far below their book value at the time of the bank's closing.[44]

The suggestion that bank failures came from bad loans and investments made in previous years must be seen as the mechanism by which failures in the panic of 1930 were correlated with previous failures. For if the loans and investments made in the 1920s did not result in failures during the 1920s, then it is hard to term them poor in quality at the time they were made. Even if they declined in value during the economic downturn starting in 1929 relative to other loans and investments, they cannot be termed poor at the time they were made unless we argue that banks should have predicted the economic downturn well before it happened. There, consequently, are only two rea-

41. Ibid., p. 308.
42. Ibid., pp. 308–09.
43. Ibid., p. 355.
44. Ibid., pp. 311, 355. This calculation will be contested below.

sons given for the bank failures in 1930: the decline in agricultural prices in 1930 and poor loans and investments made in previous years.

Several factors in the banking failures of 1930 are not explicit in this analysis. Since the composition of bank portfolios is not known in any detail, it is not possible to show the differential effect of declining bond prices on different banks. Similarly, other factors that affected the whole banking system cannot be seen in a comparison between banks. For example, it is possible that the disturbances in 1930 were not any worse than they had been at other times and that the failures were caused not by a change in the events but by a change in the banking system itself. Perhaps the strains to which the banking system was subjected in 1930 were no greater than they had been in, say, 1907, but the banking system was less stable and, therefore, less able to withstand them. This possibility was presented by Friedman and Schwartz in the course of their discussion of the bank failures of 1930, where they asserted that the existence of the Federal Reserve System was the new, destabilizing factor.[45]

This view can neither be confirmed nor denied at the present time. There does not exist a measure of the severity of the strains to which the banking system was subjected at different times. The spending hypothesis, for example, implies that the strains in 1930 were considerably stronger than those in 1907, while the money hypothesis implies the reverse. And in the absence of such a measure, it is impossible to decompose the contrast between 1907 and 1930 into a difference of the shocks and a difference of the system. It is therefore possible that the shocks to the banking system just outlined as possible reasons for the bank failures were less important than the existence of the Federal Reserve System.

A difference between the two hypothesized differential causes should be noted. The first, agricultural distress, is a part of the Depression. The argument embodying this cause therefore asserts that the banking panics were a part of the Depression.[46] The second hypothesized cause, bad loans and investments of previous years, is independent of the economic downturn. It thus makes the banking panics a possible cause of the decline in income. We therefore are choosing between the assertion that the banking panic of 1930 was the mechanism by which changes in the agricultural sector were communicated to the

45. Ibid., pp. 167–68, 311–12.
46. Lewis, 1949, p. 56.

rest of the economy and the assertion that a collapse originating within the banking system itself caused the Depression. To the extent that the bank failures were caused by the fall in bond prices or by the existence of the Federal Reserve, of course, they clearly were part of the Depression or an independent influence, respectively. But since there do not appear to be tests available to measure the effects of these overall causes, the discussion is confined to the differential incidence of the causes just outlined.

Two methods will be used to discriminate between these causes, one relating to the banking system as a whole and one relating to a single bank. If agricultural distress caused the banking panic of 1930, more banks should have failed in agricultural areas than elsewhere. Friedman and Schwartz claim that "a contagion of fear" spread from these areas to the rest of the country. This would moderate the difference between agricultural and nonagricultural areas, but it should not eliminate it. If bad loans and investments made in the 1920s caused the panic, then areas with more bank failures in the 1920s should have had more failures in 1930, where failures in the 1920s are used as a proxy for bad loans and investments. These hypotheses will be tested statistically. Then the history of the largest single bank failure in 1930, the failure of the Bank of United States, will be examined in more detail.

The data on the geographical distribution of bank failures can be organized in several ways. Since the number of banks in each state varied, the proportion of banks in a given state that failed is a good index of the severity of conditions within that state. This measure, however, has the dubious merit of weighting all states equally, that is, of weighting Arizona with its fifty banks in 1929 equally with Pennsylvania with its fifteen hundred banks. An alternate index, therefore, is simply the number of banks in each state that failed.[47] This index treats all banks alike independent of size. It weights large and small banks equally, a bias that can be eliminated by using each dollar of deposits as the unit of observation. For symmetry, the proportion of deposits in a state that were in failed banks also was used to incorporate the effect of size differences among banks when using states as the units of observation.

47. The states mentioned by Friedman and Schwartz in the passage quoted on page 85 were those in which the largest number of banks failed, and they appear to have used the individual bank as their unit of observation.

All of these variables were regressed on a set of variables for each of the years 1929, 1930, and 1931. The idea behind the variables remains the same for all the years, but the actual variables are different for the different dependent variables to keep the weighting consistent within each regression. For the regressions with the proportions of banks that failed (*PN*) and the proportion of deposits in failed banks (*PD*) as the dependent variables, the independent variables are the proportion of the state's income derived from growing cotton, the proportion derived from growing wheat, the proportion coming from other farm income, and the ratio of bank failures in 1921–29 to the number of banks in existence on June 30, 1920 ("previous suspensions"). For the regressions using the number of banks that failed (*N*) as the dependent variable, variables are the ones just listed multiplied by the number of banks in the state in 1929. The agricultural variables, therefore, equal the value of income originating in the sectors mentioned times the number of banks per dollar of total income in that state. The "previous suspension" variable equals the number of bank failures in 1921–29 times the ratio of the number of banks in 1929 to the number of banks in 1920. For the regressions using the deposits in failed banks (*D*) as the dependent variable, the independent variables are the ones originally listed multiplied by the total value of deposits in the state. The interpretation of the variables is analogous to the preceding case.[48]

The regression results are shown in Table 11. The regressions generally explain between one-quarter and one-half of the variance of the dependent variable. This is quite good for cross-section regressions, although it does emphasize the limited explanatory power of the variables being used. Our primary interest, however, is in the significance of the individual coefficients. And here we find some interesting results.

In all the regressions for 1929 the only significant variables (with one exception) are the "previous suspension" ones. This correlation is partly spurious since the independent variable contains the dependent variable among others. Nevertheless, these regressions show that the

48. The data come from *Banking and Monetary Statistics,* 1943, pp. 24–33, 284–85; *U.S. Statistical Abstract,* 1931, pp. 709–15; *Federal Reserve Bulletin,* September 1937, p. 883; and *Survey of Current Business,* Supplement, 1956, p. 207. The nature of the data on previous suspensions forces the awkward definition of this variable.

bank failures of 1929 were part of the general movement of the 1920s and that they were not more prevalent in agricultural areas than in others after correction for the overall experience of the 1920s.[49]

The picture is completely different for 1930. The "previous suspension" variables are not significant in any of the regressions; the banking failures of 1930 were not a continuation of the failures of the 1920s. The cotton variable is significantly positive in the first two regressions (where states are the units of observation); positive but less

TABLE 11 • *Regression Results on the Causes of Bank Failures, 1929–31*

Dependent Variable	Cotton Income	Wheat Income	Other Farm Income	Previous Suspensions	R^2
		1929			
PN	−.04	−.06	−.05	.18	.41
	(−.48)	(−.74)	(−.75)	(4.9)	
PD	−.06	−.06	−.04	.09	.28
	(−1.3)	(−1.1)	(−.97)	(3.9)	
N	−.07	.01	.02	.17	.43
	(−.90)	(.15)	(.35)	(2.8)	
D	−.07	−.05	−.03	.09	.42
	(−2.1)	(−.84)	(−1.7)	(5.1)	
		1930			
PN	.57	.15	.06	.07	.50
	(5.6)	(1.3)	(.68)	(1.5)	
PD	.27	.02	.10	.02	.29
	(3.4)	(.21)	(1.5)	(.53)	
N	.23	.04	.12	.11	.39
	(1.9)	(.73)	(1.4)	(1.3)	
D	−.02	−.24	.22	.00	.28
	(−.15)	(−.92)	(3.1)	(.02)	
		1931			
PN	.25	.18	.11	.01	.21
	(2.5)	(1.6)	(1.3)	(.20)	
PD	.15	.08	.10	−.02	.16
	(2.3)	(1.2)	(1.8)	(−.67)	
N	.03	−.04	.35	.12	.45
	(.19)	(−.20)	(2.8)	(.92)	
D	−.21	.26	.31	.07	.22
	(−.75)	(.49)	(2.1)	(.44)	

NOTE: *t*-statistics are shown in parentheses.

49. The one significant agricultural variable has the wrong sign: fewer dollars of deposits in failed banks were in cotton-growing states than in others.

significant in the regression for the number of failed banks; and not different from zero in the regression for deposits. The "other farm income" variable is significant only for the regression explaining the volume of deposits in failed banks. If one wants to explain the different experiences of states or of banks, therefore, it makes sense to attribute them in part to their proximity to the cotton market. The price of cotton declined rapidly, and the solvency of banks in cotton-growing areas was affected by this fall, either because they financed trade or because they were linked to cotton in some less direct way. The states for which this phenomenon was important, however, contain a relatively small share of the nation's deposits and it does not help to explain the amount of deposits in failed banks.[50]

The geographical pattern of failures in 1931 followed roughly the same pattern as it did in 1930. There was no correlation between the pattern in 1931 and the pattern of the 1920s. And there were more failures in agriculture areas than in others. Taking the states as the units of observation, cotton-growing areas again seem to have been the hardest hit. Taking banks or deposits as units makes farm income other than that from cotton and wheat into the most significant variable. The link to agriculture clearly is there, but its precise nature is by no means clear.

We conclude from this exercise that the bank failures of 1930 (and 1931) were not the result of poor loans and investments made in the 1920s and that they were caused to some extent by changes in agricultural conditions. This concentration is apparent if we look at states and also, to a lesser extent, if we look at the number of banks. It is not visible (in 1930) if we take a dollar of deposits as our unit of observation.

One reason why the location of deposits in failed banks may be hard to explain by regression methods is that a few banks accounted for a disproportionate part of the failures. The Bank of United States alone contained almost one-fifth of the deposits in failed banks in 1930. This bank was over three times the size of any other bank failing at the time and the largest bank to fail up to that time. It deserves—and got from Friedman and Schwartz—special attention. Friedman and Schwartz attempted to show, however, that the Bank of United States was an ordinary solvent bank caught in a temporary

50. The difference between the regression on *D* in 1930 echoes the difference in 1929. In both years, the influence of the cotton variable was more negative for *D* than for the other dependent variables shown in Table 11.

liquidity crisis that could have been met by a short-term loan from the Clearing House. This view of the Bank of United States is completely at variance with the facts.

The Bank of United States was formed in 1913 by Joseph S. Marcus with an initial capital of $100,000. It grew slowly until Joseph Marcus's death in late 1928, when it had a capital of $6 million and six branches in New York City. Despite the grandiose name, the bank was throughout this period a small local bank, serving a predominantly Jewish clientele in Manhattan. All of this changed when the founder's son, Bernard K. Marcus, succeeded to the presidency of the bank upon his father's death. Bernard Marcus embarked on a vigorous program of expansion and fraud that ended with the bank's failure in late 1930.

The Bank of United States merged with the Central Mercantile Bank and Trust Company in May 1928, bringing its capital up to $8.3 million and increasing the number of its branches to fifteen. It merged with the Cosmopolitan Bank in August 1928, bringing the number of its branches up to twenty. It merged with the City Financial Corporation in November 1928, bringing its capital up to $18 million. A security and investment affiliate of the bank, the Bankus Corporation, was formed at this time to take over the City Financial Corporation. The Bank of United States then merged with the Colonial Bank and the Bank of the Rockaways in April 1929, bringing its capital up to $21 million and the number of its branches up to thirty-seven. And it merged with the Municipal Bank and Trust Company in May 1929, bringing its capital up to $25 million and the number of its branches up to fifty-seven. Two branches were opened later, and the bank had fifty-nine branches at the time of its failure.

It is clear that the Bank of United States under Bernard Marcus was a very different bank than it had been under his father. In two years, Bernard Marcus had quadrupled the bank's capital stock and increased the number of its branches by a factor of ten. He had also formed the Bankus Corporation, which was investing in New York real estate and indulging in a variety of questionable and—it turned out—illegal activity. Problems with the Bank of United States apparently surfaced with a bank examiner's report in 1930 that wiped out $17 million of the bank's surplus and undivided profits. After the failure, over $50 million of other assets were cited as also "impaired." These included $25 million in loans to the bank's subsidiaries (of which almost $20 million were to the Bankus Corporation, City Financial Corporation, and their subsidiaries), $17 million in mortgages and frozen real-estate loans (of which over $8 million were second or third mortgages which were frozen due to the Depression), and $13 million of other ''slow'' loans. Almost all of these ''impaired'' assets were direct or indirect claims on real estate.

It should not be inferred that this was simply a bank that was dragged down by the general decline in the monetary value of assets during the Depression, because many of these real-estate investments were not simply illiquid, they were also illegal. Banks in New York are forbidden to own land in names other than their own. Yet the Bank of United States had several landowning subsidiaries.

This practice seems to have arisen in the following way. The bank had an excessive amount of mortgages in its assets, making it illiquid. In order to disguise the composition of its assets, the bank acquired the property on which it had mortgages and sold this property to its subsidiaries in return for short-term loans. It thereby succeeded in transforming long-term assets (mortgages) into short-term assets (accounts receivable). These loans, of course, were short-term in name only; one cannot change the nature of a loan merely by relabeling it. The activity was just the kind of fraudulent labeling of assets that the law appears designed to prevent.

Even this strategem appears not to have worked, however, because the subsidiaries found themselves with an excessive amount of debt to the bank. The bank and its subsidiaries got together and tried in a very complex and roundabout fashion—which nevertheless was detected—to erase $8 million of debt owned by the Bankus and City Financial Corporations to the bank. Marcus, together with the executive vice-president of the bank and the vice-president's son, were indicted for this illegal activity, convicted and imprisoned. Marcus and the vice-president were sentenced to three to six years; the son received an indeterminate sentence of up to three years.

In his appeal to the New York Clearing House for aid to the Bank of United States, Joseph Broderick, the New York State Superintendent of Banks, described the dangers he foresaw if the bank were allowed to fail. But he also admitted the tenuous nature of the claim these men had upon their fellow bankers. According to his later recollection, he said that "I did not like the policies and practices of the bank and that I was convinced the officers were of a type which might better never have been in the banking business, but I added that they were not the only such officers in the city and that I had to be patient with them and try as best I could to correct their errors and reform their methods." A more damning indictment in the context cannot be imagined.[51]

Friedman and Schwartz offered as confirmation of the Bank of United States's essential soundness the observation that the Bank of United States paid out 83.5 per cent of its liabilities at the time of its closing, four-fifths of it within two years. Phrased differently, the Bank of United States paid only about $.60 on each dollar of deposits within two years of its closing. Over one-fifth of this was composed of offsets, that is, simultaneous cancellations of loans and deposits. This is not compelling evidence of underlying solvency.[52]

The banking crisis of November and December 1930 seems, therefore, to have been composed of at least two quite distinct events. There was a rash of bank failures in cotton-growing areas, and a large New York bank closed due to fraud. The concomitant nature of these events may have been coincidence or it may have been the result of the declining value of assets in bank portfolios. In any case, the contrast between these events suggests that the banking panic in 1930 was caused in part by events outside the banking system and in part by events inside the system.

The former class of events appears to have been the more important. This inference derives from the observation that the initial decrease in the demand for demand deposits resulting from the bank failures preceded the failure of the Bank of United States. The rise in the public's holdings of currency, which can be used as an index of the fall in the demand for deposits, was already evident in November

51. The foregoing account has been taken from a series of articles in the *Commercial and Financial Chronicle* 131: 3815–16 (Dec. 13, 1930); 132: 971–72 (Feb. 7, 1931), 1161–63 (Feb. 14, 1931), 2319 (Mar. 28, 1931); 134: 3743–46 (May 21, 1932). Friedman and Schwartz quoted part of Broderick's appeal to the Clearing House, but not the part where he acknowledged the character of the bank's officers (Friedman and Schwartz, 1963a, p. 309n).

52. New York State, 1931, pp. 53, 148–49; *Moody's Manual of Investments*, 1932, p. 2614; and 1939, pp. 40–41.

1930, before the failure of the Bank of United States.[53] The failure of the Bank of United States was a special case, connected intimately with the personalities of its officers and speedily linked to fraud and dishonesty. There is little reason to think that holders of bank deposits generalized these character traits to all bankers as a result of this single failure. The beginning of the process initiated by the banking panic therefore cannot be attributed to it.

The money hypothesis is concerned primarily with the effects of the banking crisis, not its causes. But to the extent that the banking crisis was caused by agricultural distress and the increased riskiness of industrial bonds, the Depression cannot be attributed purely to monetary factors even by adherents of the money hypothesis. Instead, the money hypothesis and the spending hypothesis select different aspects of the initial downturn in 1929 to emphasize. The spending hypothesis asserts that the large decline in total (U.S.) consumption was the critical difference between this and other declines in income and that this aspect of the decline was the one that perpetuated the decline. The money hypothesis, by contrast, asserts that the (world-wide) agricultural decline was the distinguishing feature of this downturn, the features that produced effects that led, in turn, to the massive decline in income.[54]

To the extent that the bank failures were the result of the change in the banking system attendant on the creation of the Federal Reserve System, however, the two stories are entirely distinct. In this case, the difference between the behavior of the banking system in 1930 and other depressions cannot be traced to the events of 1930. The contrast between 1930 and 1893 or 1907 was the result of the existence of the Federal Reserve. But the contrast between 1930 and 1921 or 1938 then cries for explanation. The difference between 1930 and 1938 can be explained by the formation of the FDIC, and the consequent removal of risks to depositors.[55] But the difference between 1930 and 1921 must have been in the events of those years, as the Fed existed in

53. Friedman and Schwartz, 1963a, pp. 713, 803.

54. If the decline in consumption can be attributed to the agricultural depression, the two stories may be different aspects of a single tale. See the discussion of agriculture and consumption in Chapter V.

55. Friedman and Schwartz, 1963a, pp. 434–42.

both. Since the deflation of 1921 was even more severe than the one of 1930, the source of the difference is unclear. The precipitating factors in the money hypothesis are no clearer than in the spending hypothesis.

IV

Why the Stock of Money Fell

WE TURN NOW to the central issue of this inquiry: Did the stock of money fall because of a fall in the supply or a fall in the demand? This question, of course, is an example of the classic identification problem. For the reasons outlined in Chapter II, the usual econometric methods for dealing with this problem are not appropriate here. While the need for theory to resolve the identification problem is unabated, the theory used here concerns the adjustment mechanism of the economy, not some aspect of comparative statics. Accordingly, we begin our discussion with a brief review of the way in which autonomous changes in the money supply are thought to affect the economy.

A Sketch of the Theory

Assume that individuals and firms in the economy are content with the stocks of assets, financial and real, that they own. Let the supply of money increase for exogenous reasons—which may or may not be reasons of aggregate economic policy. Then there will be an oversupply of the asset called money; there will be more money in the economy than people want to hold at the prevailing prices. People will attempt to get rid of some of their money holdings. They will "sell" money, that is, they will buy other things with money, and the increase in the demand for these other things will raise their prices. If the other things are assets with a fixed return, this will lower the ratio of their return to their price, also known as their rate of return or their "own rate of interest."

This reaction to a change in the supply of money is known as the liquidity or portfolio effect. There is general agreement among all economists that a process like this takes place.[1] There are, however, some further delineations of the process that are necessary to our discussion. Which other things do people buy with the money they do not want to hold? And how long will this effect on rates of return last?

The most popular version of what people do with their money is what I shall call the "pebble in the pond" theory. This theory says that people use their excess money balances in the first instance to buy assets that are similar to money and then later spread out to assets that are more and more unlike money, much as ripples spread out toward the shore from the place where a pebble drops into a pond. More explicitly,

> It seems plausible that both nonbank and bank holders of redundant balances will turn first to securities comparable to those they have sold, say, fixed-interest coupon, low-risk obligations. But as they seek to purchase these they will tend to bid up the prices of those issues. Hence they, and also other holders not involved in the initial increase in the money supply, will look farther afield: the banks, to their loans; the nonbank holders, to other categories of securities—higher-risk fixed-coupon obligations, equities, real property, and so forth.
>
> As the process continues, the initial impacts are diffused in several respects: first, the range of assets affected widens; second, potential creators of assets now more in demand are induced to react to the better terms on which they can be sold, involving business enterprises wishing to engage in capital expansion, house builders or prospective homeowners, consumers—who are potential purchasers of durable consumer goods—and so on and on; third, the initially redundant money balances concentrated in the hands of those first affected by the open-market purchases become spread throughout the economy.
>
> As the prices of financial assets are bid up, they become expensive relative to nonfinancial assets, so there is an incentive for individuals and enterprises to seek to bring their actual portfolios into accord with desired portfolios by acquiring nonfinancial assets. This, in turn, tends to make existing nonfinancial assets expensive relative to newly constructed nonfinancial assets. At the same time, the general rise in the price level of nonfinancial assets tends to raise wealth relative to income, and to make the direct acquisition of current services cheaper relative to the purchase of sources of services. These effects raise demand curves for current productive services, both for producing new capital goods and for purchasing current services. The monetary stimulus

1. See Tobin, 1969, and below.

is, in this way, spread from the financial markets to the markets for goods and services.[2]

These words come from a description of the mechanism transmitting monetary changes to the rest of the economy written by Friedman and Schwartz, the prime exponents of the money hypotheses, and published at the same time as their *Monetary History*. These authors go on to say that terms like *financial markets* have to be interpreted more broadly than is usually done, but that does not alter their insistence on a path of change, from assets that resemble money to assets that don't and, further, to current services.

Now if one wants to find out if a pebble has been dropped into a pond, one may watch the water level at any point in the pond. If a pebble has fallen into the pond, the water level at each point in the pond will rise at some point. It will not rise all over the pond at the same time, nor will it rise to the same height at each spot. But it will rise everywhere at some point. One can moniter the water level anywhere in the pond, therefore, but the chances of successful observation are maximized if one observes a place near the place where the pebble fell, since the water there will rise soonest and farthest.

Similarly, if one wants to discover if the supply of money has been curtailed at some point, one can observe interest rates (interpreted broadly) at any point in the path from money to current services. The chance of a successful test are maximized, however, by watching interest rates on assets much like money. Following the analogy, these rates will rise soonest and farthest. In addition, there is less likelihood that this effect will be masked by other events if the assets chosen to be watched are very like money, both because the influences that will impinge on the price of these moneylike assets are not very different than the forces acting in the money market and because the time lag between the restriction of supply and the reaction in these markets will not be long. One would not want to say that the rise in these interest rates caused the subsequent changes in the economy any more than one would want to say that the waves lapping at the shore were caused by the rise in the water level fifty feet out. They are each part of the same process. A particular set of interest rates is isolated, like a particular spot on the pond, solely for the purposes of observation.

2. Friedman and Schwartz, 1963b, pp. 60–61. For an equivalent statement, see Friedman and Meiselman, 1963, pp. 217–22.

It is not enough for our purposes just to observe whether a few interest rates rose. We are inquiring into the causes of the Great Depression, and we want to know not simply if the supply of money fell, but if it fell far enough to explain a major movement of income. Consequently, just as one might estimate the size of the pebble falling into the pond from the size of the resultant wave (given the distance between the pebble's impact and the wave measurement), so one can estimate the magnitude of the fall in the supply of money from the magnitude of the rise in interest rates. Observation of interest rates on assets very much like money should facilitate this quantitative test, since the relation between the size of the restriction of the money supply and the change in the interest rates will be close. There will not be time for other, extraneous influences to make themselves felt. For both the qualitative and the quantitative test, therefore, we want to examine interest rates on assets resembling money, that is, on short-term, low-risk assets.[3]

The waves generated by a pebble's impact recede quickly, and the change in the level of the water at any point is only temporary. Does the analogy extend to interest rates? Most people agree that it does. Interest rates rise quickly to a peak value from which they recede in short order. People do not agree, however, on how far interest rates recede. Some people say they will return to their own level or below; others say they will remain higher. The issues can be illuminated by means of a simple graph.

Figure 1 reproduces the familiar *IS-LM* curves. Assume that the economy is at equilibrium with an interest rate of r_0 when the money supply decreases, shifting the *LM* curve from LM_1 to LM_2. The eventual equilibrium lies at the intersection of the new *LM* curve and the *IS* curve, at r_2. But since income cannot change easily in the short run, the short-run *IS* curve is vertical or close to vertical, like IS'. The economy moves in the first instance to the intersection of LM_2 and IS'

3. We must be cautious in using this analogy, as one must be cautious in using all analogies, because the parallel is not quite exact. In particular, there is no analogue of the demand for money in the story about a falling pebble. If the demand for money was falling at the same time as the supply fell, then the depressing effect of the former on interest rates might have more than offset the enhancing effect of the latter. Clearly, a rise in interest rates only shows that the supply of money has contracted more rapidly than the demand. It can only show the net effect of changes in both supply and demand, not the effects of changes in the supply alone. As noted below, this makes the test to be proposed somewhat more complicated than a simple examination of interest rates.

and then more gradually to the intersection of LM_2 and IS as the IS curve rotates counterclockwise from IS' to IS. The interest rate rises from r_0 to r_1 and then falls again to r_2.

Under what circumstances will r_2 be no higher than r_0? The answer is clear. Only if the IS curve is horizontal will r_2 equal r_0. And the IS curve will be horizontal only if either investment or consumption spending is infinitely elastic with respect to the interest rate. And while it seems to be generally accepted that spending is in fact affected by interest rates in some degree, no one maintains that it is anywhere near this sensitive.[4]

This condition therefore has not figured in the discussion of this question in the literature. The question of whether the interest rate

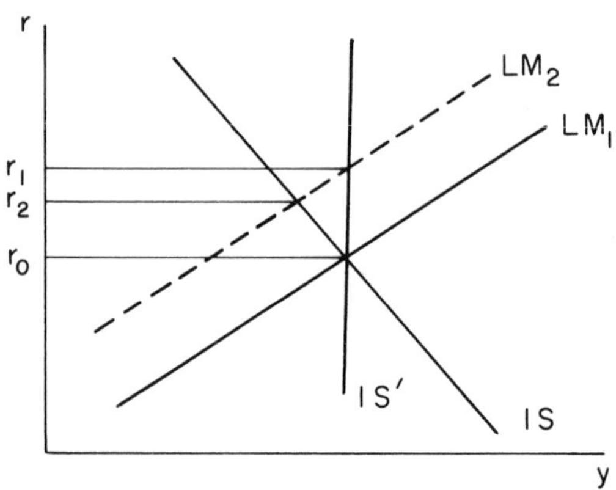

FIGURE 1. *IS-LM* Curves.

regains its old level after a change in the supply of money has been analyzed primarily from the standpoint of a rise in the supply. Explicitly or implicitly, the assumption is made that the economy is in full employment. Under these circumstances, an increase in the supply of money changes only the price level in the long run, and the interest rate is unaffected. But this result follows from the assumption of full employment, which clearly is inappropriate for the present discussion.[5]

4. I neglect the theoretical curiosity of an upward-sloping *IS* curve. The important fact that income is rising over time whenever investment is positive, which makes the static analysis problematical, will be incorporated into the analysis after the static case is considered.

5. Friedman, 1968, pp. 5–11; Cagan, 1972, p. 2.

In the absence of substantial opinion or evidence to the contrary, therefore, we may assume that the interest rate after a fall in the supply of money will be higher than the interest rate before, even after the short-run inelasticity of the *IS* curve has been allowed to evaporate. The analogy of the pebble continues to hold here, if we remember that the pebble now lies at the bottom of the pond, raising the eventual smooth water level.

The movement of the interest rate in Figure 1 from r_1 to r_2 is known as the income effect.[6] This effect describes the impact on the interest rate of the movement in income in response to the disequilibrium in the money market. Even though this disequilibrium initially affects only the money market and markets for closely related assets, the disequilibrium eventually is removed by movement of both the interest rate and income. The movement of the interest rate consequently is not as large as it would have to be if only the interest rate moved.

The discussion has been done entirely in static terms up to now. But income and the stock of money are growing over time, and most of the discussion in the literature is carried out in terms of rates of changes of these variables. To make the change, the rate of change of the money supply should be substituted for the supply of money in the preceding paragraphs. And for changes in the supply, changes in the rate of change of the supply should be read. The argument remains unchanged except for one important addition. In the static case, the price level is constant in equilibrium. The difference between the real and nominal interest rate therefore is not important. In the dynamic case, an alteration in the rate of change in the money supply could lead to a continuous change in the price level. As people begin to incorporate the rate of change of prices into their planning, they may begin to distinguish between the real and nominal rates of interest.

A decrease in the rate of change of the money supply therefore could lead to an eventual fall in the interest rate because of a third effect, the price effect. Assume that the rate of change of the money supply falls for some reason. Interest rates will rise as a result of the liquidity effect, and then spending will fall. Both income and prices then may be expected to fall. The fall in income will decrease interest rates, and the decline in the price level—if it continues long enough—will lead people to add this rate of decline to the interest rate in calculating the cost of borrowing. For a given desired cost (real inter-

6. Gibson, 1970, p. 436.

est rate), the nominal interest rate will be lowered. The liquidity and income effects therefore show how the real interest rate changes; the price effect shows how the nominal (observed) interest rate falls below the real interest rate in response to a decrease in the rate of change of the money supply. The price effect, it must be remembered, comes into play only with a lag and only if the decline in prices is expected to be sustained.

This discussion therefore leads to the following conclusion. If there was an exogenous decrease in the supply of money in 1930, then we should be able to observe a temporary rise in the rate of interest on assets bearing some resemblance to money. Following this rise, we could find a fall that eventually carried the nominal interest rate below its previous level as the deflation of the early 1930s continued.

These expectations are based on the money hypothesis. The spending hypothesis leads to a different set of expectations about the interest rate. According to this story, the supply of money did not fall in an otherwise normal situation. A decrease in spending decreased the demand for money instead. Interest rates fell as a result. Both hypotheses thus may be consistent with a fall in interest rates in the early 1930s. This fall cannot be used to discriminate between them. The money hypothesis asserts that this fall was preceded by a rise, while the spending hypothesis denies the existence of any such rise. Discrimination between the hypotheses, therefore, can come only at the beginning of the process, that is, in the months immediately following the supposed decline in the rate of growth of the money supply.

This is not strictly true because the spending hypothesis implies that interest rates fell no matter what people's long-run expectations were, while the money hypothesis implies that they fell only if people expected a continuing deflation. Accordingly, if we knew the state of expectations in 1931, a further test would be possible. Since these expectations are exceedingly hard to uncover, however, this additional test must be foregone.[7]

An idea of the usual time period between the initial change in the system and the return of the interest rate to its original level can be gleaned from the literature. Friedman, in a theoretical argument, set the time at "a year or two." One statistical inquiry using Friedman's theoretical framework and post-World War II data concluded that the

7. But see Chapter V for a discussion of these expectations.

time period was much shorter, only three to five months, but another one supported Friedman's estimate. A simulation of a large-scale flow-of-funds model showed that the interest rates on Treasury bills and three-to-five-year bonds were lower in the first quarter following a rise in unborrowed reserves than in the second quarter, but that these rates did not regain their initial level even after four years.[8] The peak of the rise in interest rates following a fall in the supply of money (or the rate of change of this supply) therefore should be reached in the first quarter following the change in the supply of money according to this literature. There is no general expectation about the time necessary to return the interest rate to its previous level. In terms of Figure 1, the interest rate goes from r_0 to r_1 in one quarter and starts back toward r_2 in the same or following quarter.

Assets that resemble money are financial assets with low risk, fixed yield, and a short time to maturity. But before we look at the paths of the interest rates on such financial securities, we must acknowledge the bewildering variety of interest-rate paths that could be observed. In the two years following the stock-market crash of 1929, short-term interest rates generally fell, yields on government bonds stayed constant, and yields on industrial bonds went up.[9] It looks at first glance as if an interest rate could be found to fit any desired pattern at all. Before examining these rates or selecting a subset to examine, therefore, we must attempt to explain the failure of interest rates to move together in 1930 and 1931.

Changes in Interest-Rate Differentials

Figure 2 shows the path of several interest rates. The diversity of these paths is easily apparent. An abrupt rise in the short-term rates in the fourth quarter of 1931 is also easily apparent. This rise appears to be a direct response to Britain's departure from gold in September 1931. As such, it represents the reaction to a stimulus other than the ones discussed so far and to a stimulus coming later in time than the

8. Friedman, 1968; Gibson, 1970, p. 453; Cagan, 1972, pp. 100–104; Bosworth and Duesenberry, 1973, p. 92. Simulation of the MPS model yielded a path for the yield on Aaa bonds that had the same shape as Bosworth and Duesenberry's path for the bill rate. See de Leeuw and Gramlich, 1968.

9. Stock prices fell, but stock yields did not simply rise as a result. See Table 4, above, and the discussion of it.

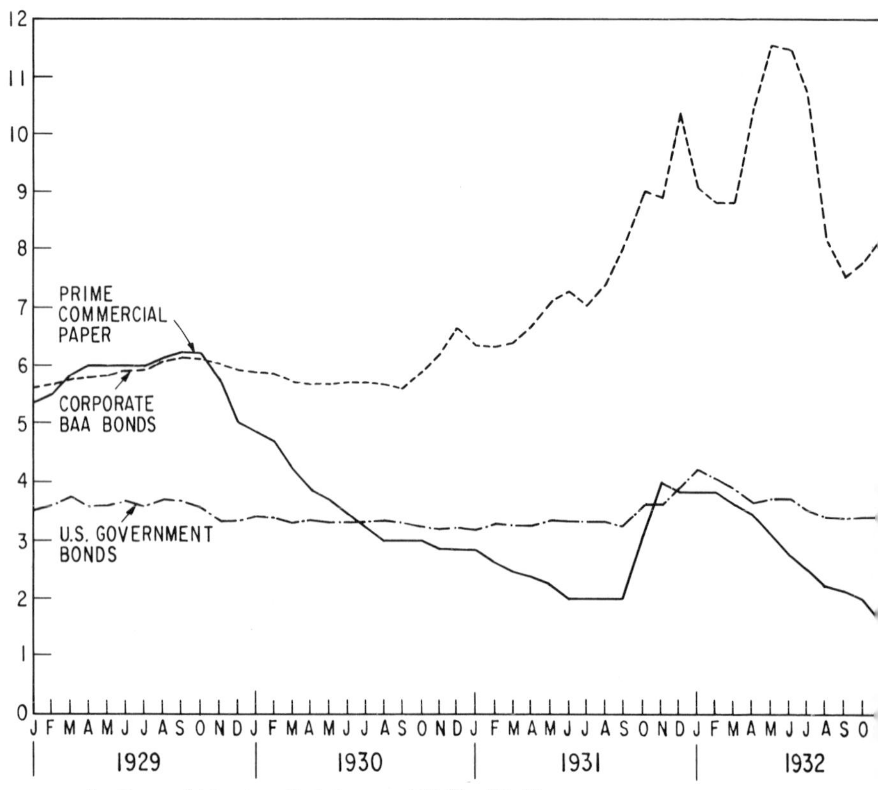

SOURCE: *Banking and Monetary Statistics,* pp. 448–51, 468–71.

FIGURE 2. Yields on Selected Assets, 1929–32.

ones discussed here. It makes sense, therefore, to discuss the path of interest rates before Britain's action.[10]

Before restricting ourselves in this way, however, we should acknowledge the meaning of the rise in short-term interest rates after September 1931. This movement is precisely the kind of evidence we are seeking to show the existence of a monetary restriction. As is well-known, the Federal Reserve responded to the British action by restrictive policies. These resulted in a temporary rise in interest rates on assets resembling money, precisely as the theory reviewed above pre-

10. See Chapter V for a discussion of the interaction between the European and American economies.

dicts. It can be seen from Figure 2 that the effect is very apparent in short-term interest rates, less apparent in the yields on government bonds, and impossible to identify in the yield on Baa bonds. This episode—which is not in dispute—shows both that the effects we seek to find can be found if the conditions are right and also that one must examine short-term interest rates to see them at all clearly. The waves lose their sharp shapes as they move farther and farther away from the falling pebble.

There are two problems to be considered in discussing the path of interest rates in 1930 and 1931 (before the last quarter). First, there appears to have been an increase in the spread between interest rates for securities of different risk of default but the same maturities. Second, there appears to have been an increase in the spread of interest rates for securities of the same risk and different times till maturity. The first observation is the sort that is interpreted as an increase in the risk premium; the second, as an increase in liquidity preference. We consider these views in turn.

As Figure 2 demonstrates, the price of lower-grade corporate bonds with a given degree of risk fell sharply in 1931. Friedman and Schwartz asserted that this price decline was the result of a scramble for liquidity by banks that started during the banking panic in late 1930, but this suggestion will not stand up.[11] As will emerge shortly, many bond prices began to fall well before the panic. And only the prices of lower-grade bonds fell; the price of high-grade corporate and government bonds stayed roughly constant.

A liquidity scramble, *ceteris paribus,* should affect the prices of all relatively liquid assets held by the illiquid parties since these people will attempt to sell some or all of these assets to raise cash without excessively unbalancing their portfolios. All of the bonds held in bank portfolios were sold on organized markets. There was no suggestion that any of them was more liquid than the others, that is, that one could be sold at shorter notice than the others. While higher-risk bonds showed more price variation over the period of the Depression than lower-risk bonds, there is no evidence that the day-to-day or the week-to-week variation was any higher.

A fall in the price of one of these assets (or one subclass of these assets), therefore, reflects a change in expectations about this asset relative to others. People will attempt to sell one asset rather than another

11. Friedman and Schwartz, 1963a, p. 312.

if they expect its price to fall relative to the other, a phenomenon that may coexist with a liquidity scramble, but which is independent of such a scramble. Therefore, the fall in the price of low-grade bonds in 1931 while the price of high-grade and government bonds stayed constant is evidence of a growing expected risk of corporate failure, not of illiquidity by bond holders.[12]

The data on net downgrading of bonds shown in Table 10, above, shows in a more direct way that the perceived risk of corporate bonds was rising, particularly in 1931. The data shown in Table 10, however, also indicate that the rate on Baa bonds—or on any other quality class of bonds—was not the same as the rate on any single bond or group of bonds in the early 1930s. Bonds were being moved from one quality class to another, and the interest rates for specific bonds must have risen more rapidly than the rate for any quality-constant group. The movements of the Baa rate therefore do not show the change in price of banks' portfolios.

This problem can be seen more clearly through the data in Table 12. The first two columns of the table show the familiar Aaa and Baa interest rates. (Yield-to-maturity is used here for the interest rate.) The third column of Table 12 shows the yield to maturity of a random sample of bonds traded on the New York Stock Exchange—where the sample remains constant over the period shown. The yield on this fixed sample of bonds rose sooner and faster than the rate on Baa bonds. The price decline in any actual bond portfolio in the early 1930s therefore was the result of two processes: the decline in the price of a given quality class and the decline in the quality ratings of the bonds in the portfolio.

The final two columns attempt to disentangle these two processes. They show the extent to which the yields on Baa bonds and on the fixed sample of bonds exceeded the yield on Aaa bonds. The difference between the two premiums is very important. The rise in the yield of the fixed sample of bonds—and therefore the rise in the premium of this yield over the Aaa yield—is a better proxy for the decline in the value of bonds actually held in bank portfolios than the rise in the yield of Baa bonds.[13]

12. Banks were net sellers of bonds in 1931 because they perceived the risk more quickly or because they were more risk averse than individuals. The fact that they sold while individuals bought is not evidence of a liquidity scramble by banks. See Goldsmith, 1955, vol. 1, p. 543.

13. In addition to showing the yield on a fixed portfolio rather than a shifting

But while the yield of the fixed sample is a better proxy for the change in the value of bank bond portfolios, it is still far from ideal. It captures the undoubted fact that banks held a portfolio of bonds and that they suffered from any downgrading of these bonds. But the bonds in banks' portfolios may have been downgraded more or less than the bonds in the random sample shown here. There is no way to know how banks selected their portfolios of bonds or whether the cri-

TABLE 12 • *Bond Yields and Risk Premiums for Different Samples, 1929–31 (percentage yield to maturity)*

	Yields			Risk Premiums	
	Aaa	Baa	Fixed Sample	Baa − Aaa	Fixed Sample − Aaa
December 1928	4.61	5.60	6.01	.99	1.40
June 1929	4.77	5.94	6.73	1.17	1.96
December 1929	4.67	5.95	7.68	1.28	3.08
June 1930	4.57	5.78	8.52	1.21	3.95
December 1930	4.42	5.71	9.26	2.29	4.84
June 1931	4.36	7.36	11.35	3.00	6.99

SOURCES: Columns (1) and (2): *Banking and Monetary Statistics,* pp. 469–70. Column (3): *Bank and Quotation Record,* 1929–31. The sample was formed by taking every tenth bond listed on the NYSE with sales of over $1 million in 1928 until twenty bonds were selected. The sample extended from firms beginning with A to firms beginning with Y. The rates are for prices at the end of the months shown.

teria they used to select bonds before 1929 discriminated well between bonds that were downgraded after 1929 and bonds that were not. If we wish to be generous toward the bank managers of the day, we could hazard the guess that the yield on the randomly selected fixed sample shown in Table 12 rose more slowly than the yield on the actual portfolios of banks. Alternatively, if loans and investments made in the 1920s were "poor," they might have risen faster.

The premium of the fixed sample began to rise well before the premium on Baa bonds. In fact, it was rising steadily throughout the period shown. Even though the change in the yield of the fixed sample

---

group of bonds, it is also free of the problem discussed below. Since the yields shown in the third column of Table 12 were derived from quoted bond prices, the changes in the yields shown in the table correspond to changes in the prices of the bonds.

in Table 12 may overstate the fall in the value of bank portfolios, it shows the timing of this fall far better than the change in the yield of Baa bonds. Since the change in the yield of Baa bonds does not correspond to the change in value of any portfolio, it would be hard to maintain that the timing of changes in this yield informed us about the timing of changes in the value of the portfolios held by banks.

The decline in the value of bank portfolios started well before the bank panic of 1930.[14] As noted already, the price decline of bonds was not the result of a liquidity scramble touched off by the bank panic. In fact, the price decline of bonds in bank portfolios undoubtedly was a cause of the bank panic in 1930. The analysis of bank failures performed in Chapter III concentrated on the differential experience of banks in different locations. It could not uncover any influence that worked on all banks equally. A decline in the value of bonds is such an influence, and it was an important one in 1930.

In the absence of other causes for the price decline, the rise in the yield of the fixed sample may be interpreted as a rise in the risk premium. It shows the implications of net downgrading of bonds on the yields of bonds. The rise in the premium of Baa bonds does not have such a similar interpretation. The bonds included in this class are supposed to be of constant quality, and a rise in the premium of this class should not reflect a rise in the riskiness of these bonds. Why then did this premium rise? Two interpretations are possible.

The first interpretation emphasizes the difference between comparative statics and a dynamic world. At a time when the riskiness of bonds was changing, it may not have been possible to maintain a list of bonds of constant quality. No matter how quick the rating agencies were to catch a change in bond quality, there must inevitably have been a lag between the decline in quality of a given bond and the change in its classification. Ratings are discreet and must change in steps. There is no suggestion that the rating agencies anticipated declines in the quality of bonds, and the step function must have lagged behind the actual rise in riskiness. Without a measure of bond quality independent of the ratings, there is no way to evaluate the magnitude

14. It appears to have started before the stock-market crash of 1929, although the proportion of bonds downgraded in 1929 was not large (see Table 10). This may be a characteristic of the particular sample chosen, and it should help remind us that the yield shown in Table 12 is only a rough proxy for the decline in value of bank portfolios.

of this dynamic effect. The discussion of Table 10 assumed it to be small.

A second interpretation is quite different. Modern portfolio theory has isolated a concept known as the price of risk. This is the premium that is received in the market for an optimal portfolio of a given risk. The riskiness of any given bond is composed of two parts: systematic and unsystematic risk. The latter represents the random element in this particular security, and it can be offset by diversification. A fully diversified portfolio therefore contains only systematic risk. The recognition of this component of risk is an admission that not all risk can be eliminated by diversification. There are some risks inherent in the economy, and no amount of diversification will offset this part of riskiness in an asset. The most common example of systematic risk is business-cycle risk, that is, the risk of loss due to a general downturn of the economy. This type of risk is precisely the risk at issue in the discussion of the early 1930s. It is also the risk left in the fixed sample shown in Table 12, since a sample of twenty bonds effectively removes all unsystematic risk.[15]

For every unit of systematic risk (usually measured in terms of the variance), there is a premium on the expected return. This premium is called the price of risk. It is a characteristic of the market, not of any individual, and it may be assumed constant in the cross-section studies that typify modern portfolio analysis. But there is no reason why this price must remain constant over time. It is possible and even probable that people's desire to take risks diminished in the early 1930s, and that a higher price was needed to convince people to hold securities of a given risk in 1931 than in 1929. The rise in the premium for Baa bonds then shows the rise in the price of a given amount of risk.

While the rise in the price of risk shown in the bond market may have been the result of a change in tastes, it need not have been. Investors hold portfolios of many assets, and very few are as liquid, that is, as easy to sell, as bonds traded on the New York Stock Exchange. If the rise in the riskiness of assets was pervasive in the early 1930s—a plausible assumption—then investors with a given taste for risk would have tried to readjust their portfolios to reduce the overall riskiness. Since the rise in riskiness was due to the economic decline, investors as a group would not have been successful in their attempt to

15. Sharpe, 1970, pp. 84, 149–50.

reduce their risk. Instead, they would have lowered the price of risky assets or, equivalently, raised the price of risk. This change would be most apparent in the prices of liquid assets, since investors could adjust their portfolios most easily by trading liquid assets. The change in the price of risk shown in the bond market then could be the result of an increase in the riskiness of other assets, not a change in tastes.

Under this interpretation, the price of risk rose in late 1930. This change in market prices then lowered the price of risky assets: The resultant downward pressure on the value of bank portfolios was a cause of the bank panic of 1930. This effect was added to the effect of the increasing risk of a given portfolio described just above. If it was the result of a change in expectations induced by the downturn in business, then it provides another reason to view the bank panic as a result of the general downturn.

Riskiness is only one attribute of bond quality; time to maturity is another. And, as noted above, the relative prices of bonds of different maturities also was changing at this time. The yield to maturity of long-term bonds and short-term securities was approximately equal in the late 1920s. After 1929, as suggested in Figure 2, the yield of short-term securities fell dramatically. This information can be summarized in terms of the familiar yield curve, which shows the yield to maturity of bonds on the vertical axis and the time to maturity on the horizontal. In 1929, this curve was flat: yields were the same for bonds of all maturities. In the early 1930s, it was rising; yields to maturity were higher for long-term bonds than for shorter-term ones.[16]

It is tempting to infer from this observation that the term structure of interest rates shows liquidity preference on the part of investors after 1929, that is, that investors were willing to pay a premium (accept a lower yield) to hold shorter-term, more liquid securities. But such an inference cannot be made without further information. All modern theories of the term structure assume that investors make plans for a specific holding period. They compare the returns on assets for that holding period, and they choose assets according to the characteristics of the return in that period.[17] There is no presumption that all investors have the same holding period, but no individual is ever thought to compare directly the yield on three-month commercial paper with

16. *Banking and Monetary Statistics,* p. 477.
17. Malkiel, 1966.

the yield to maturity of a twenty-year bond. He either compares the return on the three-month paper with the return expected to be obtained from buying and selling the long-term bond after three months, or else he compares the yield to maturity of the long-term bond with the expected yield from holding a sequence of short-term instruments. And while the holding periods of investors are not observed, it is reasonable to suppose that investors in 1930 did not compare returns to marketable securities over anything like twenty years. Many people active in these markets, in fact, must have been attempting to take advantage of all short-term opportunities.

Consider the securities of the Federal government, which may be assumed free of default risk. According to the pure expectations theory, investors have a set of expectations regarding the future course of the interest rates on these assets. In the absence of the risk of default, they invest to receive their expected return, but they are indifferent to the form of their investment. For a long-term investment, in other words, they are as willing to buy a sequence of short-term securities as a single long-term bond; and for a short-term investment they are as willing to buy and sell a long-term bond as to buy and redeem a short-term security. Arbitrage between the different forms of investment then will equalize the expected returns from these various paths to a common goal.

In a world where the existing interest rate is expected to last forever, this theory predicts that short-term yield will be the same for all government securities. Long-term bonds that were issued with this constant interest rate as their stated yield will maintain their price at par, and there will be no anticipated capital gains or losses in buying long-term bonds. Other long-term bonds will appreciate or depreciate smoothly until their maturity. Holding-period yields and yields to maturity will be the same.

But in a world where interest rates are expected to change, the capital value of long-term bonds will be expected to change when interest rates change. Since the yield from buying and selling a long-term bond consists of the interest paid out plus the capital gain (or minus the loss) coming from the change in the bond's value, the expected yield will be different both from the yield from the interest payments alone and—if the anticipated holding period is not the same as the outstanding maturity of the bond—from the yield to maturity. To uncover the pattern of expectations revealed by interest rates it is necessary to construct an estimate for the expected yields over the appropriate holding periods.

The conventional explanation for a finding that the holding-period yield on long-term securities exceeded that on short-term securities is that investors expected the short-term interest rate to rise. Investors did not all rush to buy the long-term security, driving its price down and its yield up, because they wished to be in a position to buy short-term securities when their yield rose. This view, however, abstracts from two characteristics of the early 1930s that sharply change the interpretation of such a result.

First, the conventional view does not ask how the pattern of yields came about. In the late 1920s, all yields were high. After the stock-market crash, short-term yields fell sharply. In order for long-term yields to have moved with them, the price of long-term bonds would have had to rise sharply. The result would have been high realized—although not expected—holding-period yields on long-term assets. If we found high holding-period yields for long-term bonds in 1930 and 1931, therefore, they could be the results of the adjustment to the unanticipated fall in short-term interest rates after the stock-market crash. Instead of expecting short-term interest rates to rise, investors in this view expected them to stay low long enough for long-term rates to fall also.

Second, the conventional view does not take account of risks from price fluctuation that are independent of default risk. A long-term bond without risk of default will in general experience more price variation than a similar short-term bond. This uncertainty of the price at any given moment makes the long-term bond more risky in the sense of portfolio theory, and investors can be expected to pay less for a bond with higher risk than one with lower risk. The long-term bond therefore should have a higher yield than the short-term bond, even if there is no risk of default, because there is more risk of facing a low price at some given moment when an investor wishes to sell. The price of long-term bonds in the early 1930s should not have risen to the point where the yields from holding all maturities was the same.

These two factors then work in opposite directions. The expectation that short-term rates will stay at their new low level acted to raise the price of long-term bonds. The rise would have continued for some time if the required adjustment was large and expectations did not all change at once. The greater price variability of long-term bonds acted to lower their mean price, or to arrest the price rise. Expectations of low interest rates therefore raised holding-period returns; expectations of risk lowered them.

These reactions sound counter-intuitive, and for good reason. The conventional analysis implicitly assumes that interest rates have not been changing in the recent past and that interest rates are in some kind of equilibrium configuration. This assumption does not fit the early 1930s. Short-term interest rates had dropped sharply and were continuing downward. If the yields on long-term bonds were to fall as a result, the prices of long-term bonds had to rise, producing large—but unanticipated—returns to holders of these bonds. On the other hand, if short-term rates were not expected to stay low or if investors were wary of the greater price variation of long-term bonds, the price of long-term bonds would not have fallen, and investors would not have earned large profits.

Having transformed the discussion from yields to maturity to holding-period yields, it is necessary to do the same to the data. This will be accomplished by examining the one-month holding-period yield on a few risk-free assets. Monthly bond price data were taken from the *Bank and Quotation Record* for four securities of the federal government over the period from October 1928 to December 1931. The securities consisted of two U.S. Treasury Bonds (4¼s 1947–52 and 3⅜s 1943–47), one U.S. Treasury Note (3½s December 15, 1930–32) and one U.S. Treasury Certificate of Indebtedness (various coupon rates, depending on year). These were taken to represent long-term, intermediate, and short-term securities with no risk of default. Monthly holding-period yields were then calculated as follows: the return to the investors over the month consisted of (1) any interest payments during the month, (2) any interest accrued during the month, (3) any appreciation or depreciation in the price of the security during the month. The sum of these three items was then divided by the security's purchase price.[18]

18. Accrued interest was calculated on a daily basis. If twenty-eight days elapsed between price quotations, if no coupon payments were made during the period, and if the coupon rate was, say 4¼ per cent, accrued interest over the twenty-eight-day period was $28/365 \times 4.25$. Yields were also annualized on a daily basis. The yield on a security over a twenty-eight-day period was multiplied by 365/28 to obtain the annual rates. Coupon payments were made semiannually for the bonds (April and October for the 4¼s, June and December for the 3⅜s and the notes) and once a year, at maturity, for the

Mean monthly yields and variance of yields for 1929, 1930, and 1931 are shown in Table 13 for all four securities.[19]

As expected, the variance of the bonds exceeds the variance of the notes, which exceeds the variance of the certificates (except for 1931). The negative yields for the bonds in 1931 are the result of the fall in the price of these bonds after Britain left gold late in 1931.

TABLE 13 • *Means and Variances of One-Month Yields on Government Securities, 1929–31*

	4¼ Bond 1947–52	3⅜ Bond 1943–47	3½ Notes 1930–32	Certificates
		1929		
Mean	3.41	4.29	5.73	4.50
Variance	599	149	31.1	1.97
		1930		
Mean	4.94	5.94	5.49	3.17
Variance	79.7	65.0	12.0	4.29
		1931		
Mean	−3.63	−1.63	1.77	1.87
Variance	356	280	2.81	3.86

SOURCE: *Bank and Quotation Record,* 1929–31.

The monthly yields are shown in Figure 3. Although the higher variance of the yields from the long-term securities is apparent, it is not clear by inspection whether the average yields on bonds are higher or lower than those on notes and certificates. The pronounced effect on interest rates of Britain's going off gold in September 1931 shows up dramatically in Figure 3. To eliminate any distortions from this effect, all data for the last three months of 1931 were deleted from the statistical tests as suggested at the start of this section.

In order to reduce the dependence of the results on the specific holding period examined, three periods are used. The one-month

certificates. Accrued interest was added to buying and selling prices when computing one-month yields.

19. This yield can be calculated in two ways. It can be assumed either that the investor bought at the ask price and sold at the bid price (in which case his turnaround cost is included) or that he bought and sold at the average of the bid and ask prices. The table shows returns calculated at the average price. Buying at the ask price and selling at the bid price depresses mean yields slightly but has little effect on the variance. In the statistical tests that follow, the average of the bid and ask prices are used.

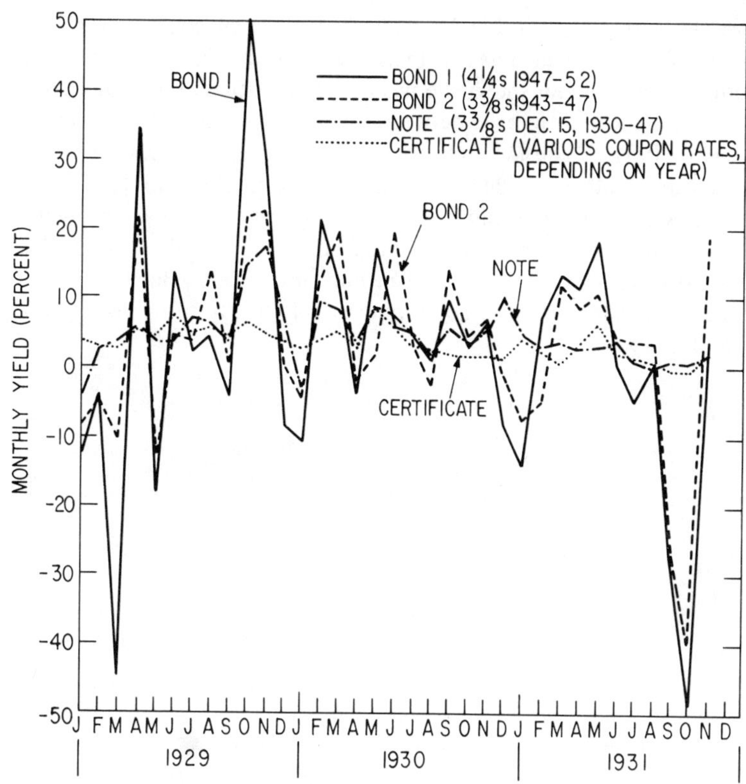

SOURCE: See text.

FIGURE 3. One-Month Yields on Government Securities, 1929–31.

yields shown in Table 13 were aggregated into monthly series of three-month and five-month yields by taking moving averages of the monthly yields.[20] Each observation can be classified by the date and by the security on which the yield was calculated; differences in yields both between different dates and different securities are of interest. These differences are shown in Tables 14 through 16 in various ways. The significance of the differences emerges through an analysis of variance.[21]

20. The moving averages are for periods ending in the denoted month.

21. The analysis of variance was carried out using the dummy variable technique (see Goldberger, 1964, pp. 227–31) and the regression coefficients represent mean val-

The first part of Table 14 shows the effect of comparing all the yields observed in each year with all the yields in other years. The first term in each column shows the mean yield for 1929. Each other entry shows the mean difference between the yield in 1929 and the yield in 1930 or 1931. There is no clear pattern of declining interest rates; the evidence is rather of stable or rising rates from 1929 to 1931. This result is simply the result of aggregating long-term and short-term yields with their diverse patterns into a single yield. It is not surprising that no pattern can be discerned in this single yield. But the lack of pattern indicates that it is not correct simply to say that interest rates fell after 1929.

TABLE 14 • *Analysis of Variance, 1929–31*

	Unweighted Observations	3-Month Moving Average	5-Month Moving Average
		1. By Year	
1929	4.48	4.04	3.18
	(3.09)	(5.10)	(5.43)
1930	.40	1.21	2.93
	(.20)	(1.08)	(3.53)
1931	−1.32	−.72	.26
	(−.58)	(−.58)	(.28)
R^2	.005	.020	.104
F	.296	1.28	7.28
(degrees of freedom)	(2,125)	(2,125)	(2,125)
		2. By Security Type	
4¼ Bond	4.15	4.19	4.27
	(2.33)	(4.28)	(5.64)
3⅜ Bond	.64	.46	.36
	(.25)	(.33)	(.34)
Notes	.65	.63	.56
	(.26)	(.46)	(.52)
Certificates	−.66	−.60	−.62
	(−.26)	(−.43)	(−.58)
R^2	.003	.008	.011
F	.123	.315	.466
(degrees of freedom)	(3,124)	(3,124)	(3,124)

NOTE: The numbers in parentheses are *t*-statistics.

SOURCE: See text.

ues for a particular cell. Coefficients for cells other than the first cell are differences from the mean for the first cell. For example, in the unweighted observations, the mean monthly yield for the 4¼ per cent bond in 1930 was 3.41 + 1.53 = 4.94 per cent.

The second part of the table shows the effect of comparing yields by security type. It emerges clearly that there are no persistent yield differentials between different securities that were maintained over these three years. As in the first part of Table 14, the first term in each column shows the mean yield on one of the long-term bonds. Each other entry shows the mean difference between this yield and the yield on another security. All of these terms are small and not significantly different from zero.

Clearly, it is necessary to distinguish yields both by year and by security. This is done in Table 15, where each entry but the first in

TABLE 15 • *Analysis of Variance by Both Security Type and Year, 1929–31*

	Unweighted Observations	3-Month Moving Average	5-Month Moving Average
4¼ Bond, 1929	3.41	3.08	1.36
	(1.14)	(1.90)	(1.17)
1930	1.53	2.49	6.07
	(.36)	(1.08)	(3.70)
1931	.64	.70	2.55
	(.14)	(.27)	(1.39)
3⅜ Bond, 1929	.88	.52	1.41
	(.21)	(.23)	(.86)
1930	2.52	3.34	5.76
	(.60)	(1.45)	(3.51)
1931	.37	.49	2.34
	(.08)	(.19)	(1.27)
3½ Note, 1929	2.32	1.89	2.79
	(.55)	(.82)	(1.70)
1930	2.08	2.55	4.86
	(.49)	(1.11)	(2.96)
1931	−1.05	.31	2.41
	(−.22)	(.12)	(1.31)
4¼ Certificate, 1929	1.08	1.43	3.05
	(.26)	(.62)	(1.89)
3¼ Certificate, 1930	−.25	2.96	2.32
	(−.06)	(.13)	(1.41)
1⅞ Certificate, 1931	−.98	−.55	1.05
	(−.21)	(−.21)	(.57)
R^2	.013	.045	.186
F	.139	.495	2.41
(degrees of freedom)	(11,116)	(11,116)	(11,116)

NOTE: The numbers in parentheses are *t*-statistics.

SOURCE: See text.

each column shows the mean deviation of the yield on a particular security in a single year from the yield on the 4¼ per cent bond in 1929. The difference between the mean yields of short-term and long-term securities in each year can be calculated from this table by subtraction. And the computations underlying the table can be utilized to provide a test of significance of these differences. Table 16 shows the difference between each of the long-term bond yields and the certificate yield in each of the years 1929, 1930, and 1931 (before the last quarter). The differences are given for the moving averages as well as the monthly observations, and the associated *t*-statistics are below the observation.[22]

In 1929 and 1931, the yields on certificates and on long-term bonds were very close to each other. In fact, they were close enough and variable enough in these two years to make it impossible to distinguish between them statistically—even if the yields are taken over three or five months at a time. The true yield curve in these years was flat.

The differences between yields were larger in 1930 than in the adjacent years, although they are not significantly different from zero unless the five-month moving average is used. There is some evidence, therefore, that the yield curve was upward sloping—long-term yields exceeded short-term—temporarily in 1930. The yield curve was either flat for these three years, or it changed its shape continuously in this short period. In any case, it did not resemble the conventional yield curve based on yields to maturity.

The first conclusion to be drawn from these results is that yields varied widely. It was impossible for most of this period to know if the average yield from holding long-term securities was higher than the average yield from short-term ones, and except for 1930, the long-term yields were not persistently above short-term yields. There is a great danger of assuming that contemporaries could have observed differences that they could not possibly have disentangled from the confusing array of yields they observed.

The second conclusion is that there does not seem to have been a movement by investors out of short-term securities into long-term bonds when the short-term interest rate fell. There is evidence in the

22. These *t*-statistics for 1930 and 1931 are not the same as those in Table 14. Standard errors of the differences in Table 15 were constructed from the variance-covariance matrix underlying Table 14, and the *t*-statistics were computed from them.

higher yield differentials for 1930 that the prices of long-term bonds were being pushed upward by such a shift, but the evidence is not persuasive, and the movement—if present—was small. There appear to be two possible reasons why investors might not have wished to purchase long-term bonds in 1930 and 1931, pushing their prices up and increasing current holding-period yields at the expense of future yields.

The first argument parallels the argument of Chapter III and seems most appropriate to 1930. Investors may not have expected the decline in short-term interest rates to have been durable. If they expected these rates to rise, there would be only a small inducement to going long. The gain in yield would have been temporary, and the added risk from going long would have offset the expected gain—at least in part.

The second argument revolves around this risk. By 1931, it does not seem likely that many investors anticipated the speedy return of pre-1929 financial conditions. The failure of long-term yields to rise as

TABLE 16 • *Excess of Average Bond Yields over the Average Certificate Yield, 1929–31*

	1929	1930	1931
1. Unweighted Observations			
4¼ Bond	−1.08	1.78	1.62
	(−.26)	(.42)	(.31)
3⅜ Bond	−.20	2.77	1.35
	(−.05)	(.66)	(.26)
2. Three-Month Moving Average			
4¼ Bond	1.43	2.19	1.25
	(.62)	(.96)	(.45)
3⅜ Bond	−.91	3.04	1.03
	(−.40)	(1.33)	(.37)
3. Five-Month Moving Average			
4¼ Bond	−3.09	3.75	1.50
	(−1.89)	(2.29)	(.75)
3⅜ Bond	−1.68	3.44	1.29
	(−1.02)	(2.10)	(.65)

NOTE: The numbers in parentheses are *t*-statistics.

SOURCE: See text.

investors bid up the prices of long-term bonds must be explained on different grounds. A possible explanation for the growing differential between Aaa and Baa corporate bonds was that investors had a growing distaste for risk in the early 1930s. In the corporate context, this distaste showed up in an aversion to bonds with a significant risk of failure. In the context of government securities, it showed up in a reluctance to buy long-term bonds and to incur the risk of short-term variation in yields due to price fluctuations.

Investors therefore may have shied away from long-term government bonds for the same reason they shied away from lower-grade private bonds: risk. The risk in governments was smaller—price variation due to interest-rate and other changes is hardly the same as the possibility of default—and the effect was correspondingly smaller. The prices of Baa bonds fell sharply, the prices of long-term governments did not change much. Instead, the rising price of risk prevented the price of long-term government bonds from rising enough to equalize yields to maturity of all government securities. And while the mean yield from holding government bonds was higher in 1931 than the mean yield from holding certificates, the large variance of this difference meant that not every investor would cash in on it. Table 16 therefore shows no significant difference, and investors did not rush out of low-yielding certificates into the apparently more profitable bonds. The windfall profits that might be expected to accrue to holders of long-term bonds when short-term interest rates fall for more than a brief period failed to materialize because the fall in short-term interest rates was accompanied by a rise in the price of risk.

The discussion here has been in terms of holding-period yields and price changes in bonds. While these are the appropriate variables for analysis, the data on them have not been collected in the published sources with the care that data on yields to maturity have been compiled. It is tempting to assert that changes in yields to maturity can be used as proxies for changes in prices and, therefore, for holding-period yields. For short periods of time, however, this assertion is not quite accurate.

The correlations between changes in the yield to maturity, as calculated in official publications, and the holding-period yields calculated here are considerably less than one. In fact, the squared correlation coefficients between the yields of each of the two bonds shown in Table 13 and the change in the yield to maturity for government bonds shown in *Banking and Monetary Statistics* are only about one-half.[23]

Empirical investigations of a period with rapidly changing interest rates therefore are in some trouble. Inferences from changes in yields to maturity about holding-period yields are not to be trusted. Since holding-period yields are the theoretically correct variables, the dilemma is serious, and not to be resolved here. In the spirit of the literature, we will attempt to side-step the problem—but with the hope that theory will be pursued to the point where this will not be necessary at some later date.[24] For short-term securities, the problem does not arise, or at least is not so serious. Since these securities normally are held to maturity, the yield to maturity is the relevant variable to enter into their decisions. Some of these securities will be sold before maturity, but this probably was a small proportion of the total, and the fluctuations in the price of the asset were restricted by its imminent maturity. These sales therefore may be ignored safely.

For present purposes, then, the importance of using short-term interest rates is twofold. They are the rates on assets which resemble money most closely, and they are relatively free of the complications introduced into the analysis of long-term rates by the growing risk of default for some bonds and the rising price of risk, which depressed the prices of all long-term assets subject to price fluctuations.

The Fall in the Demand for Money

The outstanding volume of the principal short-term credit instruments in the years around 1929 is shown in Table 17. Commercial paper and bankers' acceptances were used to finance domestic activity and international trade. Brokers' loans were used to finance purchases of other financial assets. And loans by commercial banks included both commercial loans—serving the same purposes as commercial paper—and stock exchange loans. Since most of the brokers' loans listed came from banks, there is substantial double counting in that category.

Most short-term credit was extended in these years in the form of

23. Changes in interest rates are from *Banking and Monetary Statistics,* Table 128.

24. In a recent study, Bosworth and Duesenberry, 1973, discussed the flow of funds in terms of portfolio theory and the expectations hypothesis—which concern holding-period yields—and then performed their econometric estimations with data on yields to maturity. The change was not mentioned.

bank loans. These loans were issued in a wide variety of localities and in widely varying circumstances. We cannot hope to describe fully the changes in this variety of local markets. Instead, we look at the rates on bank loans for New York City, which can be expected to reflect any monetary stringency that existed. This rate moved closely with the rates in other cities, although it is somewhat lower than rates charged by smaller banks.[25]

In addition to this interest rate, we will examine the rates on the other instruments listed in Table 17. Although the amounts outstand-

TABLE 17 • *Volume of Short-Term Credit Outstanding, 1928–32 (millions of dollars)*

			June		
	1928	1929	1930	1931	1932
Commercial Paper	503	274	527	298	103
Bankers' Acceptances	1,026	1,113	1,305	1,368	747
Brokers' Loans	4,900	7,070	3,795	1,600	335
U.S. Bills and Certificates	1,252	1,640	1,420	2,246	3,341
Loans by Commercial Banks	34,035	35,738	34,539	29,166	21,806

SOURCE: *Banking and Monetary Statistics,* pp. 19, 465–66, 494, 511.

ing of these other instruments were smaller than the volume of bank loans, the movements of rates in these markets can be expected to reflect the changes in monetary conditions in the economy. Since we are looking for evidence of stringency, not following a causal pathway from the money supply to the rest of the economy, we do not have to restrict ourselves to the short-term instruments used most widely.

These interest rates are graphed on a monthly basis for the interwar period in Figures 4 and 5. Weekly observations are available for some of the interest rates shown, but the weekly patterns do not show any movements not present in the monthly data. Three rises can be seen clearly in these rates, in 1920, 1929, and 1931. They are not present in all of the rates, but the movements of the various rates are sufficiently similar to allow us to group these three years together as periods of some monetary stringency. In addition, the magnitudes of the rises in 1920 and 1929 are sufficiently similar that there is no reason apparent in these data to think that either of these periods of str-

25. *Banking and Monetary Statistics,* p. 426.

ingency was worse than the other.[26]

It is possible, in other words, that the downturn in 1929 was caused in part by monetary stringency. The Federal Reserve was trying to tighten up in order to dampen or break the stock-market boom. Many observers, including Keynes, thought that this action would have consequences for the economy as a whole.[27] But, it must be remembered, this is the answer to the wrong question. While the downturn originating in 1929 is interesting, we are trying to discover why the downturn was so much larger and more sustained in the few years just after 1929 than in the other interwar depressions. The interest-rate rises in Figures 4 and 5 are similar in the periods just preceding the first two downturns. They suggest that the monetary stringency in 1929 was no larger than in 1920. Why should the effects have been so much larger?

This question can be posed rather differently. We have been looking for evidence of monetary restriction. Let us turn for a minute to the actual mechanism by which such a restriction causes changes in the economy. The mechanism has been specified in slightly different ways by different authors, but it always involves changes in interest rates and changes in actions in response to the changes in relative prices that the changes in interest rates represent.[28] It is hard to believe that the cause of the Great Depression was the minor change in relative prices visible in the short-term interest rates in 1929. The only large change in interest rates was in the rate for stock exchange loans which had little effect by itself on the economy as a whole. And if one looks at long-term rates, like the Aaa rate shown in Table 12, there is no evidence of a rise at all.

Even the money hypothesis does not assert that the monetary stringency in 1929 was severe enough to cause the entire depression. The argument is that an ordinary downturn was turned into a rout by the bank panic late in 1930. The monetary stringency that distinguished the Great Depression from other depressions therefore came at the end of 1930 and the beginning of 1931, according to this story. The rise in

26. The monetary restriction in 1929 may have been more severe than the one in 1920 if the demand for money was also falling at that time. As noted above, interest rates show only the net effect of the two movements. But if the demand for money was falling more rapidly in 1929 than in 1920, then this is the phenomenon that needs to be explained.

27. Keynes, 1930, vol. 2, p. 196.

28. Compare Friedman and Schwartz, 1963b, and deLeeuw and Gramlich, 1968.

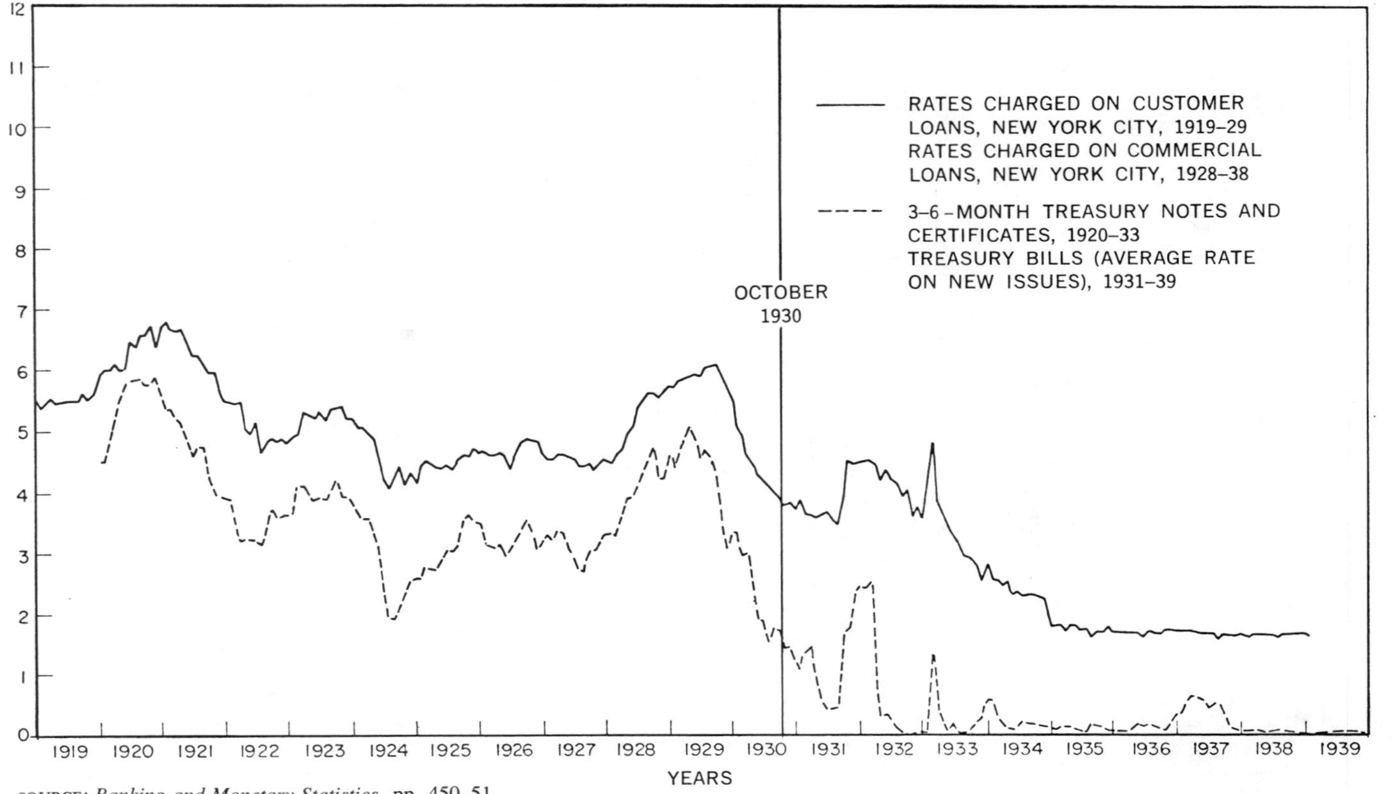

SOURCE: *Banking and Monetary Statistics,* pp. 450–51.

FIGURE 4. Three Short-Term Interest Rates, Monthly, 1919–39.

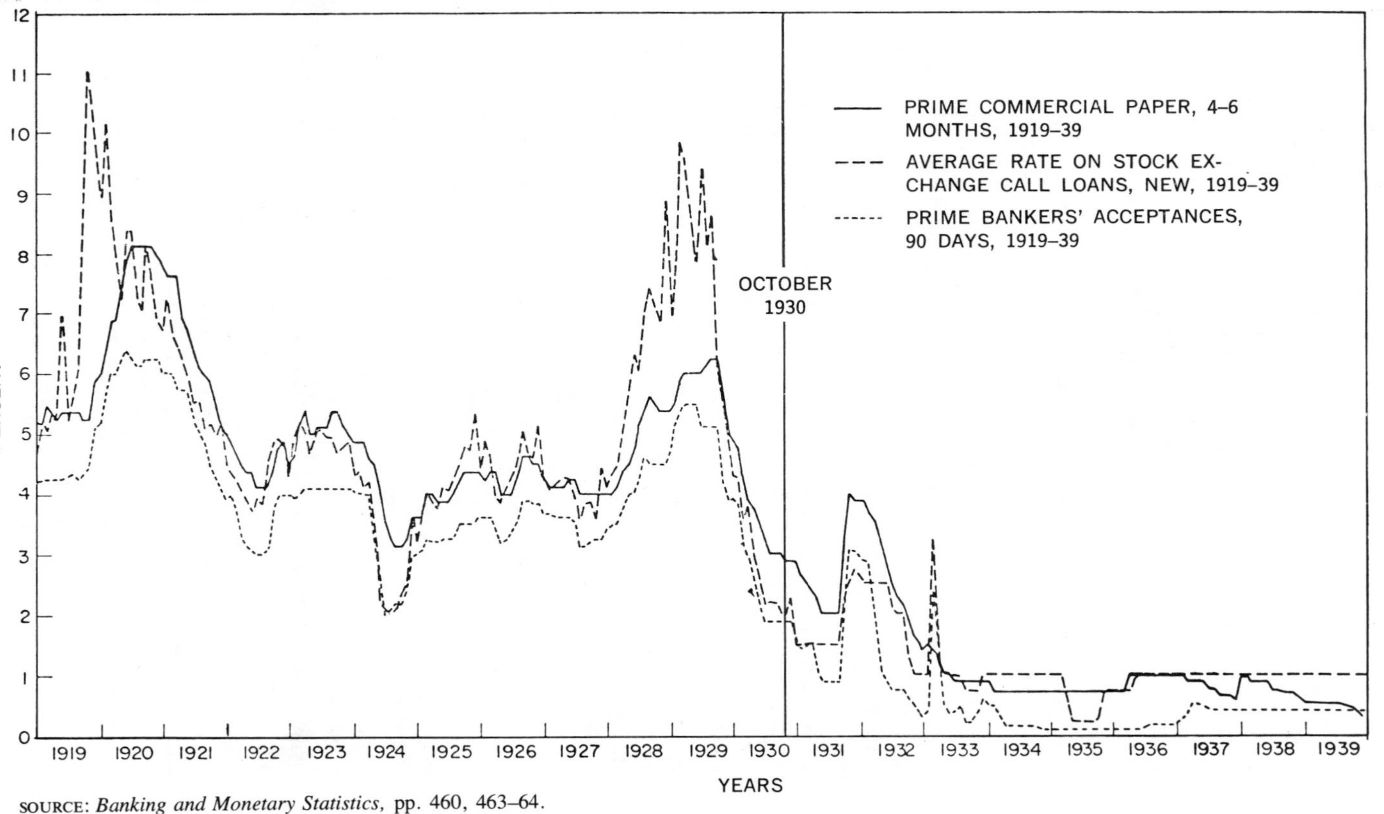

SOURCE: *Banking and Monetary Statistics,* pp. 460, 463–64.

FIGURE 5. Two Short-Term Interest Rates, Monthly, 1919–39.

interest rates that was generated by this stringency should be apparent in the data. It may not be an actual rise in the interest rates, since the decline in income in 1930, coming in part from the previous monetary stringency in 1929, was acting to lower interest rates. But we should be able to see an interruption in the downward trend of interest rates, an interruption that should be quite marked if the effects of the panic were important for the economy.

This temporary reversal of trend should be apparent even though a decline in the supply of money stemming from a banking panic is not precisely analogous to the open-market sales analyzed in most theoretical discussions. After an open-market sale, there is both a reduced supply of money and an expanded supply of government debt. The price of government securities falls for two reasons. As people try to rebuild their diminished money balances, they sell assets that resemble money, that is, government debt. And as people try to reduce their excessive holdings of government debt, they offer this debt for sale.

When the supply of money falls for other reasons, such as a banking panic, the latter influence on interest rates is absent. Interest rates nevertheless rise as people attempt to regain their lost money balances by selling other assets. While the effect on interest rates of a given reduction in the supply of money may not be as great when this change results from a banking panic as when it results from an open-market sale, the effect should be easily apparent if the reduction had any important macroeconomic impact.

Yet a glance at Figures 4 and 5 is sufficient to show that no such interruption of trend is visible at the end of 1930. There is, in other words, no evidence in the interest rates of the monetary stringency cited in the money hypothesis as the cause of the Great Depression. We must conclude that the money hypothesis has failed its most important test. There is no reason to think that the monetary stringency in 1929–30 was more severe than in other interwar depressions and no evidence that the bank failures in 1930 created such a stringency. The money hypothesis, therefore, gives no reason why the downturn following 1929 differed from the other interwar downturns.

Friedman and Schwartz appeared to recognize this, in a somewhat indirect way. They commented that "The onset of the first liquidity crisis [in October 1930] left no clear imprint on the broad economic series shown in Chart 29 [that is, personal income, industrial production, and the wholesale price index]." [29] They also said, to be sure, that the effects could be seen in the Baa interest rate, but their argument connecting the crisis and this interest rate has been shown to be invalid. They did not say where else the imprint of this crisis can be found.

There is one way, however, in which a decrease in the supply of money could have affected the economy without leaving traces behind of the sort we have been discussing. We have assumed throughout this discussion that the various markets involved were functioning properly, that is, that a condition of excess demand or supply resulted in a change in the appropriate price. But there are some markets and some times where imbalances between supply and demand are reconciled by means other than price changes. One way of dealing with an excess demand is by rationing, allocating the scarce supplies among users on some basis other than who can and will pay a higher price. It is possible that credit was being rationed in 1931, and we must ask if there is any evidence that it was.

Rationing in the credit market is always hard to detect after the fact. If we find records that a particular firm was refused a loan in early 1931, we may or may not have found evidence of rationing. Not every attempt to get more money succeeds—or should succeed—even in perfect markets. The price at which the firm wished to borrow may not have been high enough to compensate the lender for the risk involved in the loan, and the firm may not have wanted to pay a higher cost. This is how the market clears in a functioning market; demanders who cannot pay the higher price drop out of the market. The question is not whether a particular borrower could borrow at the market price. It is whether the market price could rise.

Two reasons may be given why the interest rate might not have risen in response to a shortage of credit. There might have been legal or administrative barriers to raising interest rates. Or there might have been legal or administrative barriers to furnishing credit to the people who wanted it.

It is absurd to think that there were legal or administrative reasons why interest rates could not have risen in late 1930 or early 1931. Short-term interest rates had fallen sharply in 1930 and were far below the levels of the 1920s. They could have risen again had conditions

29. Friedman and Schwartz, 1963a, p. 313.

warranted. In fact, they did so at the end of 1931 in response to the reactions of the Federal Reserve to the European currency crisis.[30]

It is equally hard to think of reasons why potential borrowers or potential sellers of assets should have been barred from doing so. We can go further than this and say that the potential demanders of money had ample supplies of other financial assets which they could have sold if they had wanted to. In addition, they bought and sold these assets in ways consistent with the existence of a free market in them. This is not to say that they could have raised all the money they wanted by selling these assets. It is probable that if everyone had decided to sell government bonds, for example, the price of government bonds would have fallen, and people would have suffered a capital loss in the course of, or perhaps even instead of, acquiring money. But in that case, their efforts to sell would have been reflected in price movements, and our previous discussion would have found evidence of them. We are looking now for evidence that people were precluded from selling financial assets or acquiring financial liabilities for reasons independent of prices.

Table 18 shows a simplified national balance sheet for 1929. The data are drawn from Goldsmith's massive studies and official banking data.[31] These data are far and away the best compilation of financial data for this period, but they are not without their problems. In order to obtain the coverage and consistency he desired, Goldsmith had to make many assumptions in his treatment of the data that readers of his work find questionable or obscure. This procedure is inevitable in any massive compilation of data, and the resultant data must always be seen as approximations or as point estimates of the true number. We do not know the variance of these estimates, and it may be quite large. We will be on safe ground, therefore, only if we restrict ourselves to questions involving large changes in the variables and gross comparisons between them.

Net worth of individuals was about $400 billion in 1929, of which roughly $150 billion was composed of tangible assets. The remaining $250 billion represents the difference between the financial assets and

30. Interest rates had not fallen much before 1929, but there is no reason to think that they could not have risen farther in that year if the pressure on the financial markets had been greater. The inference that roughly equal rises of short-term interest rates indicate roughly equal amounts of pressure thus is not negated by legal or administrative constraints.

31. See the sources for Table 18.

TABLE 18 • *U.S. National Balance Sheet, 1929 (billions of dollars)*

	Nonagricultural Individuals		Nonfinancial Corporations		Commercial Banks		Federal Reserve Banks		Federal Government		All Other	
	A	L	A	L	A	L	A	L	A	L	A	L
TANGIBLE ASSETS	157.6		121.3						5.0		138.6	
FINANCIAL INSTRUMENTS												
Cash					16.2		3.1				6.8	22.1
Currency and Demand Deposits	8.6		7.4			20.8		4.3	.2	.4		
Time Deposits	19.2					19.2						
Interbank Deposits						4.7						
Bank Float						4.0						
Other Deposits	11.3		1.4			.3			.1	.2		
Securities												
U.S. Government	5.1		3.2		4.7		.5		.1	17.5	3.9	
State and Local Government	7.6		.6		2.1						6.6	16.9
Corporate and Foreign Bonds	24.1		.5	36.3	5.6						7.9	1.8
Common and Preferred Stock	138.3		42.3		1.2						4.9	
Life Insurance	15.9										1.7	17.6
Other Securities		1.7					.4				9.8	8.5
Loans												
Discounts by Federal Reserve						.6	.6					
Consumer Loans		6.4	4.0		2.0						.9	.5
Commercial Loans				9.4	17.0							7.6
Security Loans		11.6	2.0	.6	8.3						6.0	4.1
Mortgages		18.0		11.2								7.6
Farm	3.6				.9				1.2		3.9	9.6
Residential	8.5				3.1						13.3	
Nonresidential	5.0				2.2						4.7	
Other Loans	1.2	4.1	21.9	16.1	2.5				.2		7.4	13.0
OTHER INTANGIBLES	42.1		23.4	22.8		7.4	.9	.7	1.4		1.3	
NET WORTH		406.2		131.8		8.8		.4		−9.9		120.4
TOTAL	448.1	448.1	228.1	228.1	65.8	65.8	5.5	5.5	8.2	8.2	217.7	217.7 *

* Statistical discrepancy of $12.0 billion in liability total—sum of individual items is $229.7 billion.

SOURCES: Data are from Goldsmith and Lipsey, 1963, vol. II, pp. 78–79, with the following exceptions: Commercial bank data from Goldsmith, 1955, vol. I, pp. 383, 385–86, 409; Commercial bank net worth from *Historical Statistics,* p. 632, and Federal Reserve Balance Sheet from *Banking and Monetary Statistics,* Table 86, pp. 331–32.

the financial liabilities of individuals. The money balances held by individuals were less than $10 billion if a narrow definition of money (M_1) is used and less than $30 billion if a broader definition (M_2) is used.[32] In either case, money balances constituted a small part of individuals' financial portfolios. Individuals who were short of money, therefore, had the option of selling other financial assets to get more money. We do not know that they wanted to do this, and if everyone wanted to do this, each individual would have found his ability to do so limited. Nevertheless, the possibility was there, and if people tried to use it we should observe either changes in the composition of individuals' portfolios or changes in the relative prices of financial assets or both.

Nonfinancial corporations had a net worth of approximately $130 billion in 1929, of which almost all was in the form of tangible assets. They held approximately $100 billion of both financial assets and financial liabilities. Their money holdings were less than $10 billion (whether M_1 or M_2 is meant), representing only a small part of their financial portfolios. If corporations wished to acquire more money, they had the options of selling other financial assets or increasing financial liabilities. If they exercised either of these options, relative prices might change. This could prevent them from altering the composition of their portfolio and could change prices so that they no longer desired to do so. If it did, the evidence should have been visible in the interest rates.

Tables 19 through 21 contain flow-of-funds data for the sectors distinguished in Table 18.[33] These data show the value of changes in the various portfolios, not the change in the value of the portfolios. To cite the most important example, the net additions to individuals' holdings of common stocks in 1930 and 1931 shown in Table 19 do not mean that the value of common stocks held by individuals rose. This value fell sharply in these years as the prices of stocks fell. Despite the fall in price, however, the value of total purchases of common stocks by individuals exceeded the value of total sales by individuals in these years. This difference is shown in the table.

It can be seen from Table 19 that nonagricultural individuals had

32. M_2 was only $20 billion more than M_1 in 1929 (Friedman & Schwartz, 1963a, p. 712) so only $20 billion of the $30 billion of "other deposits" could have been in M_2.

33. Unincorporated businesses are taken from the "all other" category in Table 18.

TABLE 19 • *Flow-of-Funds Data for Nonagricultural Individuals, 1927–32 (billions of dollars)*

	1927	1928	1929	1930	1931	1932
Net Financial Investment	4.9	1.7	7.9	7.9	7.2	2.5
Change in Assets	9.3	7.1	9.5	5.3	3.3	−.7
Change in Liabilities	4.4	5.4	1.6	−2.7	−3.9	−3.2
Assets						
Currency and Demand Deposits	2.7	−1.9	−.8	−.3	−1.5	−1.3
U.S. Government Securities	−2.4	−1.1	−.4	−.1	.8	.7
State and Local Bonds	.4	.4	.5	.6	1.8	.1
Corporate and Foreign Bonds	2.0	1.6	.7	.7	.6	−.4
Common Stocks	1.0	2.5	4.1	.9	.1	—
Mortgages	1.2	1.6	1.9	.8	−.2	−.2
Life Insurance	1.2	1.2	1.0	.9	.8	.3
Other	3.2	2.8	2.5	1.8	.9	.1
Liabilities						
Mortgages: 1–4 Family	1.6	1.7	1.3	.1	−.5	−1.0
Mortgages: Multifamily	.7	.8	.7	.4	—	−.1
Borrowing on Securities	1.3	1.6	−1.3	−2.1	−2.0	−1.0
Consumer Debt	.2	.8	1.0	−.7	−1.2	−1.3
Other	.6	.5	−.1	−.4	−.2	.2

SOURCES: See Appendix 2.

net financial investments of almost $8 billion in each of the years 1929, 1930, and 1931. (The last of these years was only slightly lower than the others and far above 1927 and 1938). In other words, the sum of their net purchases of financial assets and net redemptions of financial liabilities was almost $8 billion in each of these years.[34]

Despite the near-constancy of net financial investment, the net purchases of assets by individuals fell sharply in 1930 and 1931. At the same time, individuals stopped acquiring new financial liabilities and began to reduce the financial liabilities they had. They stopped increasing their borrowing against securities in 1929, against commodity purchases in 1930 (consumer debt), and against houses in 1931. They were increasing their financial leverage through 1929; they decreased it in the following years.

34. As the wealth data used in the estimation of consumption functions show, their net wealth did not increase at the same time because the net purchases were more than offset by declines in the values of assets already in their portfolio, stocks in particular.

Starting in 1928, individuals reduced their money balances in each year shown. This, of course, was a net movement. Individuals were receiving income from many sources, including sales of financial assets. They added this income to the monetary balances they held at the beginning of the year and spent the resulting balances for goods, services, and assets of all sorts. If the money left over at the end of the year was less than the amount at the beginning of the year, the entry in Table 19 is negative. Obviously we cannot say that the decrease shown in Table 19 was used to buy commodities or to buy financial assets. We can say that there does not seem to be any legal or administrative reason—as opposed to reasons derived from prices, incomes, and expectations—why they could not have attempted to increase their money balances by selling other financial assets or by refraining from purchasing as many of these assets as they did in 1930 and 1931.

In fact, the changes shown in Table 19 are quite consistent with the hypothesis that individuals were reacting to changes in prices, incomes, and expectations in this period. They reduced their leverage and their rate of acquisition of long-term financial assets in response to the increase in the risk of these assets. They reduced their money balances and their rate of acquisition of other short-term assets in response to the fall in income and the consequent need for working balances. They reduced their money balances, therefore, because their demand for money fell—not because of a restriction of supply. The evidence from quantities is consistent with the evidence from interest rates.

Nonfinancial corporations had very different financial structures than individuals. Their financial flows are shown in Table 20. They had negative net financial investment for every year shown in Table 20 except 1932. They were acquiring more financial liabilities than financial assets in these years, although this phrase must be interpreted to mean that they were reducing their financial liabilities more slowly than they were selling financial assets in 1931.

The difference in financial behavior between the late 1920s and the early 1930s that was shown in Table 19 for individuals is also visible here. Nonfinancial corporations were acquiring financial assets in the years before 1929; they were decreasing their holdings of financial assets after then.[35] Three different financial assets were affected. Con-

35. This process of simultaneously acquiring financial assets and liabilities was noted with suspicion by Eddy, 1937.

sumer loans rose in the twenties and fell in the thirties. This change can be understood as a reault of the volume of trade; it tells us nothing about the desire of corporations for financial assets. Corporations bought government securities in the 1920s and sold them in the 1930s. This movement suggests that corporations reduced their desires to hold financial assets in the 1930s, but the movement is too small and indefinite to provide a basis for such a conclusion. And corporations kept stable money balances in the late 1920s, reducing them in the early 1930s. This movement is the one we are interested in.

TABLE 20 • *Flow-of-Funds Data for Nonfinancial Corporations, 1927–32 (billions of dollars)*

	1927	1928	1929	1930	1931	1932
Net Financial Investment	−4.2	−3.0	−4.6	−2.8	−2.2	1.5
Change in Assets	.5	2.6	1.1	−1.0	−2.8	−1.1
Change in Liabilities	4.8	5.7	5.7	1.8	−.6	−2.7
Assets						
Cash	—	1.2	—	−.2	−2.1	−.4
U.S. Government Securities	.1	.3	−.1	−.5	−.3	.1
Consumer Loans	—	.5	.6	−.5	−.6	−.9
Other	.4	.6	.6	.2	.2	.1
Liabilities						
Bonds	2.1	.7	.2	1.6	.6	−.3
Common Stock	.8	2.3	3.6	1.1	.3	.1
Mortgages	.8	.8	.9	.5	−.1	−.4
Commercial Loans	−.2	.6	.3	−1.4	−1.9	−1.5
Other	1.3	1.3	.7	—	1.7	−.6

SOURCES: See Appendix 2.

The question at issue is whether corporations decreased their money balances because their expenditures were falling or whether their expenditures were falling because their money balances were falling. We have found already that the evidence of interest rates is consistent with the first alternative. We are asking here if the movements of quantities suggest that the connections between money balances and expenditures went through channels that did not affect interest rates. In short, is there evidence of credit rationing?

Commercial loans were falling at the same time as money balances. It is possible that they were being rationed. But if they were, it does not follow that this rationing would have prevented corporations from making expenditures. Corporations were issuing both stocks and bonds in 1930 and 1931. They issued more bonds in 1930 than in any other year shown except for 1927. No rationing is possible in the markets for these assets; they are organized along impersonal lines. If corporations had wanted more cash, they could have sold more stocks or bonds.

Nevertheless, it is hard to understand why businessmen preferred to sell low-priced bonds and stocks in 1930 and 1931 rather than to take out bank loans.[36] The paradox can be resolved by assuming the existence of credit rationing. Perhaps corporations did not borrow from banks in 1930 and 1931 because banks would not lend. This presumption, however, has its own difficulties. Most short-term credit was extended through bank loans, as Table 17 shows. If access to these loans was restricted by rationing, corporations would have tried to get the funds they were denied in this market from other sources. They might have sold more stocks and bonds than they would have otherwise. But these are long-term liabilities for corporations. To replace bank loans, at least some corporations would have wanted to borrow on a short-term basis. Being denied access to banks, they would have tried to sell commercial paper or bankers' acceptances. As Table 17 demonstrates, the markets for these assets was very small compared to the volume of bank loans outstanding. Even if only a few corporations switched into these markets in response to credit rationing, the increased supply of commercial paper and bankers' acceptances should have lowered their price and raised their yield dramatically. There is no reason why the interest rates in these markets could not have risen in 1930 and 1931. Their failure to do so—as shown in Figure 4—implies that credit rationing by banks was not diverting demands for funds into these markets. In fact, the fall in interest rates for commercial paper relative to interest rates on commercial bank loans is precisely contrary to what we would expect if the latter market was rationed while the former one was free. There is no evidence, therefore, of binding credit rationing by banks.

36. One possible argument is that corporations thought that short-term interest rates were going to rise. While direct evidence on these expectations is lacking, the evidence on expectations presented above suggests strongly that businessmen were not anticipating the kind of strong upsurge in business that would cause short-term interest rates to rise sharply in 1930 or 1931.

A better way out of this dilemma is to assume that corporations had separate demands for long-term and short-term liabilities. In other words, the demands for different parts of their financial portfolios were determined by different variables.[37] Corporations continued to issue bonds and stocks in 1930 and 1931 to raise long-term funds for investment. They issued fewer bonds and stocks as their capital investment fell, retiring more bonds than they issued in 1932. They decreased their bank loans in 1930 and subsequent years because of the fall in sales and inventories. And they were not subject to rationing by banks that led them to try alternative methods of raising short-term funds.

Data for the net financial flows of unincorporated businesses are shown in Table 21. Credit rationing by banks could not have been very important for unincorporated businesses for the simple reason that changes in their cash holdings and bank debt were small relative to other changes in the financial flows of these firms. As with individuals and corporations, 1929 marked a dividing line for unincorporated businesses. Accounts receivable from customers had been declining slowly before 1929; they began to fall rapidly in 1930 and continued to fall for the next few years. This movement dominates all other financial movements of these firms.

TABLE 21 • *Flow-of-Funds Data for Unincorporated Businesses, 1927–32* (*billions of dollars*)

	1927	1928	1929	1930	1931	1932
Net Financial Investment	−.5	−.7	−.6	−1.9	−2.8	−1.5
Change in Assets	−.3	−.1	−.1	−2.4	−3.6	−2.3
Change in Liabilities	.2	.6	.5	−.5	−.8	−.7
Assets						
Receivables (nonfarm)	−.2	−.2	−.2	−2.0	−2.5	−2.0
Cash	−.2	—	.2	−.3	−.9	−.1
Other	.1	.1	−.1	−.1	−.2	−.2
Liabilities						
Bank Debt	−.2	.1	.1	−.7	−.8	−.6
Other	.4	.5	.4	.2	—	−.1

SOURCES: See Appendix 2.

37. Recent work on corporate financial structures bears out this hypothesis. See Bosworth, 1971.

Negative net financial investment therefore does not mean the same thing for unincorporated businesses as it did for nonfinancial corporations. Corporations were borrowing to finance real investment. Unincorporated businesses were decreasing their lending to customers. As the total volume of purchases fell in the early 1930s, the demand for consumer credit fell also, and firms found themselves with smaller sales and smaller accounts receivable. The decrease in their bank debt and cash balances undoubtedly was a response to the decline in their business.

The data on financial flows therefore does not provide evidence of important credit rationing by banks. If individuals had wanted more cash, they could have refrained from buying the financial assets they were buying in the early 1930s. If nonfinancial corporations had wanted more cash and been refused credit by banks, they would have gone into other short-term capital markets, leaving some evidence of this displaced demand behind. The lack of such evidence in markets like the one for commercial paper shows that there was no such displaced demand. And it is highly unlikely that unincorporated businesses were displeased by the decline in bank credit extended to them. It was both small and almost certainly desired by the firms themselves in response to the fall in their sales.

This is not to say that credit rationing was absent in the early 1930s. No evidence has been presented here on the actual extent of credit rationing. But the credit rationing present in 1930 and 1931—if it existed—did not restrict the overall supplies of money available to firms and individuals by avenues independent of interest rates. Individuals were buying financial assets (other than money) throughout the early 1930s in a manner that is inconsistent with the notion that they were short of cash. Corporations were not seeking alternative sources of short-term credit as they would have done if they had been suffering from rationing by banks. And unincorporated businesses were suffering from a loss of business, not credit.

Having said this, however, it is worth saying also that the evidence on financial flows is consistent with the hypothesis that there was in fact no credit rationing in the early 1930s. Nonagricultural individuals who had been increasing their leverage in the late 1920s, reduced their leverage in the early 1930s as their expectations about the gains to be gotten from purchasing financial assets such as common stocks changed dramatically. Nonfinancial corporations reduced the rate at which they issued their long-term liabilities in response both to the decline in the prices of common stocks and in the perceived opportunities for profitable investment in plant and equipment. Unincorporated businesses found their loans to customers falling with sales. All of these groups reduced their cash balances and bank debt in the early 1930s in response to the fall in income.

We conclude, therefore, that there is no evidence that the banking panic of 1930 had a deflationary effect on the economy. Instead, the data are consistent with the hypothesis that the demand for money was falling more rapidly than the supply during 1930 and the first three-quarters of 1931. They are consistent with the spending hypothesis, not the money hypothesis about the cause of the Depression.[38]

38. It should be remembered that the data suggest that the downturn in 1929 may have been caused in part by a monetary restriction. They do not suggest that the monetary pressure in the early 1930s was more severe than the pressure in other interwar depressions.

V

The Deepening Depression

By the middle of 1931, the decline in income had continued for approximately two years. It was destined to continue for another two years before the decline was arrested. This chapter analyzes some of the events in the later stages of the decline with emphasis on its international aspects. In light of the extended duration of the decline, however, it is useful to deviate temporarily from the general plan of this inquiry and examine some events that did not take place.

The Absence of Equilibrating Forces

Most economic models contain equilibrating factors that will eventually bring the economy back to an equilibrium in which all factors, including labor, are fully employed. While these models acknowledge the possibility that the economy may not be in such an equilibrium, even for extended periods of time, they insist that economy would eventually return to such a position. We cannot hope to learn from the experience of the Depression whether the economy is of this sort or not. For even if none of these equilibrating forces were in evidence, they might have appeared at a later date if the decline in income had continued. Nevertheless, it is of great interest that none of these equilibrating forces were apparent in the early 1930s.

The demonstration that equilibrating forces did not immediately come into play can start at no better place than wages. According to classical theory, a disequilibrium in the labor market, like a disequilibrium in any market, should be corrected by a change in the price. The cure for unemployment was lower wages. But, as most economists realized by the 1930s, cutting wages was only effective by this reasoning if they could be made to fall relative to prices. And there was no way to insure that this would happen. In fact, as the data in Table 22 show, it did not happen.

Table 22 contains several estimates of the real wage in manufacturing. Prices can be divided either by the consumer price index or by the wholesale price index, and both are shown in Table 22. Use of the consumer price index shows the purchasing power of wages in terms of items that workers bought. It is the relevant index to use when discussing the effects of wage cuts on demand. Use of the wholesale price index shows the relationship between the price of labor as an input to manufacturing production and the price of the output of this production. It is relevant to a discussion of the effect of wage cuts on employment for a given level of demand.

TABLE 22 • *Real Earnings, 1925–34*

	All Manufacturing			
	Average Earnings/WPI		Average Earnings/CPI	
	Hourly	Weekly	Hourly	Weekly
1925	88.9	89.5	94.4	95.1
1926	93.0	93.8	93.9	95.5
1927	97.0	98.7	96.0	97.6
1928	97.7	98.2	99.4	99.8
1929	100	100	100	100
1930	107.7	102.5	100.1	95.3
1931	118.8	108.9	102.6	94.0
1932	115.9	100.1	99.0	85.5
1933	113.0	96.7	103.5	88.6
1934	119.5	93.4	120.5	94.2

SOURCES: *Historical Statistics,* Tables D626, D628, p. 92; Table 3, above.

Both weekly and hourly wages also are shown in Table 22. They differ because hours of work decreased for employed workers at the same time as the number of employed workers fell. The weekly wage is appropriate for discussions of purchasing power, while the hourly wage is relevant to a discussion of labor as a factor of production. It follows then that the first and last columns of Table 22, which show the hourly wage divided by the wholesale price index and the weekly wage divided by the consumer price index, are the ones to examine.

The first index rose in the early 1930s. If the indexes are accurate, the marginal physical productivity of labor rose as employment fell. This is consistent with the classical theory of factor substitution, and suggests that lowering the wage rate further might have avoided unemployment by preventing the hourly real wage from rising. But the last column of Table 22 shows that this hope is illusory. The problem in the Depression was not one of inappropriate factor proportions; it was of insufficient demand. And the effect of shorter hours and lower wages was to decrease the income of employed workers. Even had there been no unemployment, more rapidly falling wages would have led to a lower level of demand. (Of course, if the consumer price index is a better index of price movements than the wholesale price index, then the data suggest that real hourly wages did not rise before 1934 and that no part of the classical story is accurate.)

This finding, of course, comes as no surprise. One of the foundations of the Keynesian analysis that emerged from the Depression is the conviction that lowering wages will not arrest depressions.[1] This conclusion was not new with Keynes. President Hoover called in businessmen as the Depression began to impress upon them the futility of cutting wages in a general depression. In fact, his message was stronger: To the extent that relative wages could be cut, the depressing effect on demand would outweigh the expansionary effect coming from cheapening labor as a factor of production.[2] American economists echoed this view in many ways in the years between the crash on Wall Street and the publication of *The General Theory*. Both in policy pronouncements and in scholarly discussion, these economists agreed that full employment was not to be re-established by cutting wages. Keynes's contribution to the discussion in America was not to refute a powerful opposition view. It was to pull together a relatively formless discussion and to give it a shape that both permitted intensive analysis and encouraged public discussion and acceptance.[3]

In the postwar debates over the Keynesian system, one of the dominant questions was whether an unemployment equilibrium was possible. The conclusion now seems to be accepted that in the long run, it is not. If there is unemployment, the money wage rate should fall, as in the classical story. But the Keynesian story acknowledges the facts of Table 22 and infers that all prices will fall with wages. The fall in wages, therefore, will not affect relative prices; instead, it will alter the relationship between the stock of money and the quantity of goods

1. Keynes, 1936, Chapter 2.
2. Mitchell, 1947, pp. 82–84; Hoover, 1952, pp. 43–44.
3. Davis, 1971.

it will buy. As prices fall, the real value of the stock of money will rise, and this change will lead to an increase in demand which will lead back ultimately to full employment.

An implicit assumption in this argument is that the nominal quantity of money remains constant. But the discussion of the last chapter was motivated by the fact that the nominal stock of money fell in the early 1930s. It is useful now to switch our attention from the nominal quantity of money to the real value, several estimates of which are presented in Table 23. Two definitions of the money supply are divided by two price indexes in this table. No presumption exists on which estimate is the closest to the "real" real quantity of money.

TABLE 23 • *Estimates of the Real Money Supply, 1925–34*

	M_1/WPI	M_1/CPI	M_2/WPI	M_2/CPI
1925	88.8	94.3	83.3	88.5
1926	93.4	95.1	89.3	90.9
1927	97.8	96.7	96.0	95.0
1928	97.5	99.1	98.2	99.8
1929	100	100	100	100
1930	106.2	98.8	107.9	100.4
1931	116.8	100.9	117.8	101.8
1932	114.8	98.0	110.8	94.6
1933	106.5	97.3	96.2	88.2
1934	103.3	104.2	91.7	92.5

SOURCES: Tables 2, 3, above.

In general, all the series behave similarly. There is no sign of a systematic negative relation between the price level and the real quantity of money. The beginning of a massive increase in real balances that would eventually inflate demand is not apparent in these data. The nominal money supply decreased at more or less the same rate as prices in the early 1930s.

The demand for money is generally written in terms of real balances.[4] People are assumed to act on the basis of purchasing power over goods and services. The actual dollar price of something or the actual number of dollars he holds is not thought to enter into his calculations. Instead, he asks what his financial assets are worth in terms of the goods and services that he could buy with them. A simul-

4. Friedman, 1970; Goldfeld, 1973.

taneous decrease in the quantity of money and in prices therefore would be a matter of complete indifference. This is the situation chronicled in Table 23; there was no expansionary influence in the early 1930s that came from an increase in real balances.

The same data show, however, that there was also no decrease in the real stock of money in the early 1930s. The money hypothesis asserts that the decrease in the stock of money caused the Depression, but how can that be if the real stock of money—which figures in the demand function for money—did not fall? Why, in other words, should the level of real expenditures and hence of employment have been lower in, say, 1931 than in 1929 since the real stock of money was larger by all of the measures shown in Table 23?

This important question will be considered in the third part of this chapter, but a few objections to the way in which it has been posed, only one of which is important, may be noted here. The first objection is that a constant level of the real money stock represents a decrease relative to the historical trend of this stock. Population was increasing in the early 1930s, even if income was not, and the real money stock needed to increase to keep a constant real money stock per capita even if nothing else changed. A constant level of real money balances therefore indicates a decrease relative to the demand at constant prices and per capita income levels. If the real money stock is defined to be the nominal stock divided by the wholesale price index, however, the real money stock was larger in 1931 than in 1929 even when the previous trend of population and income is allowed for.

The real money stock declined in 1932 by all of the measures shown in Table 23, both absolutely and relative to any positive trend. As noted above, the monetary restriction that followed the British devaluation in September 1931 raised short-term interest rates and had a deflationary effect on the economy. While the magnitude of this effect is unknown, the direction is undisputed.

The second caveat is that money is not the only financial asset, and a broader selection of financial assets needs to be examined to see the effect of deflation on demand. In particular, if the stock of other financial assets had stayed constant, then the real value of financial assets would have risen. But as the discussion of the stock-market crash in Chapter II showed, the decline in the value of financial assets held by individuals was quite severe. The picture shown in Table 23 would not be changed by including more financial assets.

A more serious objection to this proposition is that it concerns the comparison of two steady states. In two economies, one with twice the prices and twice the quantity of money (or financial assets) of the other, everything else could be the same. But the transition from one of these steady states to the other might involve problems not apparent from the comparison of the steady states. For example, the only way to decrease the quantity of money by half in a short period of time might be to have half the banks fail. These bank failures then could have impacts on the economy that would be separate from the effect of lower prices. In addition, falling prices and lower prices are not the same thing. And if people are calculating interest rates in the same way that they are calculating their desired money balances, this difference is important. In terms of the goods and services that money will buy, money balances increase in value during a period of falling prices. In these real terms, money balances earn a positive rate of interest during deflation, rather than the zero rate we normally think of. The implications of this proposition are far reaching, and we will return to them below.

An active fiscal policy also was missing during the Depression. Neither the active commitment to this kind of policy nor the built-in stabilizers that can make this kind of policy partially automatic were present in the 1930s. President Kennedy's Council of Economic Advisers popularized the use of the "full-employment surplus" as an index of fiscal policy. The actual budget of the government is dependent partly on the government's tax and expenditure rates and partly on the level of activity in the economy. Less taxes are paid in depression than in prosperity, even if the tax rates are unchanged. To look simply at the government deficit, therefore, shows the interaction of the government's policy and the events that this policy is trying to correct. By calculating what the government's surplus would be at a given level of economic activity—full employment—the effects of policy are isolated.[5]

Brown calculated the full-employment surplus for the 1930s, well before President Kennedy took office, and his results are shown in Table 24. As Brown concluded from his analysis, expansionary fiscal policy was not tried. The expansionary trend of federal expenditures

5. Council of Economic Advisors, 1962, pp. 77–81. This measure ignores the second-order effects (in the 1930s) that come from changes in the size of the government budget even if it is balanced.

was offset by the contractionary trend of state and local governments, and the Veterans Bonus of 1931 was simply too small to materially affect the Depression. As Table 24 shows, the rise in demand in 1931 was less than 2 per cent of GNP and was not sustained.

Finally, among the things that did not happen, the rest of the world did not maintain its demand for American products. There was no

TABLE 24 • *Effects of Fiscal Policy, 1929–39 (net shift in demand as per cent of full-employment GNP)*

	All Governments	Federal
1929	1.4	−0.4
1930	1.9	0.0
1931	3.6	1.7
1932	1.8	1.0
1933	0.5	0.5
1934	1.5	2.0
1935	1.6	1.9
1936	2.6	2.5
1937	0.2	0.1
1938	1.2	1.2
1939	2.0	1.4

SOURCE: Brown, 1956, p. 865.

cushioning effect from a constant export demand. Indexes of the real quantities of exports and imports are shown in Table 25, where two price indexes have again been used. The real quantity of exports fell by more than half of its 1929 volume between 1929 and 1932.

Exports were about $7 billion in 1929, and the fall in the real quantity of exports was approximately $4 billion in 1929 prices. If we assume for the moment that this fall was independent of events within the United States, we can estimate the magnitude of the depressing effect this had on income in the United States. Most estimates of the multiplier lie between one and two, with estimates taken from simulation of the larger econometric models tending to lie in the low end of this range and the estimates derived from consumption functions alone tending toward the high end.[6] The effect of this fall therefore was to

6. One-year multipliers were used from a variety of sources. Evans, 1969, pp. 23, 65, 583, surveyed most of the standard work. Other estimates were taken from Ando and Modigliani, 1963; Modigliani, 1971; and Table 9, above.

lower income in 1933 by close to $8 billion in 1929 prices. (The high end of this range should be used because part of the fall occurred in 1930 and 1931, and the effects of the earlier falls would have expanded beyond their initial impacts by 1933.) GNP in 1929 prices fell by $30 billion between 1929 and 1933.[7] The fall in exports could have accounted for between 25 and 30 per cent of this fall.

TABLE 25 • *Real Merchandise Exports and Imports 1925–34*

	Exports/CPI	Exports/WPI	Imports/CPI	Imports/WPI
1925	91.6	86.2	93.9	88.4
1926	89.0	87.4	97.7	95.9
1927	91.7	92.7	94.0	95.0
1928	97.8	96.3	93.0	91.5
1929	100	100	100	100
1930	75.3	80.9	71.4	76.8
1931	52.1	60.4	53.6	62.1
1932	38.6	45.2	37.7	44.2
1933	42.4	46.2	43.7	47.7
1934	52.1	51.7	48.2	47.8

SOURCES: *Historical Statistics,* Tables U10, U13, p. 537; Table 3, above.

This is a substantial proportion, although it is not by any means the whole of the Depression. But it must be remembered that this estimate was derived under the strong assumption that the fall in the demand for exports from the United States was independent of events in the United States. This assumption clearly is faulty. If we make the opposite assumption—that the world Depression was caused entirely by events within the United States—then the independent effect of foreign events obviously was zero. The calculation just performed then shows one path by which the Depression spread throughout the American economy, but no clues as to its cause.

International Interactions

We now turn our attention back from what did not happen to what did happen and ask where between these extremes the reality might have been. We need to examine the relation between the Depression in

7. Table 1, above.

the United States and the Depression in the rest of the world. The analysis has two parts, which will be treated in turn. The first part concerns the world-wide agricultural Depression; the second concerns the industrial countries of Europe, and Germany in particular.

Agricultural prices fell first, fastest, and furthest of all prices. People were aware of the fall in agricultural prices long before they were aware of the general deflation, and discussions throughout 1930 were phrased in terms of the fall in specific agricultural prices rather than in the aggregate price level. The extent to which agricultural prices fell below the average of all prices is shown at the bottom of Table 26, where the ratio of agricultural wholesale prices to the wholesale price index is shown. This ratio is computed for two large nineteenth-century depressions in the rest of Table 26.

A dramatic change can be seen in the behavior of relative prices between 1900 and 1930. Agricultural prices fell much more relative to other prices in the 1930s than they did in the 1840s and 1890s. Looked at another way, nonagricultural prices fell less relative to agricultural prices in the later depression than in the earlier ones. It is hard to know which formulation is the more revealing, but the latter appears to be. Unemployment in the nonagricultural sectors of the economy was far more serious in the 1930s than in the 1840s and 1890s, while the difference in the agricultural sector is considerably less clear. It is tempting, therefore, to infer that some form of price rigidity prevented the economy as a whole from following the example of agriculture, that is, from maintaining a more or less constant level of output in the face of a lower demand.[8] Since industrial prices did fall dramatically, however, the meaning of "price rigidity" in this context is less than clear.

The comparison in Table 26 shows that what was useful behavior for agriculture in the nineteenth century may not have been so advantageous in the twentieth. Clearly, if all prices fall and real income does not, everyone is better off than if real income falls. But if real income is falling, it is not clear that any single sector benefits from a maintenance of its production. In particular, the members of the agricultural sector in the 1930s were not to be heard exclaiming how the Depression had passed them by. Their real incomes fell because the price of their output fell more than other prices, even though the volume of

8. Means, 1935.

their production did not fall. This method of reducing incomes affects the distribution of the fall within the agricultural sector—possibly by reducing the burden on farm workers who would have otherwise been unemployed—but it is unlikely that it helped the sector as a whole. In-

TABLE 26 • *Ratio of the Price of Farm Products to the Wholesale Price Index in Selected Years*

	(1910–14 = 100)	(1926 = 100)
1835	.750	
1836	.781	
1837	.730	
1838	.745	
1939	.767	
1840	.680	
1841	.696	
1842	.646	
1843	.640	
1844	.675	
1890		.897
1891		.971
1892		.948
1893		.961
1894		.931
1895		.900
1896		.852
1897		.912
1898		.926
1899		.877
1925		1.06
1926		1.00
1927		1.04
1928		1.10
1929		1.10
1930		1.02
1931		.888
1932		.744
1933		.780
1934		.872

SOURCES: Column 1, *Historical Statistics,* Series E1, E2, p. 115; Column 2, *Historical Statistics,* Series E13, E15, p. 116.

deed, if the demand for agricultural goods was inelastic, the income of the sector as a whole might have been increased by behavior more similar to that in the rest of the economy.[9]

The weakness in the markets for primary products before 1929 usually is traced to the expansion of supply during the First World War.[10] There were secular shifts in demand during the 1920s, of course, but these proceeded much more slowly than the wartime expansion of supply and, consequently, were much less important in creating the excess supply. Prices did not fall as rapidly during the 1920s as during the 1930s for two reasons. First, many prices were not free to move in response to market forces. Governmental price-maintenance boards chose to accumulate stocks rather than to let the price of their product fall. The increase in stocks is thus a better indication of excess supply than a falling price in the 1920s.[11] Second, the demand for primary products—like the demand for other products—fell sharply in the early 1930s. The result of these two forces was to make the early 1930s considerably worse for farmers and other primary producers than the 1920s had been.

The demise of price-maintenance activities has been traced to problems raising funds. The cost of carrying inventories, so the argument runs, became excessively high at the end of the 1920s, and price-support programs collapsed. If the cost of carrying inventories is interpreted to mean simply the interest rate, the argument will not stand. Interest rates rose at the end of the 1920s, but they fell dramatically in the last quarter of 1929. Short-term interest rates were lower in 1930 than they had been for several years, both inside and outside the United States. And long-term rates were no higher. If a world-wide shortage of credit resulting from the attraction of funds to the New York stock market had been the only problem with raw-material inventories, then the price breaks of 1928 and 1929 should have been eliminated by 1930.

But as the discussion of the previous chapter shows, these statements refer only to risk-free interest rates—the pure interest rates of economic theory. Actual interest rates included a premium for risk, and this premium, as Chapter IV shows, rose in 1930. In addition, the

9. This statement ignores the effects of such a change on the rest of the economy.

10. Timoshenko, 1953, pp. 12–19, 102; Kindleberger, 1973, p. 86. For an opposing view, see Malenbaum, 1953.

11. Timoshenko, 1953, pp. 25–26.

cost of holding inventories includes the anticipated capital gains or losses on the inventories themselves. In the face of conditions in 1930, we may presume that this component of anticipated costs rose sharply. The failure of the various schemes to maintain prices then must be seen as the result of the Depression rather than a cause. It was produced by changing expectations in 1930, rather than by a scarcity of credit in 1929.

It was argued above (Chapter III) that expectations did not shift sharply in 1930. People became more pessimistic than they had been in 1929, but the shift was not more extreme than in other interwar downturns. To be consistent, we must infer either that the shift in expectations was concentrated in the agricultural sector of the economy or that this "normal" fading of prospects was enough to discourage the price-support operations of the 1920s. There does not seem to be any reason why people would have changed their views on agriculture more quickly than on other sectors of the economy. The accumulation of surpluses was a well-known phenomenon, and there was no new information about the course of agricultural demand or supply in 1929 or 1930. It seems fair to opt for the latter of the two possibilities just cited. The sudden decline in agricultural prices, therefore, reflected conditions outside the agricultural sector rather than changes within it.

Rapidity of decline is one thing; extent of the fall is another. Agricultural prices fell further than other prices because the supply of agricultural goods was in inelastic supply. The output of many crops did not fall in the early 1930s; in fact, some producers were attempting to increase their production. The result was a more rapid movement along the demand curve than in other sectors.

The long-run causes of the agricultural depression as well as the peculiar form it took—falling prices without falling production—were the result of forces within agriculture itself. The timing of the deflation was the result of forces outside this sector. These, in a general way, were the causes. What were the effects for the United States?

As noted in Chapter III, the decline in agricultural prices affected the solvency of some banks. These banks were financing trade in agricultural produce, and they held bills that were secured by agricultural goods at one stage or another. When the price of these goods fell, the value of the bills fell too. The result could be bankruptcy.[12]

12. See Temin, 1969, for a parallel. No one has done a similar study of the European currency crisis, but the suggestion may be hazarded that the initial banking failures

A more direct effect of the agricultural deflation was suggested by Kindleberger. He coined the phrase "structural deflation" to describe a process by which a shift in a relative price affects the output of the whole system.[13] A fall in a price decreases the income of the producers and raises the income of the consumers of the good in question. But—according to Kindleberger—while the producers react quickly to the decrease in their income by cutting expenditures, the consumers react much more slowly to the rise in their income, due in part to money illusion and a resultant lack of perception of the effect of the deflation on their incomes. The result is a fall in aggregate demand, leading in turn to a more general deflation.

In terms of aggregate data, this penomenon would look like a shift in the consumption function, that is, a fall in consumption demand for a given total income. The argument is that any redistribution of income lowers the consumption function in the short run. Just such a shift in the consumption function in 1930 was discovered in Chapter III. Could the decline in agricultural prices have been its cause? [14]

The unexplained fall in consumption in 1930 was about 3 per cent of GNP. About 9 per cent of the gross private domestic product originated in agriculture in 1929.[15] For the fall in farm consumption to have accounted for all of the unexplained fall in consumption, farm consumption—which accounted for the bulk of farm income—must have fallen by one-third or more in that year. Such a fall, while not impossible, is unlikely to have occurred. The fall in farm income may have played a disproportionate role in the fall in consumption in 1930, but the farm sector was too small by 1930 for changes within this sector to dominate the whole economy.[16]

The effects of the agricultural depression on the level of aggregate

---

were connected in some way with the decline in the prices of agricultural goods. See Kindleberger, 1973, pp. 146, 153, 155.

13. Kindleberger, 1973, pp. 104–07.

14. We must keep in mind while discussing this question that this is not the question posed by Kindleberger. He was discussing the world Depression. It was sufficient for his argument that the demand in agricultural countries fell while that in industrial countries did not rise. Even though the United States was an exporter of agricultural goods, it stands as an industrial country in the world.

15. *Historical Statistics*, p. 140.

16. Agricultural prices fell by 7 per cent relative to all wholesale prices in 1930 (Table 26). If farmers had been operating on a 15 per cent margin in 1929 and if their costs fell only as much as the average of all wholesale prices, then the fall in farm prices

activity in the United States therefore appears to have been small. The European currency crisis in 1931 was more dramatic than the agricultural depression. We ask now about its connection with events within the United States.

In the face of the European currency crisis, the Federal Reserve chose to preserve the international value of the dollar by policies which were in conflict with the aim of promoting recovery within the United States. Almost everyone agrees that this was a poor choice, and alternative policies have been offered for the Fed to have considered.[17] The importance of these alternative policies is not in their presumed effectiveness; it is in the implicit demonstration that the rise in American interest rates in 1931 was not an inevitable result of the European crisis. It was the joint result of this crisis and the policies of the Fed.

If the European crisis was a result of events in America, then this episode was in fact not very separate from the rest of the story. Instead, it represented a chain of effects that started with changes within the United States after a delay of a year or two. If, by contrast, the European crisis originated outside the United States, then this separate event independently extended the duration of the Depression in America.

The European currency crisis followed the model of a domestic banking crisis. Since the connections between banks in Europe crossed national boundaries, the crisis involved countries and was resolved by national currency restrictions as well as restrictions by banks. Nevertheless, the mechanisms of the panic resulted from the system of fractional reserves and were the same as in a domestic crisis. Since this process is an unstable one once started, it is hard to identify the event that touched it off and perhaps unimportant to do so.[18] Instead, we ask if the depressed economic environment in Europe in 1931 was the result of conditions in the United States. To the extent that it was, events in America created conditions conducive to a banking crisis.

---

would halved farm profits. A fall in consumption by one-third might not be unreasonable in the face of this shock. But we do not know that the decline in farm income was this precipitous or that nonfarm consumption did not rise in response to the fall in agricultural prices. A fall in farm consumption by one-third in one year consequently appears unlikely.

17. Friedman and Schwartz, 1963a, pp. 395–99; Tobin, 1965.

18. Clarke, 1967.

The European country that suffered the largest fall in real income during the 1930s was Germany, and we direct our attention to it. It was important because of the magnitude of the Depression in Germany, because of the sheer size of Germany, and because the currency crisis was so closely tied to the German banking system.[19]

A view of the origins of the international financial crisis of the early 1930s was presented both in the report of the Macmillan Committee and in the analysis of the Depression written by Bertil Ohlin for the League of Nations at the time, and it continues to be repeated in academic studies today.[20] It states that the diminution of capital exports from the United States to Germany in the last years of the 1920s produced the economic decline in Germany that then spread to other European countries.

The hypothesis appears in its most extended form in Schmidt's study of the German business cycles in the 1920s, where it is part of a description of fluctuations after the stabilization of the mark in 1923. His study asserts that the recovery in 1924–25 was due to an inflow of foreign capital stimulated by stabilization and the deliberations of the Dawes Committee. The recession of 1926 was caused by a domestic credit contraction due in turn to a decrease in the rate of capital imports. The mechanism was as follows: In any country where foreign currency or gold can be used for banking reserves, the volume of the domestic money supply—and domestic credit in general—will be affected by changes in the balance of payments. If there is a balance-of-payments surplus, that is, an excess of capital imports over the deficit on current account, there will be an accumulation of foreign exchange or gold; the domestic money supply will rise, and domestic credit conditions will ease. If there is a balance-of-payments deficit, foreign exchange or gold will be lost, and domestic credit will contract. Any decrease in capital imports that increases the deficit will lead to a credit contraction.[21]

19. The following discussion is adapted from Temin, 1971.

20. Great Britain, Committee on Finance and Industry (Macmillan Committee), 1931, p. 81; League of Nations, 1931, p. 214; Angell, 1932, p. 363; Arndt, 1944, p. 29; Schmidt, 1934, pp. 49–50; Clarke, 1967, pp. 147–48; Landes, 1969, pp. 370–72.

21. Schmidt, 1934. This connection between the domestic money supply and the balance of payments, of course, is the one assumed in discussions of the price-specie-flow mechanism. It has been incorporated into Keynesian models of income determination, producing an "income-specie-flow" mechanism, by Mundell, 1968, Chapter 15; and Cooper, 1969.

This is a description of the results of an autonomous fall in capital imports; a fall in capital imports in response to, or offsetting, a decline in imports will not have these effects. If commodity imports and capital imports fall together, there will not be a deficit in the balance of payments or a shortage of credit; the decline in purchasing power will be the same as the decline in purchases, and consequently there will not be any reason for banks to contract.

Recovery from the recession of 1926 was accompanied by the resumption of the capital inflow, and the boom continued for two years accompanied by a steady capital inflow. But it could not last forever according to this story: "By late 1928 and early 1929 American banks began calling their European loans, so that net exports of capital from the United States, which had risen from less than $200 million in 1926 to over a billion dollars in 1928, plunged to $200 million again in 1929.

"This withdrawal of support put tremendous pressure on the European banking system, particularly on the great German banks, which had always followed the policy of borrowing short and lending long. The result was a brutal contraction of credit, which made itself felt in every corner of the economy." [22]

The explanation for the downturn in 1929 to be found in the literature is thus the same as the explanation advanced for the recession in 1926. The test of the explanation accordingly is the same also. A balance-of-payments deficit in 1929 led to a credit scarcity that inhibited economic activity.

Two logical difficulties with this explanation are immediately apparent. First, the withdrawal of American capital from Germany in 1928 and 1929 is said to have been caused by the profitable opportunities for investment on the New York Stock Exchange. But purchases of shares on the stock exchange do not represent investment in the Keynesian sense. They are transfers of ownership, not allocations of real resources. If people who were previously buying German stocks bought American ones instead, what did the people who sold the American stocks do with the money they were paid? If they did not send it abroad, they must have spent it at home or held it as idle balances. And if they did increase domestic spending or idle balances, it is on this that the explanation for the fall in capital export should cen-

22. Landes, 1969, p. 372.

ter, not on the stock market.[23]

Second, the withdrawal of foreign capital is supposed to have had its effect on income almost instantaneously. But the change in the balance of payments had to affect the money supply and then this change had to affect investment plans before income could be affected. Both of these processes take time, and we should be suspicious of any explanation of the fall of German income from its peak in 1928 that focuses on a change in the balance of payments starting late in 1928.

Some data on the German balance of payments are presented in Table 27.[24] The parallel between 1926 and 1929 is instructive, for the downturns of both years are said to have been caused by a fall in capital imports leading to a credit stringency. It is true that capital imports

TABLE 27 • *The German Balance of Payments, 1924–29 (million Reichsmarks)*

	1924	1925	1926	1927	1928	1929
Balance on current account	−1,664	−3,045	−39	−4,244	−3,192	−2,469
Long-term capital movements	+2,000	+1,324	+1,376	+1,703	+1,788	+660
Capital movements n.e.c.	+413	+1,704	−916	+310	+1,000	+879
Balance	+749	−17	+421	−2,231	−404	−930
Short-term capital movements	+506	+107	+147	+1,779	+1,335	+765
Gold and foreign-exchange movements	−1,255	−90	−568	−452	−931	+165

SOURCE: *Die deutsche Zahlungsbilanz der Jahre 1924–1933, Wirtschaft und Statistik,* pp. 10–11.

23. One possibility, of course, is that the increased volume of activity on the New York Stock Exchange required an increased quantity of money for transactions purposes in that market. The idea that "funds flowed into the stock market" might mean just that. But while the transactions demand for money rose in this sector, it is hard to believe that it rose very much. The market was very highly organized, and brokers and speculators did not hold large inventories of cash at the peak of the boom. Kindleberger, 1973, pp. 75–76, asserted that the stock-market boom increased idle balances, but this view is in conflict with the widespread view that idle balances were at a minimum in 1929. See Tobin, 1947.

24. The composition of "capital movements not elsewhere classified" is unclear, but they appear to include the errors and omissions in the accounts. As errors and omissions tend to be concentrated in the capital account, these miscellaneous capital movements are treated like long-term capital movements in the table. None of the qualitative conclusions of the analysis would be changed if they were included with short-term capital movements "below the line." Foreign purchases of German stocks are included in long-term capital movements.

fell in both years, but the balance of payments improved in 1926 nevertheless. Only if the decline in capital imports exceeds the fall in commodity imports can it result in a decline in domestic purchasing power and a resultant credit contraction. As noted earlier, if the decline in capital imports is offset by a fall in commodity imports, the net effect is simply the absence of the imported goods. This appears to have been the case in 1926. There was a decline in imports, presumably caused by a fall in German demand during the recession, and the capital imports by which they were financed fell with them. As the autonomous capital imports did not fall as much as the commodity imports, the overall balance moved into surplus.[25] We may reject a balance-of-payments deficit as the cause of the German recession of 1926.

Since the balance-of-payments deficit in 1929 rose with the fall in capital imports—although not as much—we cannot at this point reject it as a cause of the downturn of that year. Accordingly, we turn to the German credit market for evidence of a credit contraction caused by the balance-of-payments deficit. The movements of the stock of money are not known with precision because of the method of bookkeeping used in the German statistics. But the data suggest that the stock of money as well as the volume of credit outstanding in the economy did not fall in 1929. They did, however, grow less rapidly than in the previous years.[26]

It is tempting to attribute this decline in the rate of growth of money and credit to the deterioration in the balance of payments in 1929. Commentators on the German economy stressed the absolute dependence of German monetary conditions on the balance of payments.[27] The president of the Reichsbank complained that his hands were tied by international constraints.[28] And the magnitude of the change in the deficit in 1929 is more or less the right size to explain

25. If capital movements not elsewhere classified (n.e.c.) are placed below the line, the surplus in 1926 is shown as much larger than in Table 27, and the argument is reinforced. This change amounts to saying that all capital movements n.e.c. were balancing movements, not autonomous ones. For data on imports, see the source for Table 27.

26. The series on currency in circulation, which shows the stock of currency, indicates that this component of the money supply also did not fall in these years. For a discussion of German banking data in the 1930s see J. Klein, 1956.

27. Angell, 1932, p. 201; Guillebaud, 1939, pp. 11–12; Schmidt, 1934, pp. 88–89.

28. Schacht, 1955, p. 218.

the fall in new bank credit (since foreign exchange can be used as bank reserves) which formed the major component of the decline in the growth of total credit, and which must have been in part a fall in the rate of growth of money.

There is, however, a problem with this inference: It assumes that the domestic credit market in Germany was more closely linked to the balance of payments than it actually was. For the years in which we have data, 1925 to 1929, there is no correlation between changes in the supply of credit (or bank credit alone) and the deficit. The volume of new financing was high in 1926 when there was a balance-of-payments surplus, but it was higher in 1927 when there was a deficit. In fact, it was higher in 1927 than in 1929, although the higher deficit of the former year should have inhibited the growth of credit. Despite the protests of the president of the Reichsbank and other observers, the German credit market responded to forces other than the balance of payments.[29]

Even so, the question now remains: Did the level of German production respond to changes in the credit market? The supply of credit (and presumably that component of it classified as money) rose in 1929, albeit at a slower rate than before, while the level of production fell. Data on the net national product of Germany in constant prices are shown in Table 28. The declines of NNP in 1926 (about 1 per cent) and 1929 (about 5 per cent) are apparent in the table. Below the estimates of NNP appear various components of the NNP, each one—with the exception of exports—being a component of the aggregate in the preceding line. In addition, each one is the most volatile compo-

TABLE 28 • *The German National Product and Components in Constant Prices, 1924–29 (billion 1913 marks)*

	1924	1925	1926	1927	1928	1929
Net national product	—	46.9	46.6	53.1	54.0	51.7
Net investment	—	5.4	3.3	8.1	6.9	3.6
Net industrial investment	6.0	3.1	1.0	4.3	3.5	1.3
Inventory investment	4.8	1.2	0.6	2.2	1.2	0.4
Exports	—	6.7	7.7	7.8	8.6	9.9

SOURCE: Hoffmann, 1965, pp. 246, 258, 822, 828.

29. Hoffmann, 1965, pp. 813, 815.

nent of the preceding entry, and fluctuations in each one account for almost all of the fluctuations in its predecessor. Thus the declines of NNP in 1926 and 1929 were falls in net investment which fell by more than NNP in both years. The fall in investment was in turn primarily a fall in industrial investment, which itself was almost exclusively a fall in inventory investment. The other component of investment to show a large fall in 1929 was net agricultural investment (which fell to zero), and the fall here was also mainly a fall in inventory investment. The sum of the change in industrial inventory investment and agricultural investment exceeded the change in NNP in 1929.[30]

It should be noted that although NNP reached a peak in 1928, net investment and its components (including agricultural investment) did so in 1927. The fall in investment thus began before the withdrawal of credit from Germany and the contraction in the rate of growth of credit. Even without examining the nature of the fall, it is hard to believe that it was due to a subsequent credit contraction.

The composition of the fall, in addition, indicates clearly that it was not due to a credit contraction. For the fall in income and investment in 1929 (as in 1926) was primarily a fall in inventory investment. If the fall in NNP was the result of the credit contraction, then the restriction of credit must have caused inventory investment to fall. In terms of the call-money rate, which rose by 15 per cent from 1928 to 1929, inventory investment must have had an interest elasticity larger than eight, since it fell by over 120 per cent. In terms of less volatile long-term interest rates, the elasticity would have had to have been even higher. (If there was credit rationing, so that the volume of credit is a better indication of the state of the market than the cost of credit, then we are faced with the paradoxical picture of falling inventory investment in 1928 when the volume of credit was expanding at the fastest rate since stabilization of the mark.)

This is a high-interest elasticity under any circumstances, but it is particularly problematical for inventory investment. Recent research into the determinants of inventory investment in the United States has failed to uncover any significant or consistent relationship between credit conditions and inventory investment, much less a highly elastic

30. Hoffmann, 1965, pp. 236, 258. Public building, which has sometimes been blamed for the decline in German NNP, was quite small in this period (400 million Reichsmarks at its peak in 1928 and 1929), and it did not decline from 1927 or 1928 to 1929 (Ibid. p. 258).

one.[31] The large econometric models of the postwar United States do not even include the cost or availability of credit among the determinants of industrial inventory investment.[32] The models of the United States in the interwar years surveyed in Chapter II also fail to show a strong effect of interest rates on inventory investment. Conditions in America were not the same as they were in Weimar Germany, but present knowledge gives no reason to think that they differed in this particular area. (Present knowledge also provides no alternative sources of data sufficient to duplicate the American research.) It is therefore entirely unreasonable to hypothesize a relationship between inventories and credit conditions in Germany in the late 1920s strong enough to explain the change in the former by changes in the latter.

The traditional argument relating international capital movements and the German downturn does not stand up under close scrutiny. A new argument must be found, and two choices are immediately apparent. The contemporary observers and their followers may have been mistaken; the German difficulties may have been domestic rather than international. The steady growth in exports shown in Table 28 indicates that fluctuations in exports were not important. A decrease in the rate of growth of domestic demand with its attendant change in orders and expectations consequently stands as a probable cause of the reduction of German inventories.

Alternatively, a more sophisticated argument may be found to link international capital movements and the German downturn. For example, one could argue that as a result of the stock-market boom in New York, investors changed their preferences for financial securities. At given prices, German bonds then looked less attractive and American stocks looked more attractive. As a result of this change in preferences, the price of German bonds would fall, even if no capital was actually withdrawn or no capital inflow was actually interrupted. And as the price of bonds fell, the cost of capital to investors rose and reduced investment.

As noted in Chapter IV, any fall in income—whether caused by a credit stringency or not—can be expected to reduce the demand for credit. It follows that interest rates at the onset of the downturn must

31. See Lovell, 1964.

32. Darling and Lovell, 1965; de Leeuw and Gramlich, 1968, pp. 11–40. The Brookings model uses an interest rate as an explanatory variable for inventories in trade, but it appears in the equations with either the wrong sign or a very large standard error.

be examined to show the effect of financial variables, because the financial markets can be expected to be loose once the downturn gets under way in any case. And, as noted above, German financial markets were tight in 1929, consistent with this alternative argument.

But this story raises as many problems as it resolves. The shift in preferences that starts the process off is extraordinarily hard to verify empirically. Demand curves for financial assets are well defined theoretically, but very hard to observe. And the link between interest rates and investment in Germany does not appear to have been close. The German downturn came first in inventory investment, and empirical work has failed to show a systematic relationship between credit conditions and inventory investment. However compelling the theoretical argument linking the two may appear, there is no evidence to support its importance as an empirical matter.[33]

The European Depression and the currency crisis that was a portion of it therefore was due partly to events outside the United States. By 1931, of course, conditions in Europe were also partly a reflection of the Depression in America. We cannot hope to assess the relative weight of these factors; it is enough to acknowledge that both were present.[34]

This brief analysis of conditions in Germany thus reaffirms the view of the American credit restriction in 1931 as a separate episode in the economic decline. It was the result in part of events in the United States, both contemporaneous and earlier. But it was also the result in part of events that took place outside the United States and that appear to have been largely independent of American conditions. Further work on Germany and Europe in general may expose more connections between them and the United States, but the connection assumed universally to have been effective was not.

Provisionally, we can say that one cause of the depth and duration of the American Depression was the depth of the European Depression, which was only partly a result of the American one.

33. In an attempted refutation of my argument, Falkus, 1975, cites Trivedi, 1973, as evidence that interest rates and inventory investment are related. But this article on inventory investment in the United Kingdom does not even mention interest rates! Far from contradicting my assertion, it shows that data from England are consistent with American data on this point.

34. The political policies within Germany that encouraged the deflation there were important and independent of contemporaneous economic events in the United States. Kindleberger, 1973, pp. 138–42.

Deflation

The preceding discussion has emphasized the part of the fall in agricultural prices that represented a change in relative prices, but the decline in these prices was also part of a general deflation. The discussion of real wages and real balances emphasized their constancy, but we must remember that the nominal quantities fell. Most of the analyses of the Depression surveyed in Chapter II ignored the deflation altogether. It is time to examine the overall deflation.

In a period of changing prices, it is necessary to distinguish between nominal and real interest rates. The nominal interest rate shows the return to an investment in terms of money. If the value of money in terms of goods has changed over the time of the investment, this return will not measure accurately the return in terms of the change in command over goods. The real interest rate is the rate of return in terms of goods. It equals the sum of the nominal rate of interest and the rate of deflation.

The realized real rate of interest can be calculated for any past investment because the nominal rate of return and the rate of deflation are known. The anticipated real rate on current investments, by contrast, is not observable. Market quotations give the nominal rates at which people are buying and selling assets. They show the nominal rates of return that investors hope to get for the coming period. But their hopes for the real rate of return are not recorded, and one has to construct them from the data on nominal rates and changes in the price level.

If the rate of deflation has not changed in a long time, it is reasonable to assume that people expect the deflation to continue at the same rate. The real interest rate then can be calculated from data on present nominal interest rates and the present rate of deflation. But if the rate of deflation has been changing, the problem is much more difficult. If a deflation has just started, or has been going on for just a year or two, do people expect it to continue? Do they expect it to stop momentarily? Do they expect it to be replaced by inflation—to return the price level to its old level? No answers are possible to these questions in general. Individual historical episodes need to be examined for the answer appropriate to them.

The mild deflation of the 1920s changed in 1929 into a severe deflation that lasted until 1932 or 1933, depending on which price index is used. At the conclusion of this process, the wholesale price level was only about two-thirds of its 1929 level, and the consumer price index was three-quarters of the 1929 level. For two or three years the rate of deflation was approximately 10 per cent a year.[35]

We may assume that people were not aware of the deflation immediately. The price declines that they saw undoubtedly appeared at first to be changes in relative prices.[36] Then, as they began to discover that more and more prices had fallen, people must have realized that the price level was changing. This process often is summarized by saying that people estimate future prices from observations of a distributed lag of old prices. The length of this lag is important if we want to know how soon people became aware of the deflation, but it is exceedingly hard to estimate the length of this kind of lag with any confidence.[37] In addition, while it is convenient to assume that the length of this lag did not change in the early 1930s, there is no reason to think that this assumption is true. Prices had been drifting downward slowly for most of the preceding decade. When the rate of deflation changed in late 1929, it represented a break from the immediate past. There is no reason to think that people did not at some point change the way in which they formed expectations as a result of this break.

But while the events of 1930 were clearly different than those of the preceding years, it was not immediately apparent that they represented the start of a continued deflation. Evidence was presented in Chapter III to support the view that expectations of continued depression were not as strong in 1930 as they had been in 1921. This evidence pertained to failures, not to price changes, but the extrapolation from one to the other is immediate. Up until the middle of 1930, certainly, there was no expectation of continued deflation.[38]

This hypothesis is supported by a comparison of price behavior in 1921 and 1930. The data are presented in Table 29, following the format of the tables in Chapter III. The deflation in 1920–21 was very severe, far more severe than the deflation of 1929–30. Over the two-

35. Table 3, above.

36. For a more recent example of this confusion, see Timoshenko, 1953. He attributed the entire fall in agricultural prices in the Depression to agricultural conditions alone.

37. Griliches, 1961.

38. The evidence from the contemporary press supports this view. Writers in the trade press did not distinguish between rises in the quantity of production and rises in prices. They talked of values, which could mean changes in prices or in quantities.

year periods shown in the bottom half of the table—which net out the large rise and fall in prices during 1920—the picture is mixed, but the price fall in 1930 was not clearly larger than the price fall in 1921. There was no evidence in the price data that the deflation would extend for more than a year or two.

We may infer from this evidence that people did not revise their expectations about the future course of prices until sometime late in

TABLE 29 • *Changes in Prices in Three Periods (percentage change)*

	1920–21	1929–30	1937–38
GNP Deflator	−14.9	−4.0	0
WPI	−36.8	−9.3	−8.9
CPI	−10.9	−2.6	−1.8
	1919–21	**1928–30**	**1936–38**
GNP Deflator	−2.8	−4.0	+1.2
WPI	−29.6	−10.7	−2.7
CPI	+3.4	−2.6	+1.7

SOURCE: Table 3, above.

1930. This implies that the fall in interest rates during 1930 shown in Figures 4 and 5 was a fall in anticipated real as well as nominal interest rates.

If we assume that people began to expect the deflation to continue late in 1930 or early in 1931, then their estimates of real and nominal interest rates began to diverge at this point. The anticipated real rate must then have risen over 10 per cent, since this was the rate of deflation current in 1931 and 1932. In other words, all real interest rates rose during the Depression, under this assumption. The explanation of the increase in interest-rate differentials given in Chapter IV is unaffected by this assumption, but the context is different. In terms of real interest rates, the problem becomes why some interest rates rose more than others rather than why some interest rates fell while others rose.

A glance at Figures 4 and 5 reveals that all the interest rates shown were well below 10 per cent during the 1920s, with the sole exception of the call-money rate in two short periods. If the real short-term interest rate rose above 10 per cent for two years or so in the 1930s, this surely would have depressed business. And if we add 10 per cent to the estimates of long-term interest rates as well, then the picture of business deterred by high interest rates is clear.

In 1932, the deflation slowed or stopped. But people who had reluctantly adopted deflationary expectations presumably would not have rapidly scrapped them, particularly in the face of the monetary stringency of 1932. Anticipated high real interest rates then would have continued into 1933, when we may presume that they fell back toward the level of nominal interest rates. The dramatic rise in expected real interest rates in late 1930 or 1931 must have been balanced by an equally dramatic fall in expected real interest rates in late 1932 or 1933. The depressing effect of the former on business should have been more or less offset by the expansionary effect of the latter. The deflation—according to this line of thought—was an important determinant of the length and severity of the Depression.

Two questions are raised by this discussion of real interest rates which must be answered before the importance of the deflation can be assessed. Did people actually think in these terms? And does this discussion provide any clues about the mechanisms that produced and then terminated the deflation? Neither question appears to have a clear-cut answer, as we shall see.

Economists routinely make the distinction between nominal and real interest rates, but it is hard to find even a mention of this distinction outside the professional literature. While it seems obvious to economists that people must have been thinking in these terms, a reading of the trade press does not support that idea. And it is not even clear that an individual in the early 1930s had that much to gain from thinking in these terms.[39]

Assume that it took approximately a year for this individual to change his price expectations. In other words, he lived through a year of different price behavior before he both acknowledged that the course of the price level had changed and decided that the new rate of change would endure. The 10 per cent rate of deflation lasted only two or three years, depending on which price index is used. This individual would not have estimated the real rate of interest correctly in the

39. Lewis argued for the importance of deflation without introducing the concept of real interest rates. He said the deflation "checked confidence in recovery, and persuaded businessmen to 'wait and see' rather than to make new investments." As noted in Chapter III, expectations about recovery are hard to observe and even harder to explain. Accordingly, it is not clear how to test Lewis's formulation of this process. See Lewis, 1949, p. 56; Kindleberger, 1973, p. 142.

first year of this deflation, so he would have gained only one or two years of correct predictions. But the picture is worse than this. When the deflation stopped, this individual would have taken a year to realize that it had stopped and to change his expectations. He then would have overpredicted the real interest rate for the year following the end of the deflation. Assuming that the losses from this incorrect prediction balanced the gain from the correct prediction for the same length of time, he would have profited by his ability to distinguish real and nominal interest rates in at most only one year and possibly not at all. The gains were small.

Individuals who made up their minds more quickly than this hypothetical individual had more to gain, the man who correctly anticipated all price changes having the most. But few people could have changed their expectations significantly more rapidly than this. The evidence presented in Chapter III suggests that there was no general expectation of continued depression before late 1930. And common sense supports the idea that people wait and see for at least a few months before extrapolating present trends blithely into the future.

Arguments such as these do not settle historical questions. People often do things that yield only a little profit. And the absence of public mention of something is both hard to prove and hard to evaluate. Nevertheless, these arguments create a presumption that nominal interest rates rather than some estimates of real interest rates were important in the early 1930s.

Of course, if people were thinking in terms of real interest rates, then the rise in the real interest rate would have been a powerful deterrent to investment. It could even have been a sufficiently important factor to dominate all other explanations of the fall in investment. The Depression, then, would have been caused by the combination of deflation and the institutional constraint that the nominal rate of interest not be negative. Together, these conditions meant that all real rates of interest had to be above 10 per cent.

The problem with this argument is that it explains too much. There were many periods of sharp deflation before the early 1930s. In all of these periods the nominal rate was constrained to be positive. The real interest rate calculated by the means just outlined then must have been high; investment should have been choked off, and there should have been massive unemployment as a result. Yet the Depression of the 1930s was a unique event; the prior deflations do not seem to have had this effect. If high real interest rates in the early 1930s caused the Depression, then we have to explain why—in light of the data in Table 24—the deflation of the early 1920s did not produce a depression then.[40]

The mechanisms that produce deflation are the same as the mechanisms that produce declines in output. The arguments given in Chapter IV about the latter therefore apply to the former as well. If a monetary restriction had produced the deflation, then the deflation should have been preceded by a rise in interest rates. The rise in interest rates in 1929 therefore may have helped to start the deflation, although the importance of the role they played is not known. The rise in interest rates in 1931 played a similar role, adding to the deflationary forces already present. In the interval between these rises, there is no evidence of monetary pressure.

This argument needs some modification if the assumption that people more or less correctly anticipated the course of real interest rates and acted on this basis is accepted. In terms of real interest rates, calculated to show the effects of price changes with a lag, the argument goes as follows. The initial rise in interest rates in 1929 is unaffected because it precedes the deflation. The rise of nominal interest rates in 1931 becomes less significant beside the much larger rise of real interest rates in 1930 or 1931. Real interest rates fell in 1929 and 1930, then rose rapidly in 1930 or 1931 to new heights, where they stayed until 1933 or so.

The rise in real interest rates emphasized in this story cannot be attributed to the contemporaneous bank failures; they were the results of the previous deflation. Given the deflation of 1930 and the low level of nominal interest rates at the end of the year, expected real rates had to rise in late 1930 or 1931 under the assumption being used here. If there had been no bank failures, they would still have risen. Unless nominal rates could have gone below zero, the expectations created by the deflation of 1930 (under our assumption) had to create a rise in anticipated real interest rates. The conclusions of Chapter IV are unaffected; the bank failures of 1930 did not have strong macroeconomic effects.

At the end of the deflation, the process was the reverse. If mone-

40. This argument applies as well to any alternative mechanism—such as a change in expectations—by which the deflation is presumed to have reduced investment expenditures in the early 1930s. See Lewis, 1949, p. 56.

tary ease caused the deflation to end, then a fall in interest rates should have been apparent. Since the expected rate of deflation was not changing at the time the deflation stopped (due to the delay in forming expectations), any change in the real interest rate would be apparent in the nominal interest rate as well. It does not matter whether we assume people thought in terms of real or nominal rates for this argument.[41]

As Figures 4 and 5 show, short-term interest rates did fall in 1932. But the fall seems only to balance the rise in 1931, and the quantity of money fell between 1932 and 1933. The fall in short-term interest rates in 1932 therefore reflects the easing of the monetary pressure imposed by the Federal Reserve after the European currency crisis of 1931. It signaled a return to the conditions of mid-1931, not the conditions of 1929. The gradual fall in interest rates in 1933 that is apparent in some of the series shown in Figures 4 and 5 may show the effects of monetary ease, but the record of such ease that they provide is hardly clear.

If we assume that investors thought in terms of real interest rates in the early 1930s, the resulting story is no more favorable to the money hypothesis than the story told without this assumption. The argument about the effect of bank failures given in Chapter IV is unaffected by the change; both bank failures and the further decline in economic activity in 1931 were results of the deflation, not causes. The spending hypothesis, by way of contrast, provides an explanation of the fall in demand in 1931—the extraordinary fall in consumption in 1930—that could explain continued deflation as well as continued depression.

In fact, there is a further difficulty with the money hypothesis under the assumption that people realized the implications of the price changes of the early 1930s. As Table 23 demonstrates, the real stock of money did not fall in these years.[42] If the demand for money can be written in real terms, that is, if the demand for real balances is a stable function of the level of real income, then there does not seem to have been any contractionary pressure on real income from the supply of money. This, clearly, is inconsistent with the money hypothesis.

The paradox can be approached in two ways, neither of them satisfactory. The assumption that prices do not matter for the demand for

41. The fall in anticipated real interest rates that followed the end of the deflation obviously provides no clues about the cause of this ending.

42. The discussion of Table 23 emphasized the failure of real balances to rise in the early 1930s. Here we are interested in their failure also to fall.

money could be abandoned. But since Friedman is a strong proponent both of this assumption and of the money hypothesis, the merit of this resolution is unclear.[43] Alternatively, it could be asserted that the monetary contraction caused the deflation. The resulting story, however, is not a convincing one.

The monetary pressure that caused the contraction according to this story must have been imposed in 1929 and 1928 when interest rates rose. As the arguments just given and in Chapter IV have shown, the bank failures of 1930 could not have caused the deflation. They followed the onset of the deflation, and they did not give rise to any signs of monetary pressure. In addition, the deflation caused by monetary pressure, according to this story, was sufficiently rapid to remove the sources of pressure. An initial decline in real balances was eliminated by the resulting fall in prices. But if this means of eliminating the pressure created by a fall in real balances worked so well, why did real income fall at all? This story neither identifies properly the source of monetary pressure as given by the money hypothesis nor provides a mechanism whereby this pressure led to a reduction in economic activity.

Neither Friedman and Schwartz nor the postwar econometric investigations of the Depression payed much attention to the deflation.[44] Its presence was acknowledged from time to time, but it was never incorporated into the analysis. The evident difficulties in bringing it into the money hypothesis have just been explored. The spending hypothesis, since it sees nonmonetary causes for the Depression, has no similar difficulties. Bringing the deflation to center stage for a minute, therefore, strengthens the argument for the spending hypothesis.

Analysts of the international Depression have spent much more time on the deflation than historians of the United States alone. Kindleberger's hypothesis about the effects of structural deflation has already been noted.[45] He asserted that the unevenness of the deflation created strains on the economy that intensified the Depression. These strains were said to be characteristic of deflation, and they were greater for larger deflations than for small. The presence of such strains cannot be doubted, but their importance within the United States is unclear. As Table 29 shows, prices fell at least as rapidly in

43. Friedman and Schwartz, 1963a; Friedman, 1970.
44. See Chapter II.
45. See the preceding section of this chapter and Kindleberger, 1973, pp. 104–07.

1921 as nine years later. What offsetting forces prevented the resulting strains from causing a Great Depression then? The structural-deflation hypothesis is intriguing, but seriously incomplete at this stage in its development.

This discussion of deflation has helped us discriminate between the spending and money hypotheses. The spending hypothesis explains the deflation by the same arguments used to explain the fall in income. And if investors expected the deflation to continue, the implied rise in the expected real interest added to the deflationary pressure. The money hypothesis, by contrast, accommodates the possibility of these expectations only with difficulty. The macroeconomic effects of the banking panic of 1930 are absent in this expanded story—particularly since the acceleration of the deflation preceded the panic. And the failure of the real money stock to fall suggests either that the hypothesized monetary restriction was not large or that prices were sufficiently flexible to eliminate any real effects. The money hypothesis does not appear to be consistent with either the interest-rate or the price data. But adding the deflation to the list of events to be explained has complicated the story enormously. Neither hypothesis can be said to have successfully incorporated the deflation into the resulting narrative of the Depression.

VI

Conclusions

DID MONETARY FORCES cause the Depression? To this question a partial answer may now be given: There is no evidence of any effective deflationary pressure from the banking system between the stock-market crash in October 1929 and the British abandonment of the gold standard in September 1931.

The evidence for this answer is in two parts. First, if there had been deflationary monetary pressure, it would have had to be visible in the financial markets. This is not to say that the monetary pressure would have had to work exclusively through financial interest rates, although it might have. It is only to say that the pressure could not have bypassed the financial markets entirely. And, as argued in Chapter IV, this pressure would have shown up sharply in short-term interest rates. At the time when the monetary pressure was applied to the economy, a temporary rise in these interest rates should have been visible. If the pressure was strong—strong enough to send the economy into its deepest depression—then the rise should have been dramatic and obvious.

Yet there was no rise in short-term interest rates in this two-year period. The path of short-term interest rates is perfectly clear. They declined steadily from the stock-market crash to the end of the gold standard in the fall of 1931. Other rates of return moved in other directions, but these contrary movements appear to have been related to the increase in risk that accompanied the Depression and a decrease in people's desire to hold risky assets. The presence of various kinds of risks in the markets for these other assets makes them poor vehicles to use in spotting a monetary contraction. The relevant record for the purpose of identifying a monetary restriction is the record of short-term interest rates.

Second, although the nominal stock of money fell in 1930 and 1931, prices fell also. They fell so rapidly, in fact, that the stock of real balances did not fall; it was higher in 1931 than in 1929 by a variety of measures.[1] If the fall in the nominal stock of money was deflationary, prices were sufficiently flexible to absorb this pressure. In the absence of other influences, nominal income should have fallen, but not real income.

This point can be stated more formally. The deflationary impact of a reduction in the money supply is communicated to the economy through a stable demand function for money. This demand function relates the demand for real balances to the level of real income, interest rates, and other variables. A change in the overall price level is not thought to have any impact at all on it.[2] If the real supply of money did not fall, it follows that it could not have caused the level of real income to fall by means of this relation.

For these two reasons, then, the proposition that monetary forces caused the Depression must be rejected. But as noted above, the rejection is only partial, confined in time to this short—albeit critical—period. There is evidence of monetary restriction before the stock-market crash in 1929 and after Britain left gold in late 1931. Interest rates were high in 1929, although the real quantity of money continued to grow. Interest rates rose in late 1931, and even though they did not approach the levels of 1929, the real stock of money fell from 1931 to 1932. The extent to which these deflationary movements affected the economy is not known, but the direction is clear. Rises in the interest rate and decreases in the stock of real balances have depressing effects on real income.

The economic history of the Depression, then, seems to have gone something like this: A recession started in 1929 due to some combination of factors which cannot be disentangled. Financial markets were tight as a result both of the expectations built up around the stock-market boom and the efforts of the Federal Reserve to arrest that boom. There were a variety of imbalances in particular markets, of which the apparent oversupply of housing at current prices was the most obvious. These and other factors made for a drop in income, but

1. See Table 23, above.

2. It is worth noting that this formulation is agreed to by economists who hold widely differing views on other matters. See, for example, Friedman, 1970; Goldfeld, 1973.

they would not by themselves have led to a major depression.

To these forces, several other identifiable deflationary factors were added. The stock-market crash was the most dramatic of these, and it has been discussed most widely. However, it is equally incorrect to say that the crash caused the Depression by itself and that the Depression owed nothing to the crash. The crash was one of several deflationary factors, although hardly the largest. For all the discussion of the crash by historians looking back on the 1920s and 1930s, it does not seem to have altered people's anticipations about the overall level of activity of the economy. Expectations appear to have changed rather slowly as events unfolded. It was not until a year after the stock-market crash that observers in general saw that the Depression at hand was not the same as previous falls in income.

The stock-market crash did have two observable effects, however. First, the fall in stock-market prices reduced wealth in the hands of consumers. This, in turn, reduced consumption expenditures by these consumers. Second, the change in stock-market prices led to changes in the financial activities of individuals and firms. Both nonagricultural individuals and nonfinancial corporations (taken as groups) had been increasing their financial leverage during the late 1920s, that is, they were borrowing in order to lend or to invest in financial assets like equities. They began to reduce their leverage in 1930; a process of disintermediation—as it came to be called during the credit crunches of the 1960s—began.

The decrease in consumption due to the decline in wealth was perceptible but small. While it is impossible to measure the size of this decline precisely, it was less than one-fifth of the fall in consumption in 1930, and quite possibly a lot less.[3] The effects of the altered financial policies are impossible to know. They may have restricted the flow of funds into some areas, or they may have played a part in the

3. See Chapter III. Recent work by Frederic Mishkin suggests that the change in consumers' balance sheets noted in the previous paragraph may have caused consumption to decline in 1930 by more than the calculations based on (net) wealth indicate. The fall in the value of financial assets after the stock-market crash not only decreased people's net wealth; it also increased their leverage (ratio of debt to assets). Part of the reduction in leverage after 1929 was a reaction to this unexpected rise. And—in addition—people seem to have reduced their consumption as a result of the increased leverage. The rise in leverage increased the possibility of bankruptcy or forced sale of illiquid assets, and consumers reduced their purchases of consumer durables to reduce this risk. See Mishkin, forthcoming, for the general argument. An application to the Depression is in progress.

recurrent bank failures of the early 1930s, but they have left few traces in the data.

A separate depressing influence came from agriculture. The 1929 harvest was a poor one in America and other exporting regions, but not in the importing areas of Europe. Production and revenue both fell in the United States as a result. For the one-fifth of the labor force employed in agriculture, the Depression started with these events. To the extent that people engaged in agricultural occupations decreased their consumption as a result of their decreased income, this had a deflationary impact on the economy as a whole which must be added to the impact of the stock-market crash on consumption. But since most income was earned outside of agriculture, the effect could not have been large.

Consumption fell too far in 1930 to be explained by these forces alone. In addition to the fall in income, the collapse of the stock market, and the poor harvest in 1929, something else happened to depress consumption in 1930. At the current stage of our knowledge, the unexplained fall in consumption is larger than the part we can explain, but the magnitude of the total fall is incontrovertible. The large decline in consumption expenditures for both durable and non-durable goods in 1930 had a profoundly depressing effect for the economy.

It is worth emphasizing that the fall in consumption was unusually large in 1930, because the conventional literature assumes that it was investment that experienced the unusual fall. But although the composition of the fall in investment differed in 1930 from the composition in other shorter depressions, the magnitude of the fall was not larger. Investment fell in 1930, as it falls in all recessions, but it did not fall more than usual. The Depression was not caused by a dramatic collapse of investment.

The large fall in consumption in 1930, deriving from a variety of diverse and as yet still incompletely delineated sources, prevented recovery in that year. Goods that could not be sold were not produced. The fall in aggregate demand spread throughout the economy. And as the fall of 1930 wore on and business did not recover, as might have been expected from observation of previous reductions in business activity in the twentieth century, businessmen lost the confidence that underlies private investment. The economy continued to decline.

The decline appeared to stop in early 1931, but there is no way of knowing if this was the beginning of potential recovery or simply a random deviation from a downward trend. The European currency crisis in the summer and fall of 1931 caused the Federal Reserve to raise interest rates and tighten financial markets in the United States in late 1931. The resultant financial stringency and further discouragement of hopeful expectations acted to prolong the Depression.

The origins of the European crisis are too complex to be described here, but the conventional attribution of these difficulties exclusively to the cessation of American lending in the late 1920s must be rejected. The argument is not that Americans withdrew funds from the Credit Anstalt, but that prior reductions in lending had weakened the European economies. While a reduction in lending is never good for the borrowing countries, the weakness of Germany—which experienced the largest fall in real income of the European economies—derived from domestic rather than foreign influences. The decline in investment—which here was the key—came at the wrong time and was concentrated in the wrong type of investment to be explained by the fall in American lending. The European crisis must then be regarded as partly a coincident event to the American, and partly the effect of the American decline, rather than simply as the result of events in the United States.

These statements pertain to the history up to 1931 only. After that time the story becomes so complex and the interactions so numerous that it is no longer possible to envisage separate movements in different parts of the world. World-wide influences such as harvest failures tied different economies together to some extent before the Depression was well underway. And as the Depression continued and deepened, its impact spread across countries through commodity and capital markets. A world-wide perspective, as opposed to a national one, is needed to analyze the events after 1931.

What can we say about the role of macroeconomic policy in this story? It is clear from the fact that the Depression occurred that effective countermeasures were not used. Those countermeasures that were tried clearly were ineffective; the Depression took place. To show that a macroeconomic policy can be effective, a historian is forced into the uncomfortable position of attempting to prove that it was not used. If it was used, it did not work. Only if it was not used can it emerge from the debacle of the 1930s unscathed.

But it is hardly the same to say that a policy was not discredited and to say that a policy has been shown effective. It is for this reason that the position of the historian of policy is uncomfortable. The historical record can only show that a policy was not shown to be ineffective; the record does not show how the Depression was cured by the administration of this or that prescription.

A totally different kind of analysis is needed to show that a policy would have worked had it been tried and—by extension—that it will work if used today. To show this, the structure of the economy needs to be exposed. One cannot answer the question of what might have been if history had been different from the narrative of historical events alone. One must make inferences from these events about the underlying structure that tied them together. But as shown in Chapter II, the data for the interwar period are not rich enough to indicate a unique underlying structure. More than one structure can be used to explain the data for this period, and the choice between these structures must be made on other grounds.

Two separate attributes of macroeconomic theory contribute to this difficulty. The first characteristic of the theory is its extensive use of unobserved variables whose behavior is not assumed to be governed by strict laws. Many theories depend critically on the behavior of variables which cannot be observed, such as expectations and interest rates on nonmarketed assets, and which are not clearly functions of observed magnitudes.

The discussion of consumer expectations in Chapter III, of risk perceptions in Chapter IV, and of the real interest rate in Chapter V, all represent attempts to come to grips with unobserved variables in this study. But the account of the Depression given here has deemphasized the role of nonobserved variables. In order to test the competing hypotheses, observations were needed on which to perform tests, and the exposition consequently centered on observable components of the hypotheses, that is, on observed variables and unobserved variables whose movements can be inferred unambiguously from observed changes.

Most of the literature on the Depression, however, is replete with assertions about unobserved and unpredictable magnitudes. According to Wilson, "The succession of sensational [bank] crashes had a disastrous effect on confidence, which raised the risk premium on long-term securities on the one hand, and made businessmen reluctant to borrow on the other." According to Lewis, "The surprisingly rapid fall of agricultural and other raw material prices . . . checked confidence in recovery, and persuaded businessmen to 'wait and see' rather than to make new investments.'' And Gordon said, after describing the economy's ''weaknesses'' in 1929, ''Some of these developments may be described as the result of the belated and rough working of the acceleration principle, although it should be emphasized that we can trace no simple correlation between the short-period changes in the rate of increase in output and in the demand for capital goods.'' [4]

How is one to verify or disprove these assertions? In the absence of a theory of expectations and a testable formulation of the acceleration principle, there is no reason why one cannot say that neither bank failures nor deflation changed expectations and that the acceleration principle was absent. There is no way to prove these statements wrong. The presence of unobserved variables whose behavior does not obey strict laws at the heart of most narratives of the Depression means that the narratives appear to give more of an explanation than they in fact offer. For if the Depression had not occurred, but all the antecedents had, then the story would have been the same except for the unobserved variables. There need be no inconsistency in such a hypothetical course of history.

The same point may be stated a little differently. The presence of one or more unobserved and unconstrained variables in the macroeconomic theory underlying a historical explanation allows that explanation to encompass a wide variety of events. By suitable assumptions about the movements of the unobserved, unconstrained variables, the historian can interpret the theory to fit almost any observed sequence of events. But by the same token, there is no way to falsify this explanation of the events, for the difference between this and competing narratives will involve different assumptions about the movements of the unobservable, unconstrained variables, assumptions which by their nature cannot be tested. It follows that one cannot choose between competing explanations of the same events.

This problem is not apparent when macroeconomic theories are used to generate policy recommendations. For this purpose, the underlying state of the economy—including both observed and unobserved variables—is assumed static, and the effects of changes in governmental actions are examined. Since the unobserved variables are

4. Wilson, 1942, p. 170; Lewis, 1949, p. 56; Gordon, 1974, p. 44.

assumed constant, it does not matter that they are not observed. But the policies are appropriate only so long as the observed and unobserved variables assumed to be constant actually remain constant. And, obviously, it is impossible to know when this condition holds true if variations in the unobserved variables are not subject to known laws.

The second important characteristic of macroeconomic theories is their complexity. The theories involve several variables and a variety of functions expressing the interrelations between these variables. A large body of data is needed to estimate the parameters in these functions and to test for the presence or absence of hypothesized effects. During the period in which these data originate, the underlying relationships must remain constant or they cannot be estimated.

But how long can these underlying relationships in the economy be assumed to have remained constant? The twentieth century has been marked by a series of cataclysmic events, and it would be remarkable if they had left the structure of the economy unaffected. The world wars and their attendant mobilizations, the restriction of immigration after the First World War, the change in government macroeconomic policy after the Second World War, the Great Depression itself and the policies designed to alleviate it, all represent dramatic events in our economic (and social) history. It would be very strange indeed if the structure of the economy had not been altered by any of these remarkable occurrences.

In addition, the data have to show movement within the economy to trace out the relevant functions. Periods in which no variables change do not provide information about the interconnections of these variables. In order to estimate the parameters in a macroeconomic theory or to discriminate between alternative hypotheses, a period is required in which there is some change—to generate data for a variety of configurations of the economy—but not too much change—so that the values of the parameters being estimated or the shape of the functions being tested do not change. And this period must be long enough to generate enough data of this proper sort for the hypothesized regularities in the economy to be apparent.

Appropriate periods, it seems obvious, are going to be hard to find. The postwar period has generated a large amount of data, particularly since the advent of quarterly data. It has also been free of cataclysmic events that might have changed the basic structure of the economy. But by the same token, it has also lacked a richness of economic experience; it may not have encompassed enough variation for alternate theories to be tested.[5]

The interwar period has more problems than the postwar period when it comes to generating suitable data. The period itself is only two decades long. At either end stands a world war, within which the structure of the economy may be presumed to have changed. In the middle, of course, stands the Great Depression, which may or may not have altered the structure of the economy also. In any case, the period breaks down into three periods, within which there is not very much variation. The 1920s, the period of the economic decline analyzed here, and the period from 1933 on, were all different from each other. But the variation within each period was much, much smaller than the variation between the periods. For many purposes, such as the evaluation of the effects of bank failures in Chapter II, only the variation between periods is large enough to be useful.

For other variables, the events of the interwar years that generated observable changes are the depressions. And as has been noted repeatedly during this inquiry, there were three such movements in the interwar period. As we have seen, three is better than one, and the comparison of these movements has yielded useful information. But three is still a small number, and the comparisons are of only limited usefulness.

The interwar period therefore does not contain a plethora of data for the testing of macroeconomic hypotheses. It is only two decades long, and much of the relevant data is on an annual basis. Compilation of quarterly data would relieve this problem to some extent, but it would not solve it. The variations within the period are dominated by a few sharp changes which dwarf the other movements of the variables, and there are not enough of these changes to test complicated hypotheses. All of the econometric models of Chapter II, different though they are, appear to fit the data tolerably well.

The historian who attempts to use the record of the Depression to gather clues about current policies therefore is doubly hampered. The underlying theories appeal to unobserved and unconstrained variables

5. The current inflation with unemployment appears to offer a different experience than the typical one of the postwar years. It may, therefore, provide an opportunity to test alternative theories. But it is worth noting that our present macroeconomic theories have not served us well in the explanation of this combined inflation and unemployment.

at critical points in the argument, and the movements of the observed variables in the interwar period are too limited to provide enough information to test alternate macroeconomic hypotheses about them. This study has shown that the spending hypothesis fits the observed data better than the money hypothesis, that is, that it is more plausible to believe that the Depression was the result of a drop in autonomous expenditures, particularly consumption, than the result of autonomous bank failures. This is of great interest. But, for the reasons just stated, the economist who uses this conclusion or any other conclusion about the Depression as a basis for economic policy recommendations essentially is performing an act of faith.

APPENDICES ON DATA

BIBLIOGRAPHY

INDEX

APPENDICES ON DATA

1. Data for Tables 8 and 9

THE NONDURABLE CONSUMPTION variable used in Tables 8 and 9 is the annual expenditures on perishables, services, and semidurables as estimated by Swanson and Williamson (1972). For 1929–41, the Swanson and Williamson data is that of the United States Department of Commerce. For 1919–28, Kuznet's (1961) data were revised to conform to the 1966 Department of Commerce definitions. The Swanson and Williamson revisions are largely those suggested by Kendrick (1961) except that Kendrick used the 1954 Department of Commerce data, whereas Swanson and Williamson used the 1966 Department of Commerce estimates.

Alternative consumption variables were tried to see if the regression results were sensitive to the choice of data. Depreciation on consumer durables was estimated crudely, and a series for nondurable consumption plus use value from durables was constructed. No drastic changes in parameter values (and, therefore, residual patterns) resulted. This alternative consumption variable was abandoned because of the low quality of the estimate for the use value from consumer durables—inadequate data forbade accurate determination. Total expenditures by consumers was tried as the consumption variable with some, often minor, quantitative changes in the regression results. This variable is inappropriate because theory suggests that durable and nondurable expenditure decisions are not made in the same manner. Nevertheless, results using this variable are shown in Tables 8 and 9 for comparison with the conceptually preferable results.

The disposable income data also came from Swanson and Williamson. Their income series is based on computations suggested by

Goldsmith (1955, vol. 3), except that more recent data were utilized.

Two wealth series were used. They both were derived from Goldsmith's data by essentially similar methods. The differences between them are matters of methodological taste rather than ideological disagreement, and they may be regarded as two approximations of whatever reality underlays Goldsmith's estimates for benchmark years.

The first wealth series was constructed to conform to the benchmark calculations of Goldsmith (1955, vol. 1, Tables W1, W22, W27). The items included in private nonfarm household nontangible assets are currency and commercial bank deposits; deposits in other financial institutions; farm and nonfarm mortgages; private pensions and retirement funds; corporate and foreign bonds; U.S. government, state, and local securities; common and preferred stock; equity in financial nonprofit institutions; and life insurance reserves. Accruals and mortgages are included in nonfarm household liabilities. Items included in farm household nontangible assets are currency, bank deposits, life insurance reserves, U.S. government securities, farm mortgages, equity in cooperatives and veterans' funds. Private net wealth was calculated by subtracting farm and nonfarm household liabilities from the total farm and nonfarm tangible and nontangible assets. For the benchmark year 1922, data for the individual items included in net wealth were taken from Goldsmith (1955, vol. 3, Tables W22, W27). Values for the included items for all other years were obtained for year *i* by adding to the total in year *i-1* the acquisitions in year *i* (adjusting for relative price changes). The subsequent totals are end-of-year stocks. Acquisitions for individual items and price indexes were obtained from a variety of sources (including, of course, Goldsmith).

Several of the items included by Goldsmith in his benchmark calculations had to be excluded from the constructed wealth series due to insufficient data for nonbenchmark years. Government pension and retirement funds, receivables from business, equity in financial nonprofit institutions (and "other") were excluded from assets of nonfarm households. Payables to financial intermediaries, payables to other businesses, borrowings on securities, bonds and notes (and "other") were excluded from nonfarm-household liabilities. Agricultural assets excluded government pension and retirement funds, equity in financial nonprofit institutions and in government corporations, and other intangibles. None of the above excluded items were very large. However, the cyclical movement of the excluded items (and their movement relative to included items)—which is crucial to determining the bias the use of such a series imposes on subsequent estimations—is not known. The ratio of the constructed wealth series to Goldsmith's benchmark totals are:

1922	1929	1933	1939
91%	99%	96%	99%

While the constructed series will always fall short of the more inclusive Goldsmith benchmark figures, there is no obvious pattern to the size of the deviations. Surprisingly, the constructed series tracks the Goldsmith estimates least well in 1922, even though the 1922 benchmark figures for component items were taken directly from Goldsmith, and not derived, as for all other years, by successive application of savings data. More disturbing, the benchmark and constructed series differ noticeably in 1933, a depression year and, therefore, of particular interest.

Ando and Brown (1963) constructed a wealth series for the years after 1929. Starting with the same data used in the wealth estimate just described, Ando and Brown derived their annual series in three steps. First, they repriced Goldsmith's benchmark data to correspond with midyear prices. Second, they interpolated the intermediate observations on the basis of personal savings, capital gains on financial and nonfinancial assets, and minor adjustments. (The interpolators were more complete, although not necessarily more accurate, than those used in the derivation of the new wealth estimate.) Third, the series constructed by moving forward from any one benchmark year was averaged with the series constructed by moving backward from the next benchmark year to get the final estimates.

The series for wealth consisting of the new series through 1928 and Ando and Brown's thereafter was used as an alternate estimate. Its use did not significantly alter coefficient estimates or residual patterns for consumption function regressions. This is not surprising, since both series utilize the Goldsmith benchmark and savings data. The excess of Ando and Brown's wealth series over the new one is:

1929	1%	1933	−8%	1937	7%
1930	6	1934	−7	1938	0
1931	7	1935	−10	1939	1
1932	8	1936	−1	1940	−2

The comparison suggests that the new series might underestimate wealth during the height of the Depression and overstate wealth before and after the Depression.

The functional form of the consumption function used here follows the one used by Ando and Modigliani (1963) in an early formulation of the "life-cycle hypothesis." Nominal consumption was regressed on nominal disposable income and nominal private net worth. The theory postulates that persons save to spread purchases over a lifetime of variable earnings and, in its simplest form, that all people have an average and marginal propensity to consume with respect to life income of one. Given the poor quality of the data for the interwar period, this last assumption was not imposed on the regressions in Table 8.

The residuals shown in Table 9 were derived from the regressions reported in Table 8. Given the problems with the underlying estimation, it was necessary to see how sensitive the results were to the size of the estimated coefficients. Accordingly, the same calculations were done using the postwar coefficients shown at the bottom of Table 8, and the results are shown in Table A-1.[1] As can be seen, the residual pattern is not very different from the pattern shown in Table 9, even though the assumed effect of changes in wealth on consumption is three times as large. The change in the residual from 1929 to 1930 is smaller than the analogous changes reported in adjacent columns by roughly the same amount as shown in Table 9. (The greater dispersion of the residuals in Table A-1 is the natural result of using coefficients estimated for one period on data of another.) The results shown in Table 9 are not sensitive to the choice of parameters in the consumption function.

An alternate formulation of the consumption function was proposed by Friedman (1957). He postulated a "permanent-income hypothesis" in which, as in the life-cycle hypothesis, the consumer is assumed to be optimally allocating his total resources to each period, but the time over which the consumer is assumed to be optimizing is infinite. Consumption is proportional to the return on the consumer's total

1. The wealth coefficient was larger when a constant was included in the postwar regressions than when it was suppressed. The coefficient used to calculate Table A-1, therefore, is a relatively high estimate.

TABLE A–1 • *Residuals from Consumption Functions Involving Measured Wealth: Postwar Coefficients (billions of dollars)*

	R_{21}	R_{30}	R_{38}	R_{21}–R_{20}	R_{30}–R_{29}	R_{38}–R_{37}
Nondurable consumption						
Temin data	8.56	−.88	4.32	3.99	−.26	2.66
Ando-Brown data	8.56	−1.25	2.62	3.99	−4.16	.74
Total consumer spending						
Temin data	13.9	6.28	10.0	2.72	−2.25	1.41
Ando-Brown data	13.9	5.92	8.31	2.72	−6.18	−.50

SOURCE: See text.

wealth—that is, permanent income—and therefore proportional to the maximum income that could be consumed forever. Permanent income is empirically estimated as a weighted average of past realized income, and real consumption per capita is regressed on real permanent income per capita to evaluate the constant of proportionality. The permanent income series used here is due to Friedman and Schwartz, as kindly supplied by Schwartz.

Table A-2 shows the residual pattern from permanent-income consumption functions. Four estimates are shown. Both nondurable consumption and total consumer spending were used. And residuals derived from coefficients estimated for the interwar period were compared with those derived from postwar coefficients. As can be seen from Table A-2, the residuals in 1930 were lower than the residual in other interwar depression years, but the changes in the residuals from 1929 to 1930 were not different on average from the other changes shown. The picture shown here, therefore, is mixed. The permanent-income consumption function underpredicts the fall in consumption in 1930, but it also underpredicts the fall for the other years shown. So, while part of the fall in consumption in 1930 is unexplained, it is no more mysterious than the changes in 1921 and 1938. Yet the level of consumption in 1930 was lower than would have been expected from examining other interwar depressions.

TABLE A–2 • *Residuals from Permanent-Income Consumption Functions*

	R_{21}	R_{30}	R_{29}	R_{21}–R_{20}	R_{30}–R_{29}	R_{38}–R_{37}
Interwar coefficients						
Nondurable consumption	.21	−5.17	3.13	−3.40	−4.07	−2.52
Total consumer spending	−.81	−1.94	2.00	−6.91	−1.95	−2.80
Postwar coefficients						
Nondurable consumption	−6.82	−13.4	−3.29	−1.49	−3.76	−2.69
Total consumer spending	−2.31	−3.93	.39	−6.92	−1.89	−2.84

SOURCE: See text.

2. *Sources for Tables 19–21*

All data are from Goldsmith (1955, vol. 1).

Table 19

Row 1. line 2 minus line 3
2. sum of lines 4–11
3. sum of lines 12–16
4. p. 359, col. 6
5. p. 360, col. 15
6. p. 360, col. 16
7. p. 360, col. 17
8. p. 473, col. 6
9. p. 720, sum of cols. 4–7
10. p. 360, col. 11, adjusted to maintain internal consistency
11. p. 359, cols. 7, 8 plus p. 360, cols. 12, 13, 14 plus p. 361, col. 19 plus p. 473, cols. 5, 7, 8
12. p. 361, col. 20
13. p. 361, col. 21
14. p. 361, col. 22
15. p. 361, col. 23
16. p. 361, col. 24 plus col. 27

Table 20

Row 1. line 2 minus line 3
2. sum of lines 4–7
3. sum of lines 8–12
4. first differences of (p. 382, col. 2 plus p. 385, col. 4 plus p. 386, col. 4 plus p. 391, col. 1) adjusted to exclude cash holdings of financial corporations
5. p. 536, col. 28
6. first differences of p. 703, cols. 3, 4, 6, 7, 8, 9, 12 minus first differences of p. 705, cols. 1, 2, 4, 5, 6, 7, 8, 9.
7. p. 575, col. 3, first differences plus p. 749, col. 5, first differences plus p. 1085, col. 2

8. p. 487, col. 2
9. pp. 496–7, cols. 2, 3, 4, 6, 7, 8, 10, 13, 17, 18, 19
10. (p. 731, col. 1, first differences, minus p. 587, col. 6) plus (p. 732, col. 1, first differences, minus p. 591, col. 3) plus .75 times (p. 733, col. 1, first differences) minus (p. 595, col. 3) plus .25 times (p. 733, col. 1, first differences) minus (p. 599, col. 6)
11. p. 859, col. 1, first differences plus p. 651, col. 6 minus p. 859, col. 6
12. p. 1035, Table F26, col. 3 plus p. 494, cols. 3, 6, 7 minus p. 493, col. 12

Table 21

Row 1. Line 2 minus line 3
2. Sum of lines 4–6
3. Sum of lines 7, 8
4. p. 857, col. 9
5. p. 853, col. 1, first differences
6. p. 853, col. 2, first differences plus p. 853, col. 5, first differences
7. p. 859, col. 6
8. p. 597, cols. 3, 4, 6 plus p. 599, col. 6

BIBLIOGRAPHY

Allen, Frederick L. *Only Yesterday*. New York: Harper and Brothers, 1931.

Ando, Albert, and E. Cary Brown. "Lags in Fiscal Policy." In *Stabilization Policies*. Studies for the Commission on Money and Credit, pp. 97–163. Englewood Cliffs, New Jersey: Prentice-Hall, 1963.

Ando, Albert, and Franco Modigliani. "The 'Life Cycle' Hypothesis of Saving: Aggregate Implications and Tests." *American Economic Review* 53 (March 1963): 55–84.

———. "The Relative Stability of Monetary Velocity and the Investment Multiplier." *American Economic Review* 55 (September 1965): 693–728.

Angell, James W. *The Recovery of Germany,* Rev. ed. New Haven: Yale University Press, 1932.

Arena, J. J. "Capital Gains and the 'Life Cycle' Hypothesis of Saving." *American Economic Review* 54 (March 1964): 107–11.

Arndt, H. W. *The Economic Lessons of the Nineteen-Thirties*. London: Oxford University Press, 1944.

Bank and Quotation Record. New York, 1928– .

Banking and Monetary Statistics. See, Board of Governors.

Board of Governors of the Federal Reserve System. *Banking and Monetary Statistics*. Washington, D.C.: United States Government Printing Office, 1943.

Bolch, Ben, Rendigs Fels, and Marshall McMahon. "Housing Surplus in the 1920's?" *Explorations in Economic History* 8 (Spring 1971): 259–83.

Bolch, Ben, and John Pilgrim. "A Reappraisal of Some Factors Associated with Fluctuations in the United States in the Interwar Period." *Southern Economic Journal* 39 (January 1973): 327–44.

Bosworth, Barry. "Patterns of Corporate External Financing." *Brookings Papers on Economic Activity* 2 (1971): 253–79.

Bosworth, Barry, and James S. Duesenberry. *A Flow of Funds Model and Its*

Implications. In The Federal Reserve Bank of Boston. *Issues in Federal Debt Management*. Monetary Conference (June 1973), pp. 39–149.

Brainard, William C., and James Tobin. "Pitfalls in Financial Model Building." *American Economic Review* 58 (May 1968): 99–122.

Brown, E. Cary. "Fiscal Policies in the Thirties: A Reappraisal." *American Economic Review* 46 (December 1956): 857–79.

Burck, Gilbert, and Charles Silberman. "What Caused the Great Depression?" *Fortune* 51 (February 1955): 94–99, 204, 206, 209–11.

Burns, Arthur, and Wesley C. Mitchell. *Measuring Business Cycles*. New York: National Bureau of Economic Research, 1946.

Business Week. New York, 1929–.

Cagan, Phillip. "Discussion" of Green, 1971. In The Federal Reserve Bank of Boston. *Consumer Spending and Monetary Policy: The Linkages*. Monetary Conference (June 1971), pp. 222–28.

———. *The Channels of Monetary Effects on Interest Rates*. New York: National Bureau of Economic Research, distributed by Columbia University Press, 1972.

Chandler, Lester V. *America's Greatest Depression 1929–1941*. New York: Harper and Row, 1970.

Clark, Colin. "A System of Equations Explaining The United States Trade Cycle, 1921 to 1941." *Econometrica* 17 (April 1949): 93–124.

Clarke, Stephen V. *Central Bank Cooperation: 1924–1931*. New York: Federal Reserve Bank of New York, 1967.

The Commercial and Financial Chronicle. New York, 1865– .

Cooper, Richard N. "Macroeconomic Policy Adjustment in Interdependent Economics." *Quarterly Journal of Economics* 83 (February 1969): 1–24.

Council of Economic Advisers. *The Annual Report of the Council of Economic Advisers, January, 1962*. Washington, D.C.: United States Government Printing Office, 1962.

Cowles, Alfred, and Associates. *Common Stock Indexes 1871–1937*. Bloomington, Indiana: Principia Press, 1938.

Darling, Paul G., and Michael G. Lovell. "Factors Influencing Investment in Inventories." In James Duesenberry et al. *Brookings Quarterly Econometric Model of the United States*. Chicago: Rand McNally, 1965.

Davis, J. Ronnie. *The New Economics and the Old Economists*. Ames: Iowa State University Press, 1971.

Die Deutsche Zahlungsbilanz der Jahre 1924–1933, Wirtschaft und Statistik. Sonderheft 14. Berlin, 1934.

Dorfman, Nancy. "The Role of Money in the Investment Boom of the Twenties and the 1929 Turning Point." Unpublished Ph.D. dissertation,

University of California at Berkeley, 1967.

———. "The Role of Money in the Investment Boom of the Twenties and the 1929 Turning Point." *Journal of Finance* 23 (September 1968): 683–84.

Duesenberry, James. *Business Cycles and Economic Growth.* New York: McGraw-Hill, 1958.

Easterlin, Richard A. *Population, Labor Force, and Long Swings in Economic Growth.* New York: National Bureau of Economic Research, 1968.

Eddy, George A. "Security Issues and Real Investment in 1929," *Review of Economics and Statistics* 19 (May 1937): 79–91.

Evans, Michael K. *Macroeconomic Activity: Theory, Forecasting, and Control.* New York: Harper and Row, 1969.

Falkus, M. E. "The German Business Cycle in the 1920's." *Economic History Review* 28 (August 1975).

Fisher, Franklin M. *The Identification Problem in Econometrics.* New York: McGraw-Hill, 1966.

Foley, Duncan, and Miguel Sidrauski. *Monetary and Fiscal Policy in a Growing Economy.* New York: Macmillan, 1971.

Friedman, Milton. "The Quantity Theory of Money—A Restatement." In Milton Friedman, ed. *Studies in the Quantity Theory of Money,* pp. 3–21. Chicago: University of Chicago Press, 1956.

———. *A Theory of the Consumption Function.* Princeton: Princeton University Press, 1957.

———. "The Lag in the Effect of Monetary Policy." *Journal of Political Economy* 69 (October 1961): 447–66.

———. "The Role of Monetary Policy." *American Economic Review* 58 (March 1968): 1–17.

———. *The Optimum Quantity of Money, and Other Essays.* Chicago: Aldine, 1969.

———. "A Theoretical Framework for Monetary Analysis." *Journal of Political Economy* 78 (March/April 1970): 193–238.

Friedman, Milton, and David Meiselman. "The Relative Stability of Monetary Velocity and the Investment Multiplier in the United States." In *Stabilization Policies.* Studies for the Commission on Money and Credit, pp. 168–268. Englewood Cliffs, New Jersey: Prentice-Hall, 1963.

Friedman, Milton, and Anna J. Schwartz. *A Monetary History of the United States 1867–1960.* Princeton: Princeton University Press, 1963a.

———. "Money and Business Cycles." *Review of Economics and Statistics* 45 (February 1963b): 32–78.

———. *The Great Contraction 1929–1933.* Princeton: Princeton University Press, 1965.

Galbraith, John Kenneth. *The Great Crash, 1929*. London: Hamish Hamilton, 1955.

Galster, George C. "Immigration Restrictions and Construction Activity in the 1920's." Mimeographed. Cambridge, Mass.: M.I.T., 1972.

Gandolfi, Arthur E. "Stability of the Demand for Money during the Great Contraction—1929–1933." *Journal of Political Economy* 82 (September/October 1974): 969–83.

Gibson, William E. "Interest Rates and Monetary Policy." *Journal of Political Economy* 78 (May/June 1970): 431–55.

Goldberger, Arthur S. *Econometric Theory*. New York: Wiley, 1964.

Goldfeld, Stephen M. "The Demand for Money Revisited." *Brookings Papers on Economic Activity* 3 (1973): 577–646.

Goldsmith, Raymond W. *A Study of Saving in the United States*. 3 vols. Princeton: Princeton University Press, 1955.

Goldsmith, Raymond W., and Robert E. Lipsey. *Studies in the National Balance Sheet of the United States*. 2 vols. Princeton: Princeton University Press, 1963.

Gordon, Robert A. "Business Cycles in the Interwar Period: The Quantitative-Historical Approach." *American Economic Review* 39 (May 1949): 47–63.

———. "Cyclical Experience in the Interwar Period: The Investment Boom of the 'Twenties.' " In Universities-National Bureau Committee for Economic Research. *Conference on Business Cycles,* pp. 163–215. New York: National Bureau of Economic Research, 1951.

———. "Investment Behavior and Business Cycles." *Review of Economics and Statistics* 37 (February 1955): 23–34.

———. "Types of Depression and Programs to Combat Them." In Universities-National Bureau Committee for Economic Research. *Policies to Combat Depression,* pp. 7–25. Princeton: Princeton University Press, 1956.

———. *Economic Instability and Growth: The American Record*. New York: Harper and Row, 1974.

Great Britain, Committee on Finance and Industry (Macmillan Committee). *Report*. London: H.M.S.O., 1931.

Green, George D. "The Economic Impact of the Stock Market Boom and Crash of 1929." In The Federal Reserve Bank of Boston. *Consumer Spending and Monetary Policy: The Linkages*. Monetary Conference (June 1971), pp. 189–220.

Griliches, Zvi. "A Note on Serial Correlation Bias in Estimates of Distributed Lags." *Econometrica* 29 (January 1961): 65–73.

Guillebaud, Claude W. *The Economic Recovery of Germany From 1933 to the Incorporation of Austria in March 1938*. London: Macmillan, 1939.

Hahn, Frank H. "Professor Friedman's Views on Money." *Econometrica* 38 (February 1971): 61–80.

Hansen, Alvin H. *Fiscal Policy and Business Cycles*. New York: Norton, 1941.

———. "Was Fiscal Policy in the Thirties a Failure?" *Review of Economics and Statistics* 45 (August 1963): 320–23.

Hempel, Carl G. "The Function of General Laws in History." In *Aspects of Scientific Explanation and Other Essays in the Philosophy of Science*. New York: The Free Press, 1965.

Hendershott, P. H., and F. de Leeuw. "Free Reserves, Interest Rates, and Deposits: A Synthesis." *Journal of Finance* 25 (June 1970): 599–614.

Hickman, Bert G. "What Became of the Building Cycle?" In Paul David and Melvin Reder, eds. *Nations and Households in Economic Growth: Essays in Honor of Moses Abramovitz*. New York: Academic Press, 1973.

———, ed. *Econometric Models of Cyclical Behavior*. New York: Columbia University Press, 1972.

Hickman, W. Braddock. *Corporate Bond Quality and Investor Experience*. Princeton: Princeton University Press, 1958.

———. *Statistical Measures of Corporate Bond Financing since 1900*. Princeton: Princeton University Press, 1960.

Historical Statistics. See, United States Bureau of the Census, 1960.

Hoffmann, Walther G. *Das Wachstum der deutschen Wirtschaft Seit der Mitte des 19. Jahrhunderts*. Berlin: Springer-Verlag, 1965.

Hoover, Herbert H. *Memoirs: The Great Depression*. New York: Macmillan, 1952.

Jorgenson, Dale W. "Econometric Studies of Investment Behavior: A Survey." *Journal of Economic Literature* 9 (December 1971): 1111–47.

Keller, Robert. "Factor Income Distribution in the United States during the 1920's: A Reexamination of Fact and Theory." *Journal of Economic History* 33 (March 1973): 252–73.

Kempson, Kenneth E. "An Examination of Klein's Simple Model of the United States Economy." Unpublished B.S. thesis. M.I.T., 1972.

Kendrick, John. *Productivity Trends in the United States*. Princeton: Princeton University Press, 1961.

Keynes, John Maynard. *Treatise on Money*. 2 vols. New York: Harcourt Brace, 1930.

———. *The General Theory of Employment, Interest, and Money*. New York: Harcourt Brace, 1936.

Kindleberger, Charles P. *The World in Depression 1929–39*. London: Allen Lane, 1973.

Kirkwood, John B. "The Great Depression: A Structural Analysis." *Journal of Money, Credit, and Banking* 4 (November 1972): 811–37.

Klein, John J. "German Money and Prices, 1932–1944." In Milton Friedman, ed. *Studies in the Quantity Theory of Money,* pp. 121–59. Chicago: University of Chicago Press, 1956.

Klein, Lawrence R. *Economic Fluctuations in the United States, 1921–1941.* New York: Wiley, 1950.

———. *The Keynesian Revolution,* 2d ed. New York: Macmillan, 1966.

Kuznets, Simon. *Capital in the American Economy: Its Formation and Financing.* Princeton: Princeton University Press, 1961.

Landes, David S. *The Unbound Prometheus.* London: Cambridge University Press, 1969.

League of Nations. *The Course and Phases of the World Economic Depression.* Rev. ed. Geneva, 1931.

de Leeuw, Frank, and Edward Gramlich. "The Federal Reserve-M.I.T. Model." *Federal Reserve Bulletin* 54 (January 1968): 11–40.

Leijonhufvud, Axel. *On the Keynesian Economics and Economics of Keynes.* New York: Oxford University Press, 1968.

Lewis, W. Arthur. *Economic Survey 1919–1939.* London: Allen and Unwin, 1949.

Lovell, Michael C. "Determinants of Inventory Investment." In Conference on Research in Income and Wealth, 28, *Models of Income Determination,* pp. 177–224. Princeton: Princeton University Press, 1964.

Lundberg, Eric. *Instability and Economic Growth.* New Haven, Yale University Press, 1968.

Malenbaum, Wilfred. *The World Wheat Economy.* Cambridge, Mass.: Harvard University Press, 1953.

Malkiel, Burton G. *The Term Structure of Interest Rates.* Princeton: Princeton University Press, 1966.

Means, Gardiner C. "Price Inflexibility and the Requirements of a Stabilizing Monetary Policy." *Journal of the American Statistical Association* 30 (June 1935): 401–13.

Meltzer, Allan H. "The Demand for Money: The Evidence from the Time Series." *Journal of Political Economy* 71 (June 1963): 219–46.

Mercer, Lloyd J., and W. Douglas Morgan. "Alternative Interpretations of Market Saturation: Evaluation for the Automobile Market in the Late Twenties." *Explorations in Economic History* 9 (Spring 1972): 269–90.

Mishkin, Frederic S. "Illiquidity, Consumer Durable Expenditure and Monetary Policy." *American Economic Review,* forthcoming.

Mitchell, Broadus. *Depression Decade: From New Era through New Deal 1929–1941.* New York: Harper and Row, 1947.

Modigliani, Franco. "Monetary Policy and Consumption." In The Federal Reserve System of Boston, *Consumer Spending and Monetary Policy: The Linkages,* Monetary Conference (June 1971), pp. 9–84.

———. "The Life Cycle Hypothesis of Saving Twenty Years Later." Proceedings of the AUTE Conference, University of Warwick, England (March 1973).

Moody's Investors Service. *Moody's Manual of Investments: American and Foreign 1909–1954*. New York.

Morishima, Michio, and Mitsuo Saito. "A Dynamic Analysis of the American Economy 1902–1952." *International Economic Review* 5 (May 1964): 125–64.

Mundell, Robert A. "A Fallacy in the Interpretation of Macroeconomic Equilibrium." *Journal of Political Economy* 73 (February 1965): 61–66.

———. *International Economics*. New York: Macmillan, 1968.

New York State. *Annual Report of the Superintendent of Banks for the Year Ending December 31, 1930*. New York, 1931.

Norman, Morris R. "The Great Depression and What Might Have Been: An Econometric Model Simulation Study." Unpublished Ph.D. dissertation, University of Pennsylvania, 1969.

Phelps, Edmund S., et al. *Microeconomic Foundations of Employment and Inflation Theory*. New York: Norton, 1970.

Pilgrim, John. "The Upper Turning Point of 1920." Unpublished Ph.D. dissertation, Vanderbilt University, 1969.

Schacht, Hjalmar. *My First Seventy-Six Years*. Translated by Diana Pyke. London: Wingate, 1955.

Schlesinger, Arthur M., Jr. *The Crisis of the Old Order, 1919–1933*. Boston: Houghton Mifflin, 1964.

Schmidt, Carl T. *German Business Cycles, 1924–1933*. New York: National Bureau of Economic Research, 1934.

Schumpeter, Joseph. *Business Cycles*. 2 vols. New York: McGraw-Hill, 1939.

Sharpe, William F. *Portfolio Theory and Capital Markets*. New York: McGraw-Hill, 1970.

Slutsky, Eugen. "The Summation of Random Causes as the Source of Cyclic Processes." *Econometrica* 5 (April 1937). 105–46.

Sobel, Robert. *Panic on Wall Street*. New York: Macmillan, 1968.

Standard and Poor's. *Trade and Securities Statistics*. "Security Price Index Record." 1974 ed. New York: Standard and Poor's, 1974.

Stein, Herbert. *The Fiscal Revolution*. Chicago: University of Chicago Press, 1969.

Swanson, Joseph, and Samuel Williamson. "Estimates of National Product and Income for the United States 1919–1941." *Explorations in Economic History* 10 (Fall 1972): 53–73.

Temin, Peter. *The Jacksonian Economy*. New York: Norton, 1969.

———. "The Beginning of the Depression in Germany." *Economic History Review* 24 (May 1971): 240–48.

Timoshenko, Vladimir P. *World Agriculture and the Depression*. Ann Arbor: University of Michigan Press, 1953.

Tinbergen, Jan. *Statistical Testing of Business-Cycle Theories,* 2, *Business Cycles in the United States of America 1919–32*. Geneva: League of Nations, Economic Intelligence Service, 1939.

Tobin, James. "Liquidity Preference and Monetary Policy." *Review of Economics and Statistics* 29 (May 1947): 124–31.

———. Unpublished Monetary Theory Manuscript. Mimeographed. New Haven, 1959.

———. "The Monetary Interpretation of History." *American Economic Review* 55 (June 1965): 646–85.

———. "A General Equilibrium Approach to Monetary Theory." *Journal of Money, Credit, and Banking* 1 (February 1969): 15–29.

———. "Money and Income: Post Hoc Ergo Propter Hoc?" *Quarterly Journal of Economics* 84 (May 1970): 301–17.

Trivedi, P. K. "Retail Inventory Investment Behaviour." *Journal of Econometrics* 1 (March 1973): 61–80.

United States Bureau of the Census. *Historical Statistics of the United States, Colonial Times to 1957*. Washington, D.C.: United States Government Printing Office, 1960.

United States Department of Commerce. *The National Income and Product Accounts of the United States, 1929–1965*. Washington, D.C.: United States Government Printing Office, 1966.

Warburton, Clark. "Monetary Theory, Full Employment, and the Great Depression." *Econometrica* 13 (April 1945): 114–28. Reprinted as Chapter 5 in Clark Warburton. *Depression, Inflation, and Monetary Policy, Selected Papers 1945–1953*. Baltimore: Johns Hopkins Press, 1966.

Wicker, Elmus R. *Federal Reserve and Monetary Policy 1917–1933*. New York: Random House, 1966.

Wilson, Thomas. *Fluctuations in Income and Employment*. London: Pitman, 1942.

INDEX